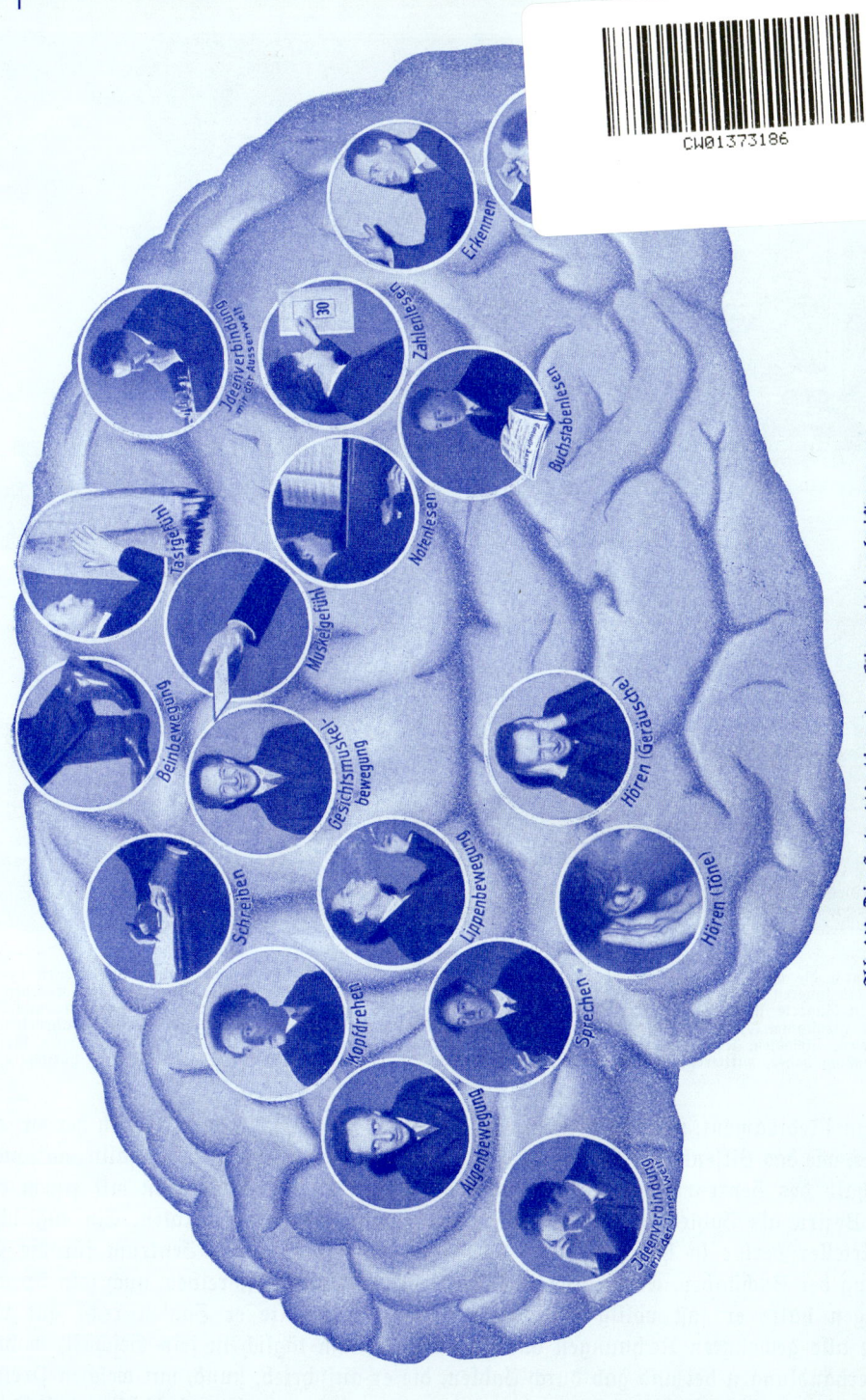

Abb. 144. Die Lokalisation der Hirnrindenleistungen.

Die Leistungen der Hirnrinde sind an ganz bestimmte Zentren gebunden, die in der hier dargestellten Weise über die Hirnrinde verteilt sind. Die Zahl erst ein geringer Teil entdeckt ist, muß außerordentlich groß sein, denn für jede einzelne Spezialleistung des Hirns ist ein spezielles Zentrum hier dargestellten Spezialzentren ist wieder in Unterzentren für Einzelleistungen gegliedert. (Vgl. Abb. 137, 140, Taf. XX.

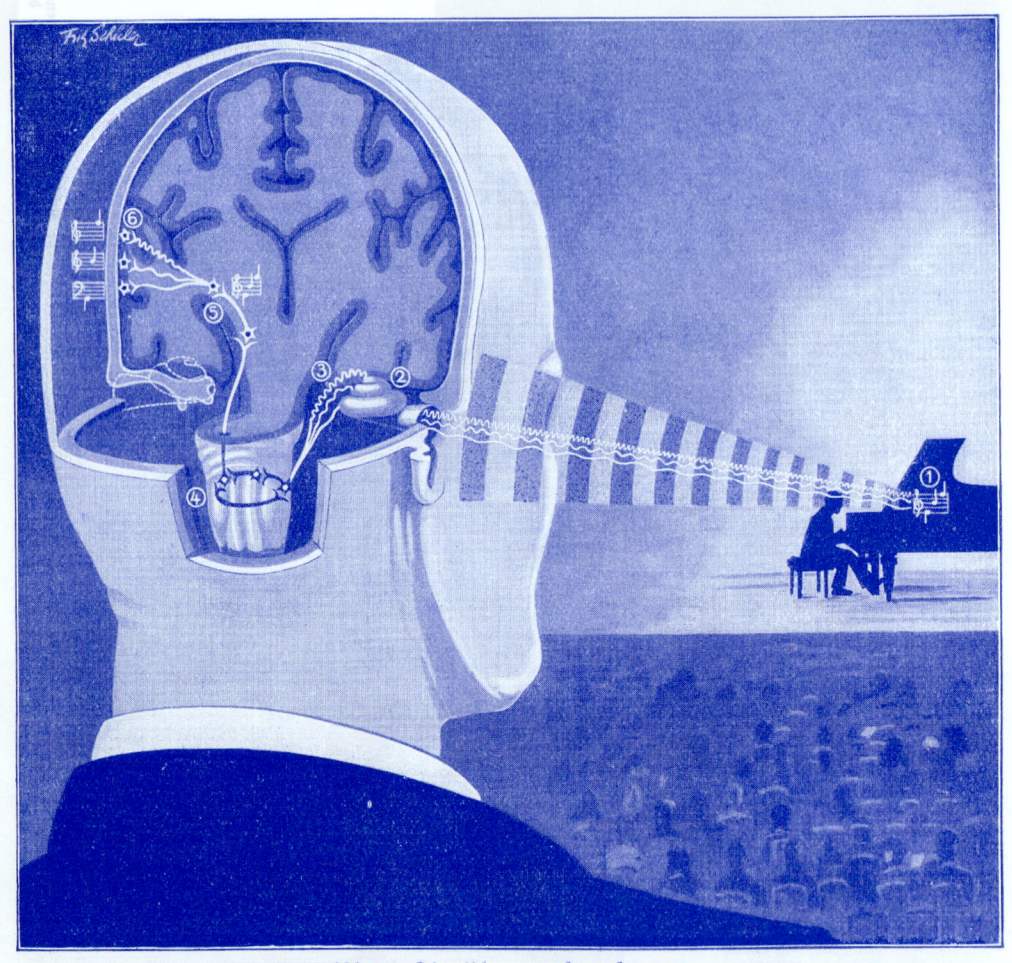

Abb. 140. Die Klangwahrnehmung

erfolgt durch die dem aufnehmenden Ohr gegenüberliegende Hörsphäre im Schläfenlappen. Der Ton (1) wird in der Schnecke des inneren Ohres (2) von den Hörzellen in Nervenerregung transformiert und wandert durch den Hörnerven (3) in das verlängerte Mark (4), läuft über mehrere ringförmig angeordnete Schaltungen auf die Gegenseite und hier durch den Hirnstamm (5) in die Hörsphäre des Schläfenlappens (6). Hier gibt es getrennte Bezirke für die Wahrnehmung von Worten, Melodien, Rhythmen und Tönen, und innerhalb der Tonreihe wieder getrennte Unterabteilungen für die Wahrnehmung hoher, mittlerer und tiefer Töne. Der Dreiklang (1) wird an drei verschiedenen Stellen der Hörsphäre (6) wahrgenommen.

denn ein Medikament, wie das Wurmmittel Santonin, ruft isoliertes Gelbsehen hervor, ein anderes, wie das Bilsenkraut, Rotsehen, ein drittes, wie der Haschisch, Violetthalluzinationen. Innerhalb des Zentrums für Formenwahrnehmung sehen wir Buchstaben mit einem anderen Bezirk als Zahlen und diese wieder mit einem anderen als Noten. Ein englischer Industrieller verlor in höherem Alter durch eine Hirnblutung das Zentrum für die Erkennung der Buchstaben. Er konnte kein Wort mehr lesen oder schreiben, auch sein Sprachvermögen hatte er fast völlig eingebüßt. Dagegen erkannte er Zahlen recht gut und konnte alle gewohnten Rechnungen durchführen. Er kam täglich in sein Geschäft, wohnte den Verhandlungen bei und gab durch Zahlen, die er aufschrieb, kund, mit welchen Preisen er einverstanden sei. Sieben Jahre nahm er so an der Leitung seines Geschäftes teil. Dann

VERSTEHEN

Durch häufige Wiederholung dringt die Hörwahrnehmung über das Hörzentrum hinaus in ein Nachbargebiet und prägt sich hier als dauernder Eindruck, als Erinnerung (D) ein. Nunmehr wird bei Wiederholung des Eindrucks dieser über das Hörzentrum hinaus bis zum Erinnerungszentrum geleitet und hier als schon vorhanden wiedererkannt, „verstanden". Nunmehr „kennt" das Kind den Laut mama.

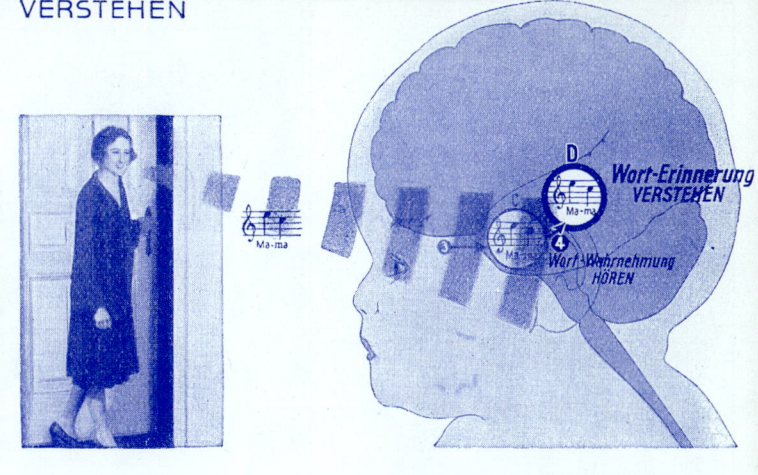

BILD-WORT-VERBINDUNG

Indem das Kind wiederholt darauf hingewiesen wird, daß der Bildeindruck Mutter identisch ist mit dem Worteindruck mama, bildet es eine Verbindungsfaser, eine Assoziationsfaser zwischen der Bilderinnerung Mutter und der Klangerinnerung mama (5). Nunmehr assoziiert das Kind den Klang mama mit dem Bild Mutter (es sucht beim Hören des Wortes mama die Mutter) und assoziiert umgekehrt beim Anblick der Mutter den Wortklang mama, kann diesen aber noch nicht ausdrücken, sondern hört ihn nur innerlich.

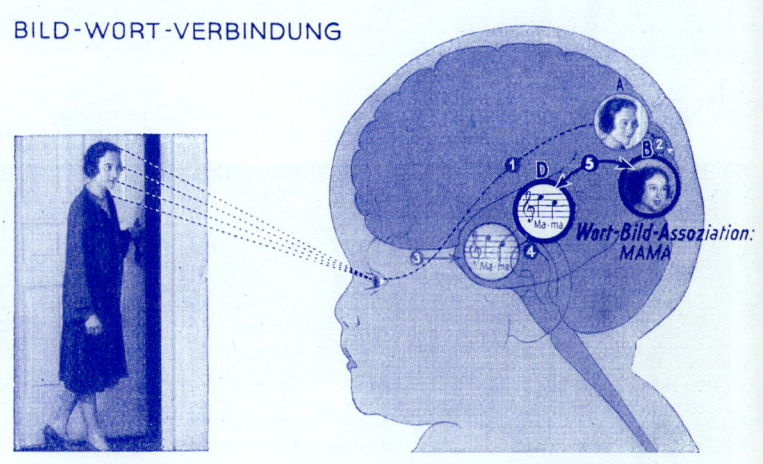

VERSUCH DER WORT-FORMUNG

Beim nunmehr einsetzenden Sprechunterricht lernt das Kind mit Hilfe des Seh- und des Hörzentrums die Mund- und Atembewegungen der ihm vorsprechenden Mutter nachahmen. Die Zusammensetzung der zum Sprechen notwendigen Kombinationsbewegungen erfolgt in einem speziellen Sprechbewegungs-Kombinationszentrum, dem Zentrum für die Wortformung oder Artikulation (E), identisch mit dem von Broca entdeckten motorischen Sprechzentrum.

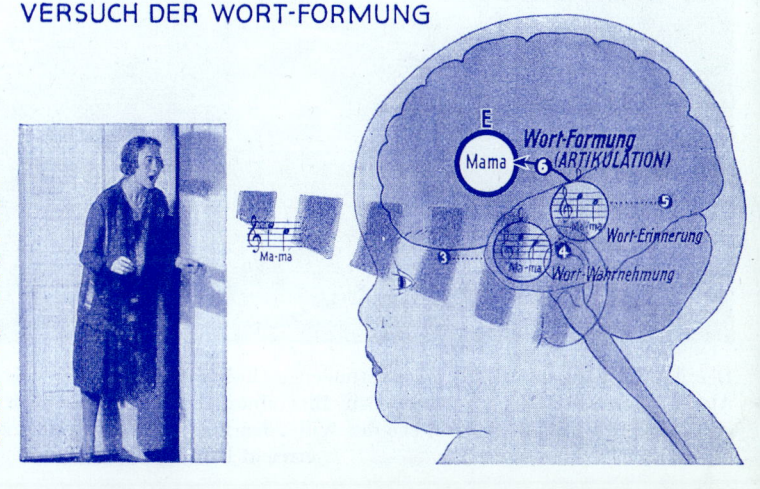

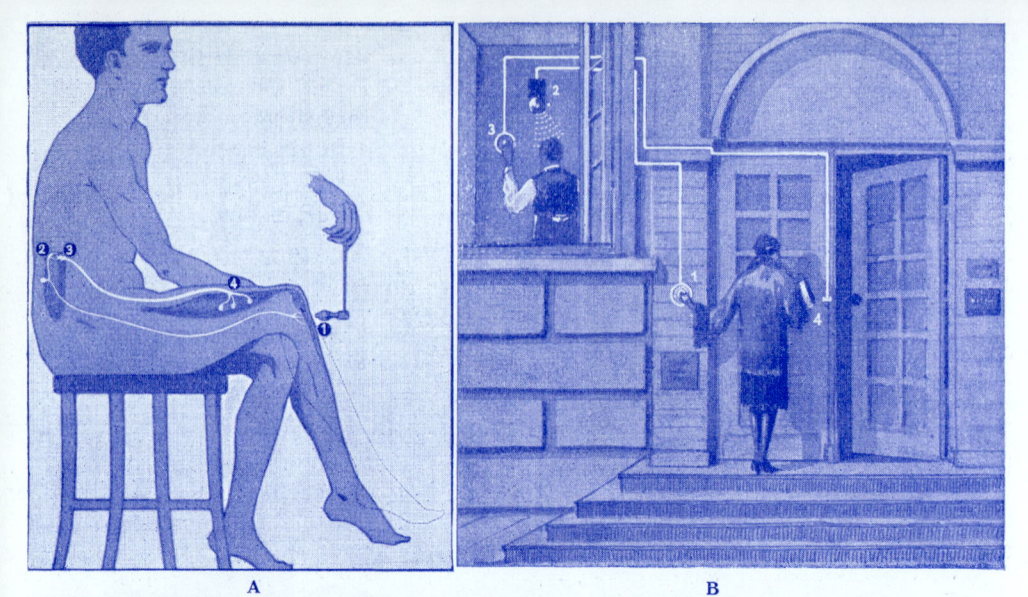

Abb. 68. Die Neuronenlehre I. Beispiel einer Zwei-Neuronen-Leitung: Die Reflexbahn Haut—Rückenmark (1, 2) = Rückenmark—Muskel (3, 4), demonstriert am Kniesehnen-Reflex A und verglichen mit einer „Zwei-Neuronen-Leitung" der Elektrotechnik B, einer Hausklingel (1, 2) und einem Türöffner (3, 4).

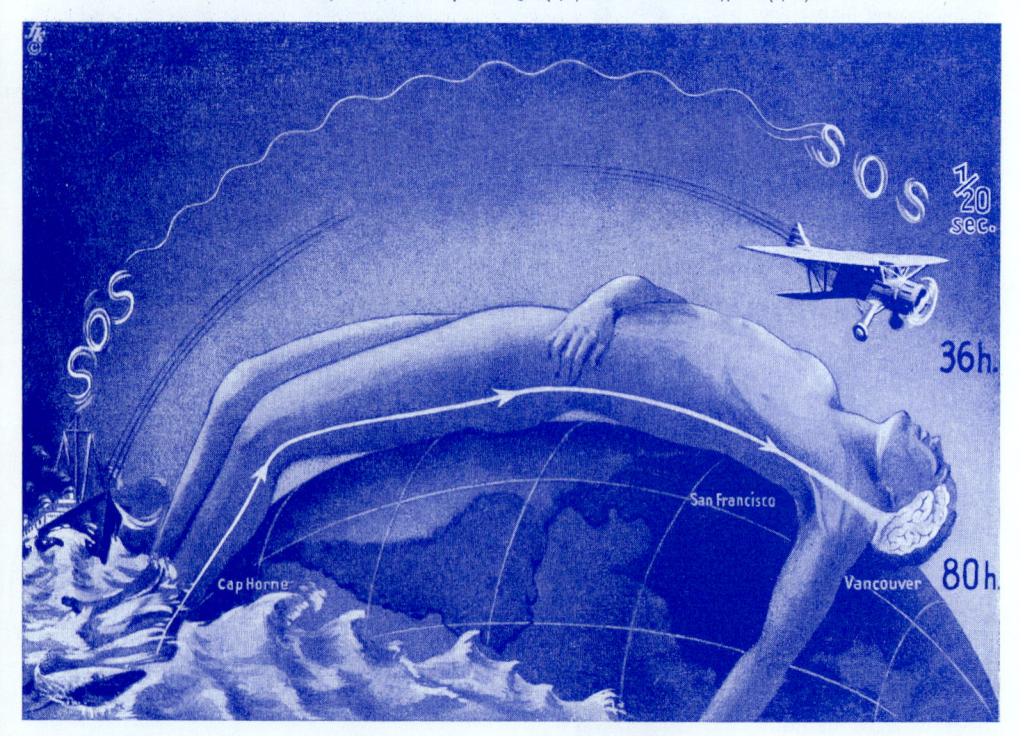

Der Nervenstrom läuft mit einer Stundengeschwindigkeit von 250 km. Ein von Kap Hoorn bis Alaska reichender Mensch würde den Biss eines Haifisches erst nach 80 Stunden fühlen, und ebenso lange würde es dauern, ehe der Wille, den Fuss zurückzuziehen, vom Gehirn her die Zehen erreicht hätte.

Selbstfahrer zu vermieten Fernruf 8493" oder „Drei=Röhren=Apparat, großes Wellen=
bereich ohne Spulenwechsel, mit Sperrkreis, Anodenbatterie und Lautsprecher zu ver=

DER WEG DER ENTWICKLUNG

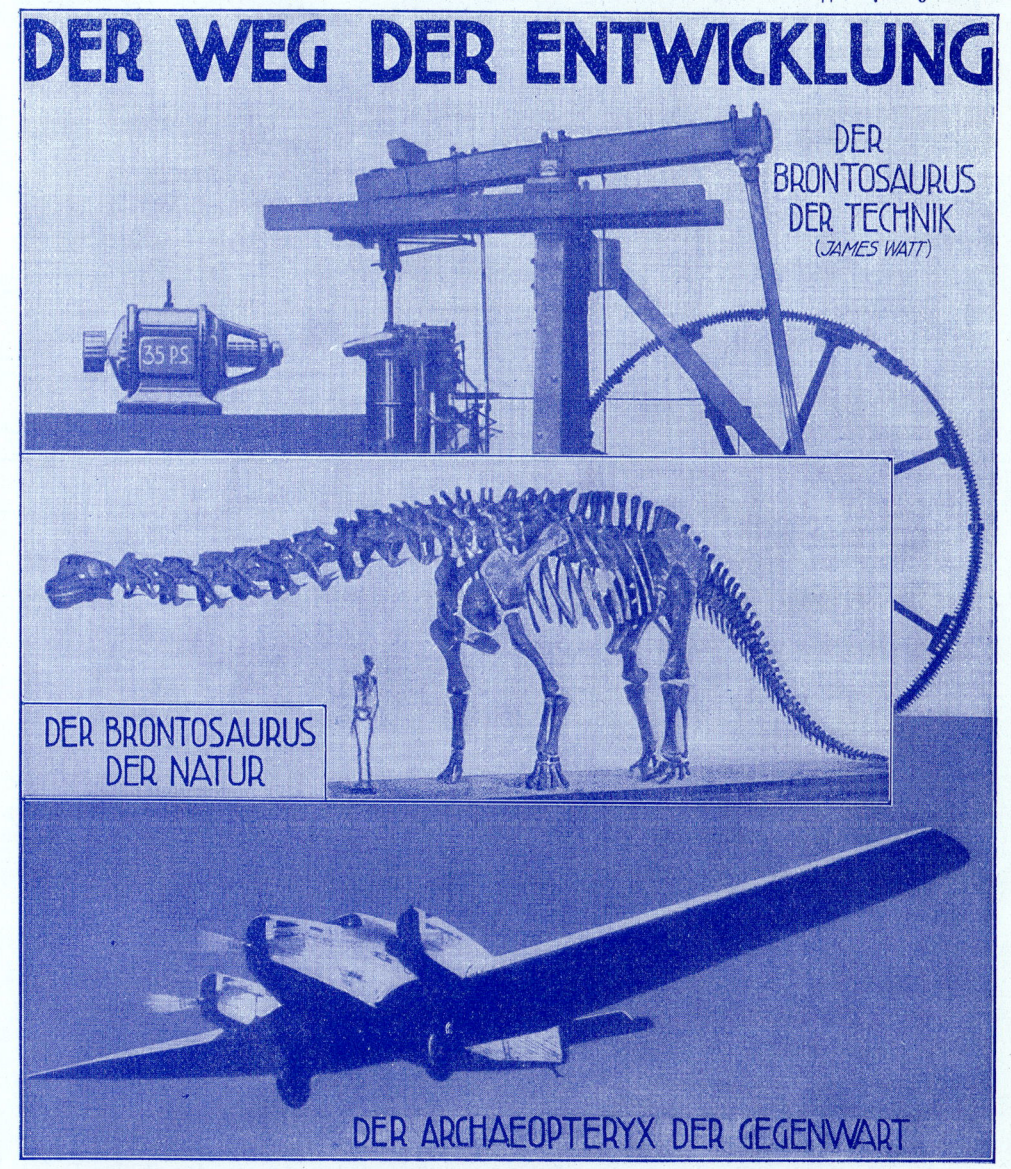

DER BRONTOSAURUS DER TECHNIK (JAMES WATT)

DER BRONTOSAURUS DER NATUR

DER ARCHAEOPTERYX DER GEGENWART

Abb. 145. Der Weg der Entwicklung führt in Technik wie Natur von gigantischen Riesenformen zu konzentrierten Kleinmaschinen von erhöhter Leistung. Den Verlust der Körpergröße ersetzt der Mensch durch Schaffung von Flug=, Lauf=, Schwimmaschinen, in denen er nun als ein „Saurier mit Menschenhirn" dahinrast. Die „organische" Entwicklung erfolgt im Rahmen der Kulturgeschichte außerhalb des Menschenkörpers — mit Ausnahme des Gehirns.

kaufen" oder „8=Zimmerwohnung mit Zentralheizung, Warmwasser, Gasherd und elektr.
Licht, Telephon, Fahrstuhl und Garage zu vermieten". Er versteht es nicht, kann es nicht
verstehen, denn in seinem Hirn fehlen jene zahllosen Begriffe, um die das Normalhirn des
heutigen Menschen gegen das des damaligen bereichert ist. Denn alles, was das Jahr=
hundert erfunden und gedacht, geschaffen und durch seine Wundermaschinen täglich in un=

Ein Erwachsener sagt Auto. Sehen, erkennen und sprechen bilden die Haupttätigkeiten unseres geistigen Lebens. Auch indem wir dieses Buch lesen, vollziehen wir diesen geistigen Prozess des Sehens, Erkennens und lauten oder leisen Sprechens, denn Lesen heisst ja nichts anderes als mit seinem inneren Sprachzentrum ohne Bewegung der Lippen das gelesene Wort nachsprechen. Vereinigt man diese drei Prozesse zu einem Bild und demonstriert die Vorgänge, die sich hierbei in uns abspielen, durch bekannte technische Verfahren, so erhält man eine Darstellung wie jene der Abb. 144. In der Sehleitung (1—4) vollzieht sich ein photographischer, in der Sprechleitung (5—8) ein musikalischer Prozess. Das Bild des Autos (1) wird auf die lichtempfindliche Scheibe des Augenhintergrunds projiziert (2), im Sehhügel entwickelt und durch das nächste Neuron zum hinteren Pol des Gehirns in die Sehsphäre geschickt und hier vom Photographen betrachtet (3). Er sieht es; um aber zu erkennen, was es vorstellt, projiziert er es auf die Tafel des Bildarchivs und bringt es hier mit einem abgelagerten Erinnerungsbild in

Abb. 144 a

Deckung (4). Hat er das entsprechende Bild aus dem Schatz der „dunklen Erinnerungen" gefunden, so leuchtet es als „Erkenntnis" auf, und gleichzeitig leuchtet auch der Name des Bildes in der nächsten Abteilung der Worterinnerung auf: Auto (5). In der Kammer des Sprachschatzes lebt wieder eine Bewusstseinszelle, die aber kein Photograph sondern ein Musiker ist. Dieser sieht das Wort Auto leuchten und drückt nun auf der Tastatur seiner Sprechorgel, die ein Silbenklavier ist, die beiden Silben nieder: Au - to. Durch den Druck der Tasten werden im motorischen Zentrum bestimmte Gruppen von Zellen in Erregung versetzt, und diese senden durch die Rückenmarksleitungen (6) der Sprechorgel im Kehlkopf die notwendigen Aktionsströme zu, damit sie die Tonfolge Au - to zum Ausdruck bringt (7).

Was wir hier im Lauf von 5 Minuten langsam gelesen und im Bild verfolgt haben, spielt sich in unserem Nervensystem im Bruchteil einer Sekunde ab. Wenn wir im Zeitraum von etwa 2 Minuten eine Buchseite heruntergelesen haben, so laufen rund 300 solche

Was sich in unserem Kopf abspielt, wenn

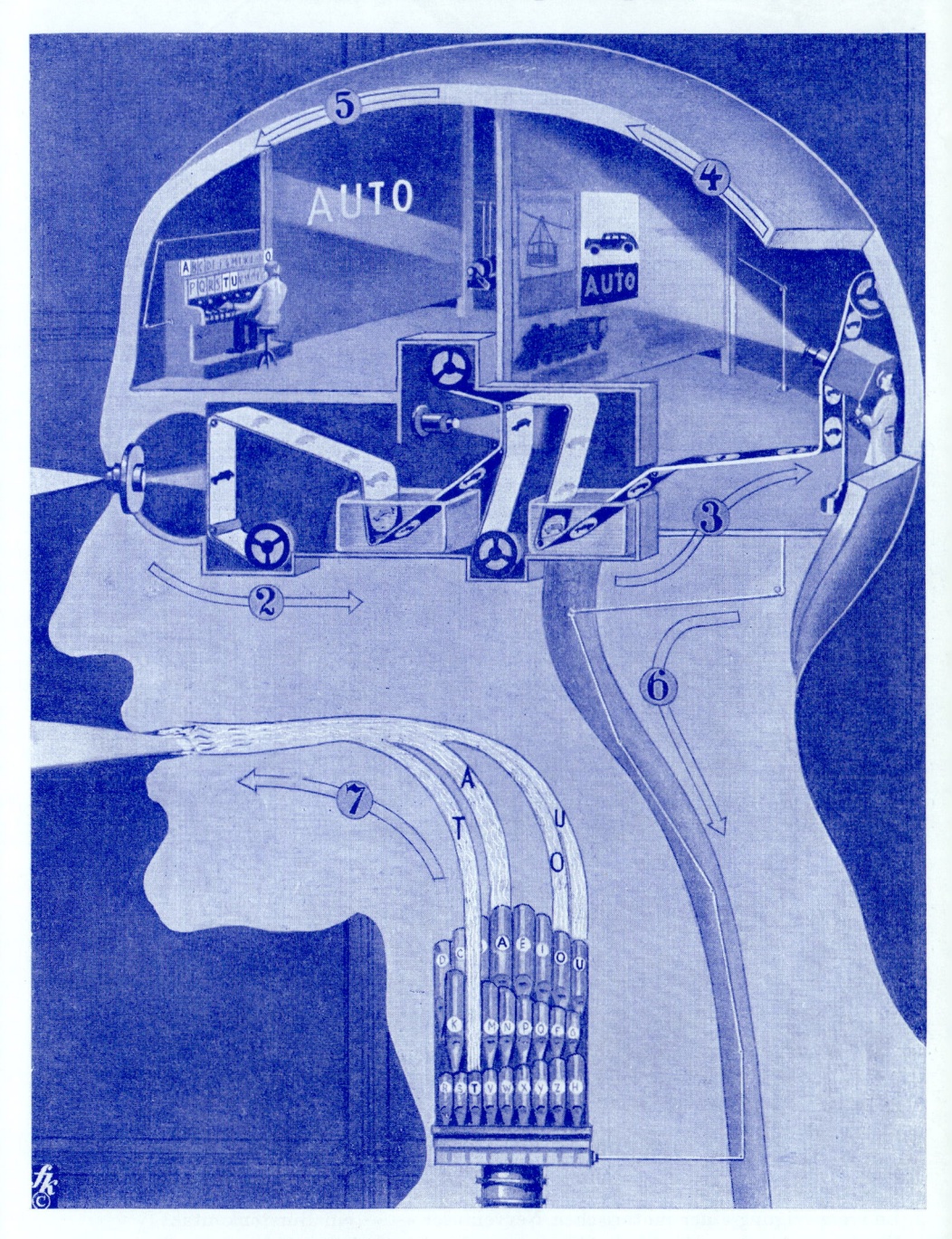

wir ein Auto sehen und „Auto" sagen.
Abb. 144b

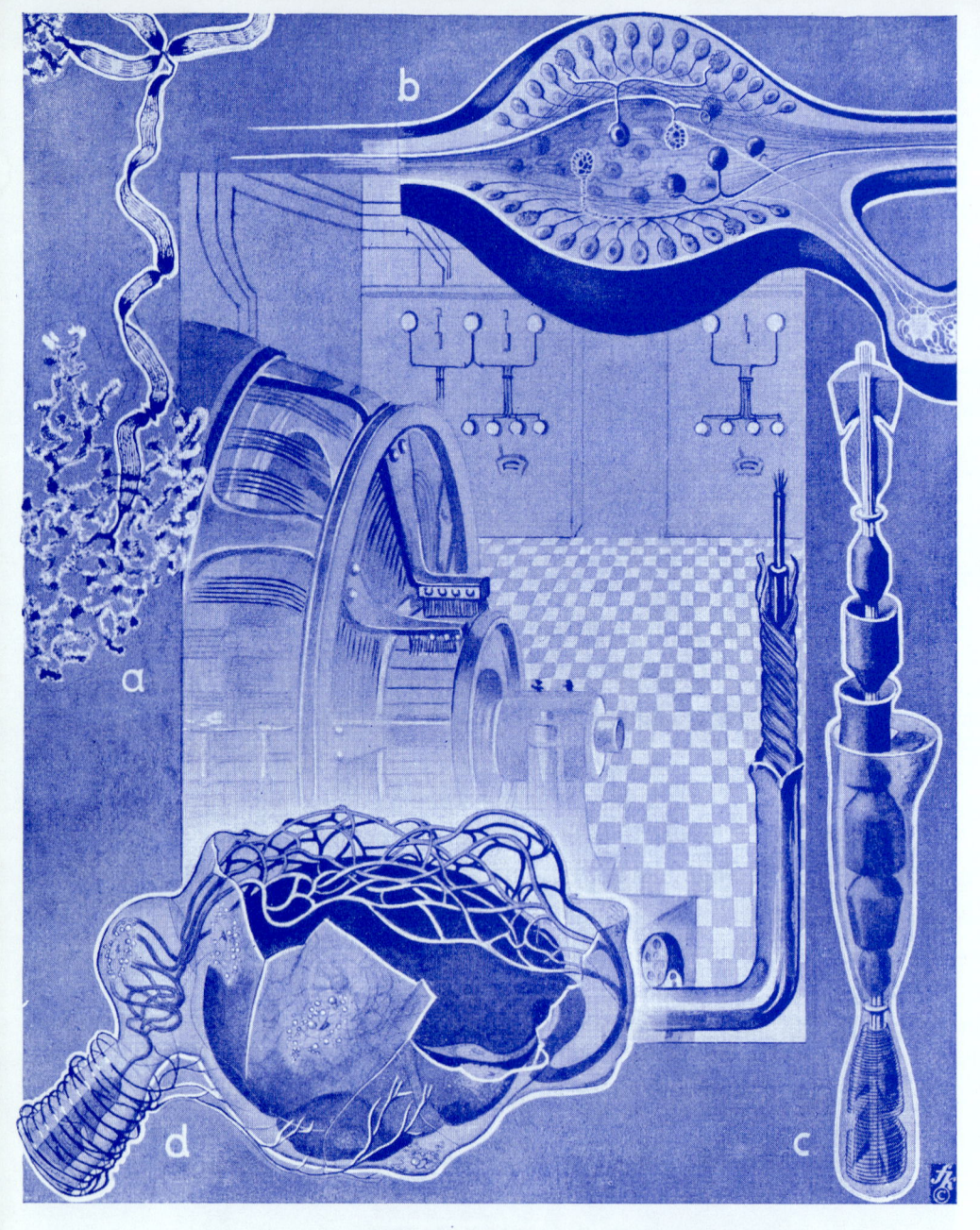

Abb. 102 Ist das Nervensystem eine elektrische Anlage?

a Endverzweigung einer motorischen Nervenfaser — — ein Bürstenkontakt?
b Ein Nervenknoten mit Schaltzellen — — ein elektrischer Schaltapparat?
c Eine Nervenleitung mit Isoliermaterial — — ein elektrisches Kabel?
d Sensible Zelle — — ein Empfänger mit Schwingungskreisen und Widerstandsdrähten?

Abb. 43. Der Blinde Fleck.

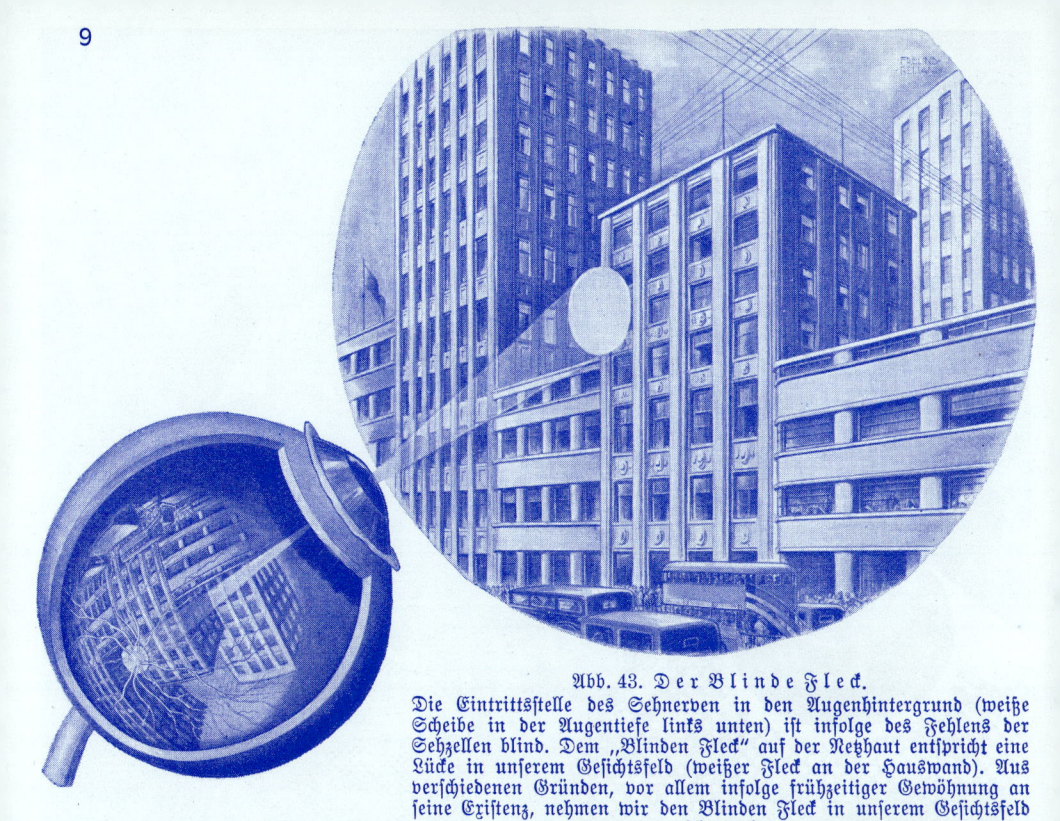

Die Eintrittsstelle des Sehnerven in den Augenhintergrund (weiße Scheibe in der Augentiefe links unten) ist infolge des Fehlens der Sehzellen blind. Dem „Blinden Fleck" auf der Netzhaut entspricht eine Lücke in unserem Gesichtsfeld (weißer Fleck an der Hauswand). Aus verschiedenen Gründen, vor allem infolge frühzeitiger Gewöhnung an seine Existenz, nehmen wir den Blinden Fleck in unserem Gesichtsfeld nicht wahr.

Abb. 13.

Die Verlängerung der Sehzellen in der Einfallsrichtung der Lichtstrahlen ermöglicht das Auffangen optischer Bilder verschiedener Entfernung. Durch die Stäbchenform der menschlichen Sehzellen (0,06 mm Länge) werden Objekte von ∞ bis auf 6 m Annäherung von den Netzhautzellen aufgenommen. Der Flieger a, die Turmuhr b und das Auto c projizieren sich noch scharf in der Sehzellenschicht. Das etwa 80 cm entfernte Bild des Geschwindigkeitsmessers d dagegen liegt hinter der Netzhaut und erscheint folglich unscharf.

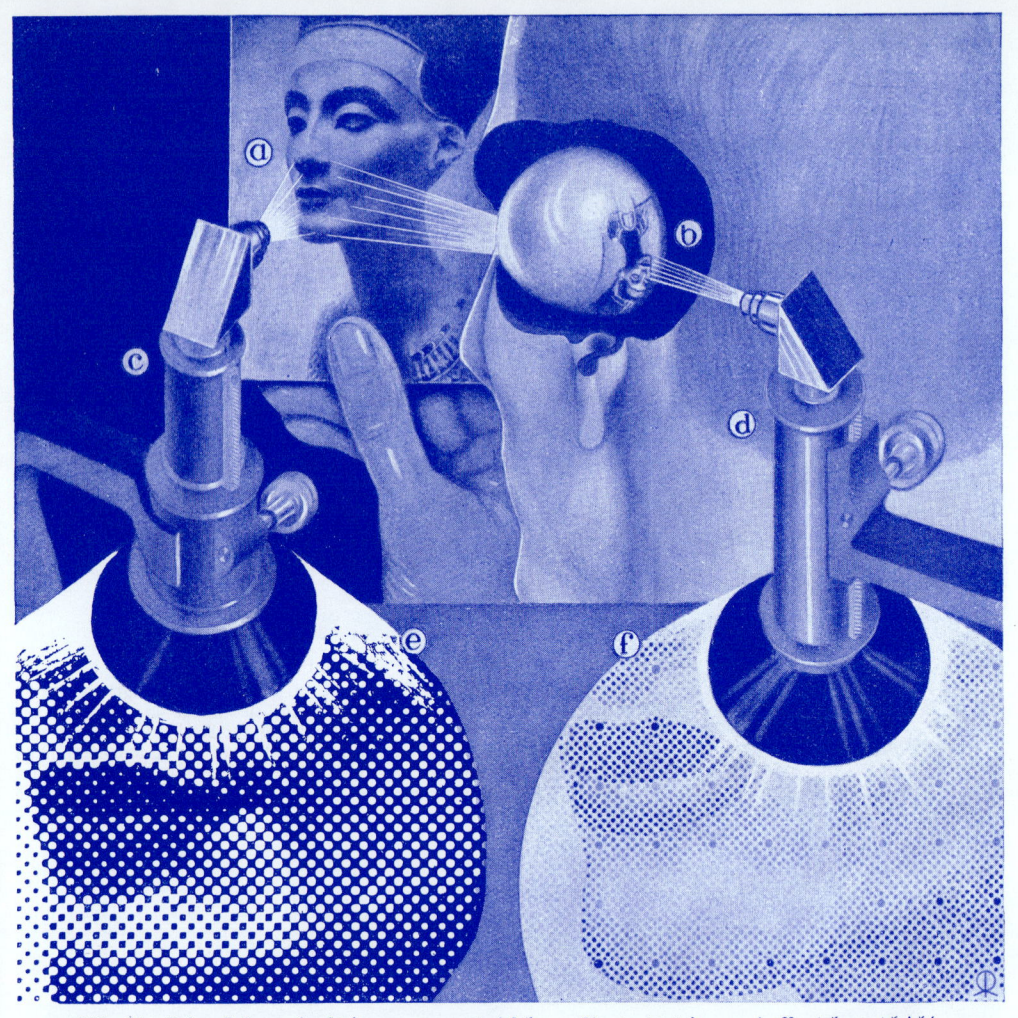

Abb. 34. Die Übereinstimmung zwischen Autotypie und Netzhautbild.
Natur wie Technik lösen das Problem der Bildübertragung durch die Aufteilung des zu übertragenden Bildes in Einzelpunkte. Im Druckverfahren geschieht die Bildauflösung durch den Raster (f. Abb. 32), im Augenhintergrund durch das Zellenmosaik der Netzhaut. Bei vergrößerter Betrachtung würde man sowohl am Druckbild (a) wie am Bild des Augenhintergrundes (b) den Punktcharakter erkennen (e u. f). In e entspricht jeder schwarze Punkt einer Sieböffnung des Rasters, in f je einer vom Licht gereizten Sehzelle der Netzhaut.

systeme. In der Netzhautperipherie sind 100—130 Sehzellen durch Assoziationssysteme zu Einheiten verbunden. Da hierdurch die Lichtreize von 100 Zellen zu einer Einheitsempfindung summiert werden, ist die Netzhautperipherie lichtempfindlicher als die zentrale Sehgrube, eine Tatsache, die zu ebenso merkwürdigen wie biologisch wichtigen Konsequenzen führt. Durch die Vereinigung von 100 zerstreuten Lichtreizen wird zwar die Lichtempfindlichkeit gesteigert, denn das Licht einer hundertmal größeren Fläche sammelt sich zu einem Reiz, aber die Qualität des Bildes muß natürlich leiden. Denn während in der Sehgrube jede Zelle isoliert ihren Punktreiz an das Großhirn sendet, laufen durch die Leitungen der Peripherie die Sammelreize von 100 Zellen zu einer Empfindung vereint. Die optischen Meldungen des Netzhautzentrums sind Solovorträge. Die Eindrücke der Peripherie gleichen

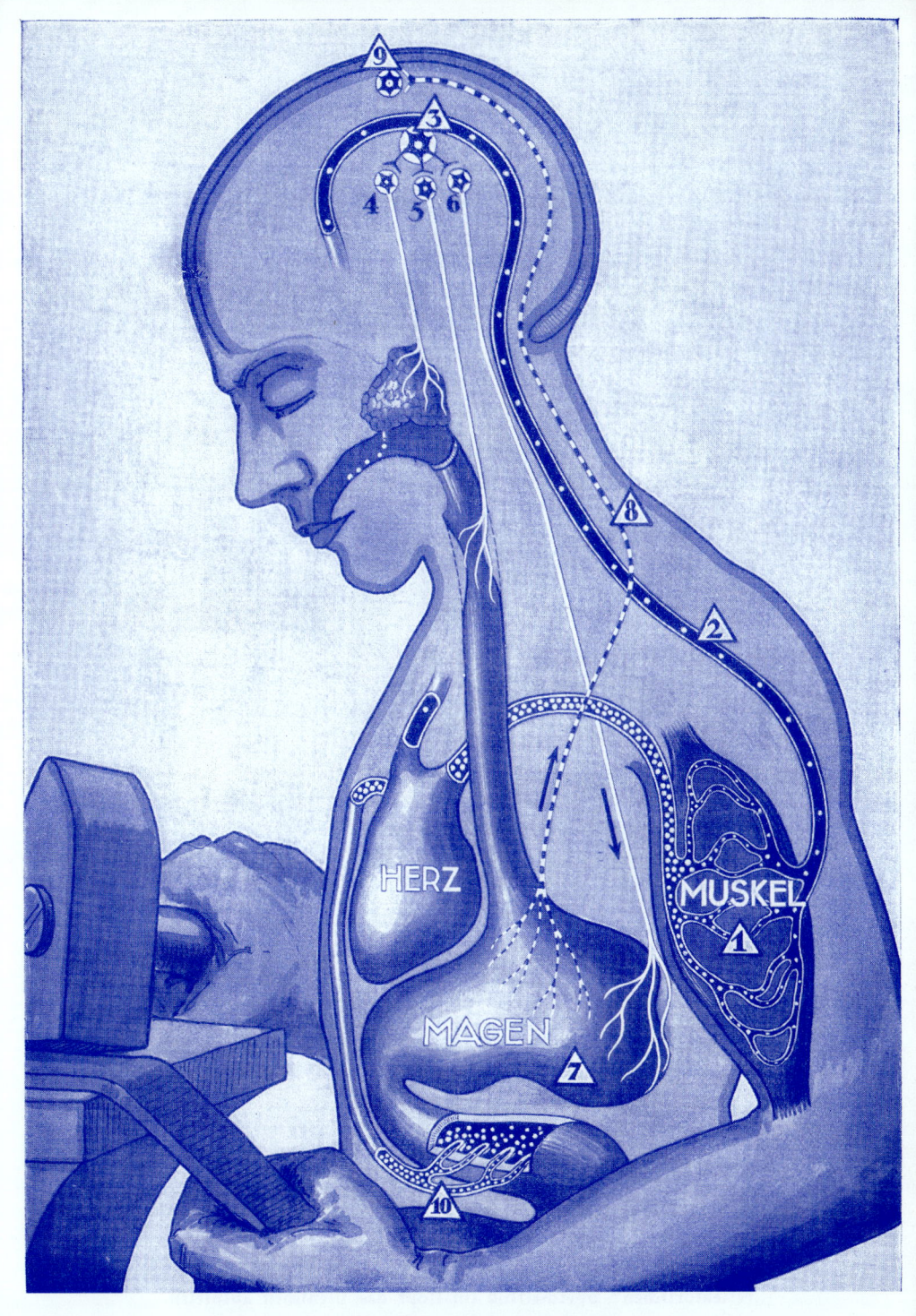

Die Entstehung des Hungergefühls

BIOLOGIE DES BRATENDUFTES

Bildliche Darstellung der Vorgänge, die sich zwischen der Geruchsempfindung und dem „reflektorischen" Speichelfluß im Kopf des Menschen abspielen.

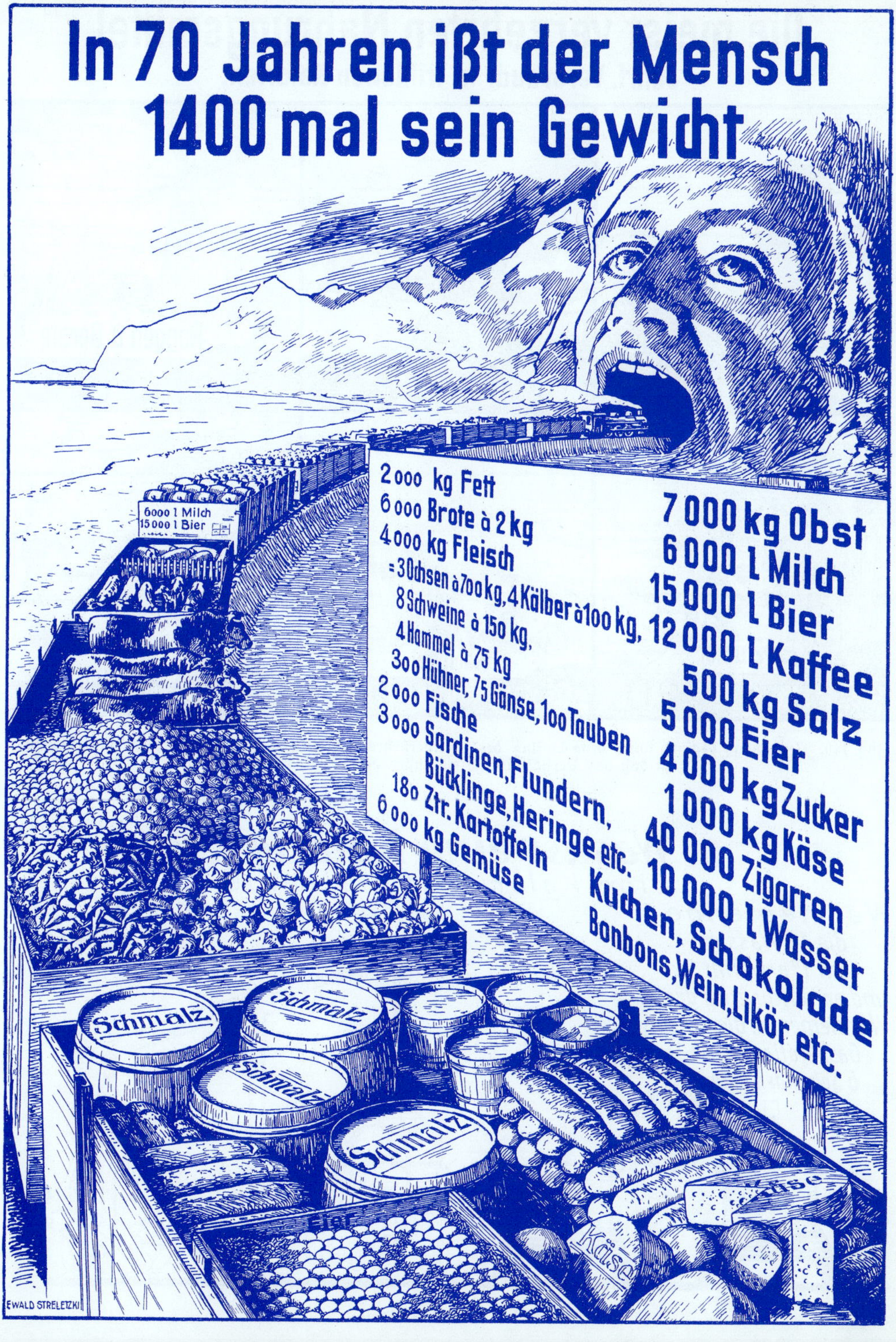
In 70 Jahren ißt der Mensch
1400 mal sein Gewicht
6000 l Milch
15000 l Bier
2000 kg Fett
6000 Brote à 2 kg
4000 kg Fleisch
= 3 Ochsen à 700 kg, 4 Kälber à 100 kg,
8 Schweine à 150 kg,
4 Hammel à 75 kg
300 Hühner, 75 Gänse, 100 Tauben
2000 Fische
3000 Sardinen, Flundern, Bücklinge, Heringe etc.
180 Ztr. Kartoffeln
6000 kg Gemüse
7000 kg Obst
6000 l Milch
15000 l Bier
12000 l Kaffee
500 kg Salz
5000 Eier
4000 kg Zucker
1000 kg Käse
40000 Zigarren
10000 l Wasser
Kuchen, Schokolade
Bonbons, Wein, Likör etc.
Schmalz
Schmalz
Schmalz
Schmalz
Eier
Käse
Käse
EWALD STRELETZKI

Die meist verzehrten Nahrungsmittel
Jährl. Verbrauch in Trillionen Kalorien.

Reis	Weizen	Roggen u. Gerste
900	385	305

Zucker	Kartoffel	Fleisch
220	100	60

EWALD STRELETZKI.

Abb. 149. Neuerdings beginnt unter dem Einfluß des Weltverkehrs der Weizen den Reis in Asien zu verdrängen, so daß das Verhältnis sich zugunsten des Weizens ändert.

Was ist eine Kalorie?
Eine Kalorie ist diejenige

Wärmemenge, die 1ℓ Wasser um 1° erwärmt und entspricht etwa der Wärmemenge, die eine Gasherdflamme in 6 Sekunden liefert.

Energiemenge, die 327 kg 1m hoch hebt.

Abb. 9 Die Kalorie

Ausstellg   1922   Malaria

100 Kinder Kranken.. 16 sephard.

Schularzt

ginge fröhlich
fort

47   53 gesund
vergr. Milz   schwere gibt
                      Chinin
Mannung detentig.
System
Petrol.   40-60 h eg
Chlor.

                        1930
                        dasselbe
Chlb. Frisch.   170 Kauk

Ausstellg Schulhygiene

Schulhyg.

Kind → Schatten i. Uls. → Schulschwester
"Kind kommt halbkrank i. d. Schule"

Schularzt i. d. Sch.

Specialarzt

Specialarzt

ובחרת בחיים

אל תושיבו את הילדים צפופים כי

צפיפות יתרה מביאה לידי עלית־חום

האדם והצמח

זווג מן השמים

האדם והפרימוס
שניהם מכונות שריפה
ומוצרים
חום
קיטור
וחומצה פחמית

לוח הטפול בשנים
2X
ביום
נקוי
השנים
2X
בשנה
בדיקה ע"י
רופא שנים
אב
אדר
Copyright
F. Kohn

תנועה
בשעת
ההוראה

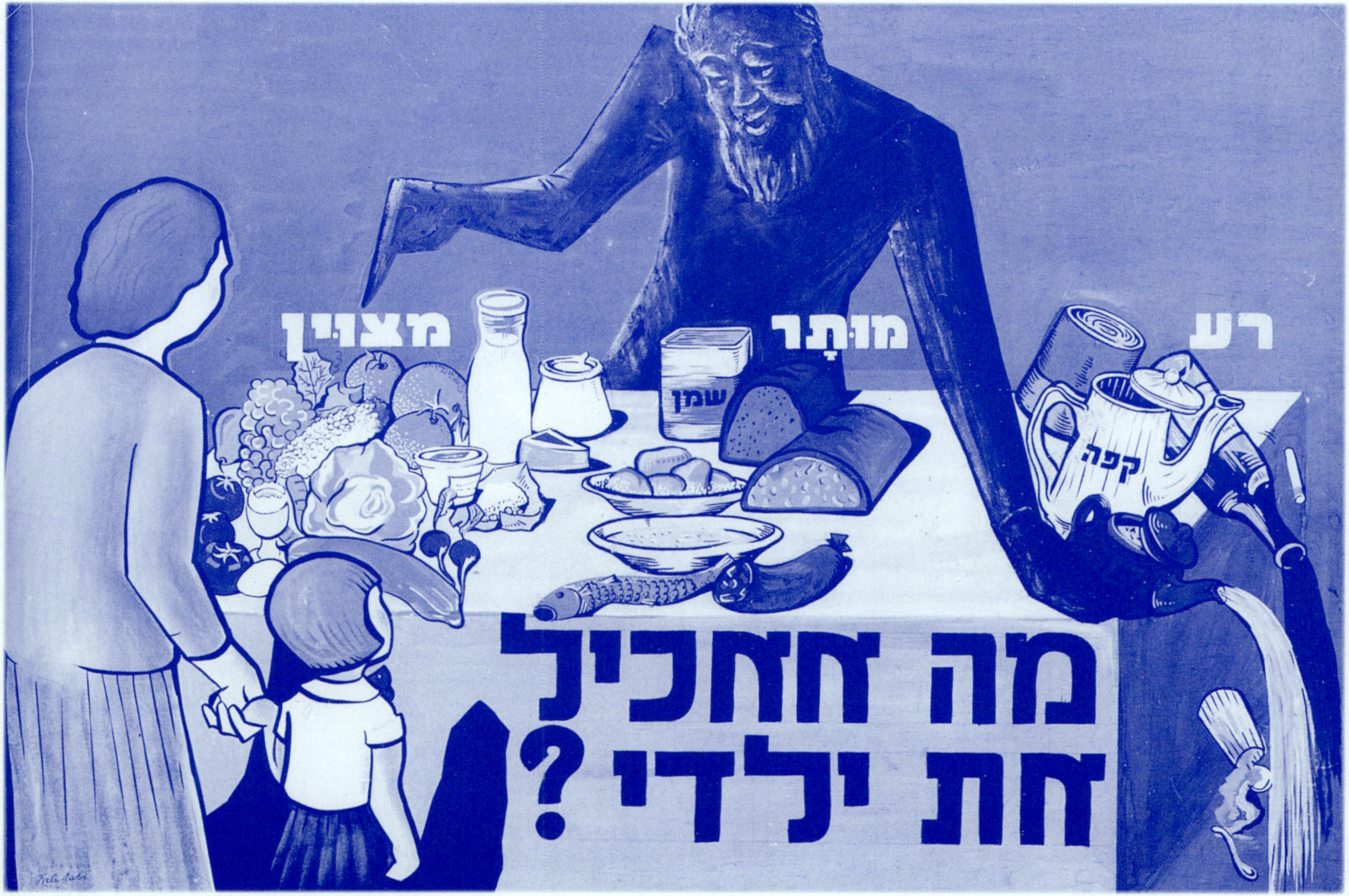

רע
מותָר
מצוין
קפה
שמן
מה אאכיל
את ילדי?

המסעדות מחלקות בבי"הס:
ביצים
275.000
ירקות
25.000
רוטל
לחם
פירות
10.000
רוטל
חלב
17.000
רוטל.
שמן
1.600
רוטל
דגים
גריסים
וסוכר
7.000
רוטל.
חמאה
400
רוטל
COPYRIGHT

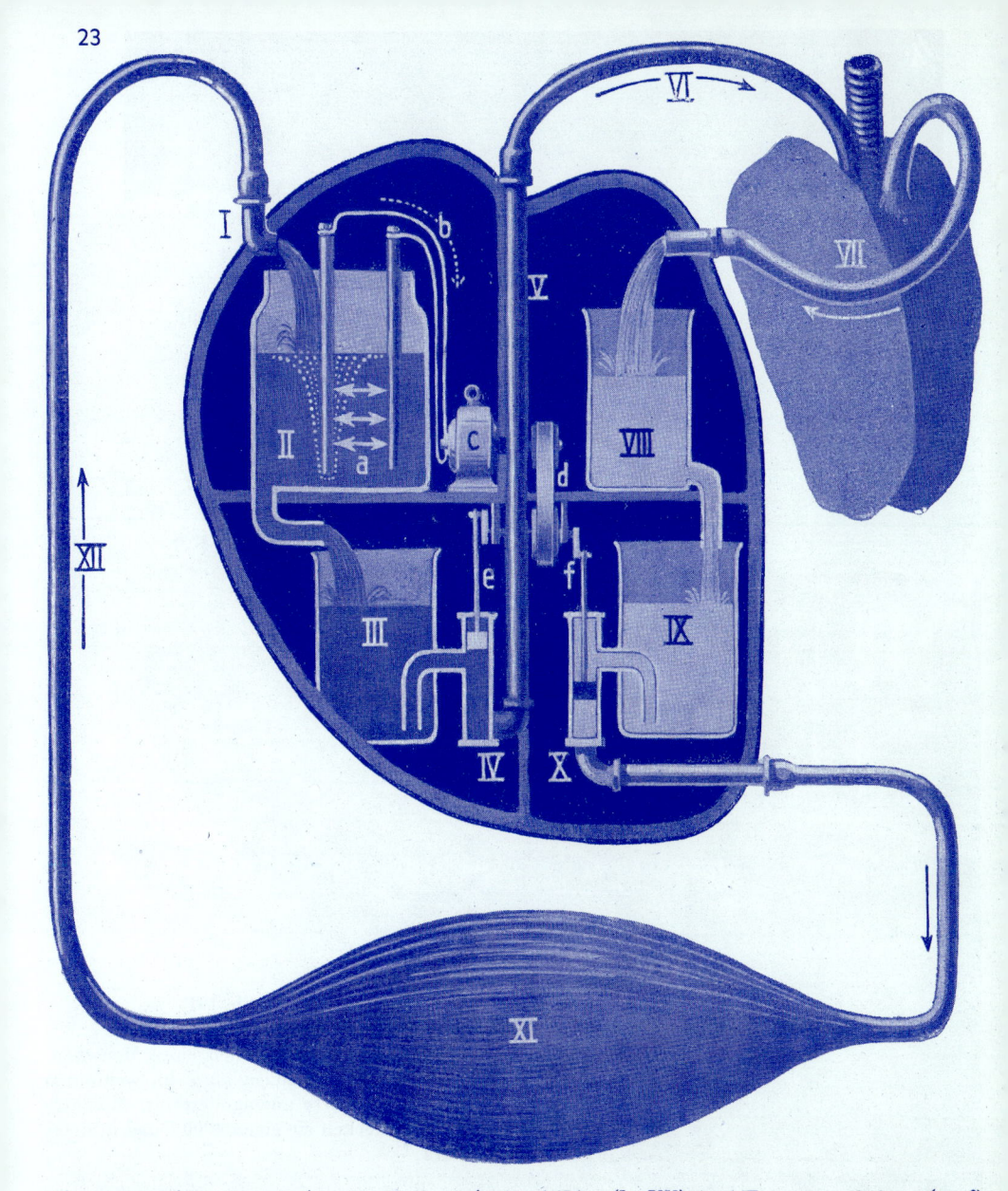

Die automatische Regulation der Herzarbeit durch Blut (I—XII) und Herznervensystem (a—f)

Zum Verständnis des Bildes verfolge man zunächst unter Nicht-Berücksichtigung der Buchstaben den Kreislauf des Blutes an Hand der römischen Zahlen von der Einmündungsstelle der großen Hohlvene I über II rechte Vorkammer, III rechte Kammer, IV, V, VI Lungenader, VII Lunge, VIII linke Vorkammer, IX linke Kammer, X Körperader, XI Blutverteilung im Körper, XII Rückfluß des Blutes durch die Venen zum Herzen. Sodann betrachte man unter Nicht-Beachtung der römischen Zahlen an Hand der Buchstaben den Triebapparat des Herzens, der hier als ein elektro-technisches System dargestellt ist. Das in die rechte Vorkammer einströmende Venenblut erzeugt durch seinen Gehalt an Kohlensäure an den Zink-Kohle-Elektroden einen elektrischen Strom a. Dieser fließt durch die Drähte b in den Elektromotor c, der den Strom in mechanische Bewegung verwandelt und die

24

Abb. 191
Viermal um den Erdball!
reichen die Blutzellen eines Menschenkörpers, 25 Billionen an Zahl, wenn man sie zu einer Kette aneinanderreiht. Mit ihrer Oberfläche bedecken sie einen 4000 Quadratmeter grossen Platz.

Während eines vierwöchigen Aufenthalts im Hochgebirge wird der Kurgast um Billionen reicher — — wenigstens an Blutzellen (Abb. 192).

Da die Blutzelle keinen Kern mehr besitzt und kein Eigenleben führt, sondern ein „toter" Sauerstoffballon ist, hält sie sich nur 20 Tage. In 20 Tagen muss der Körper 25 Billionen Blutzellen neu ersetzen, d. h. in jeder Sekunde mehr als 10 Milliarden. Würden die Blutzellen das Knochenmark wie die Automobile die Fabrik am laufenden Band verlassen,

Der Mechanismus der Bogengangsfunktion

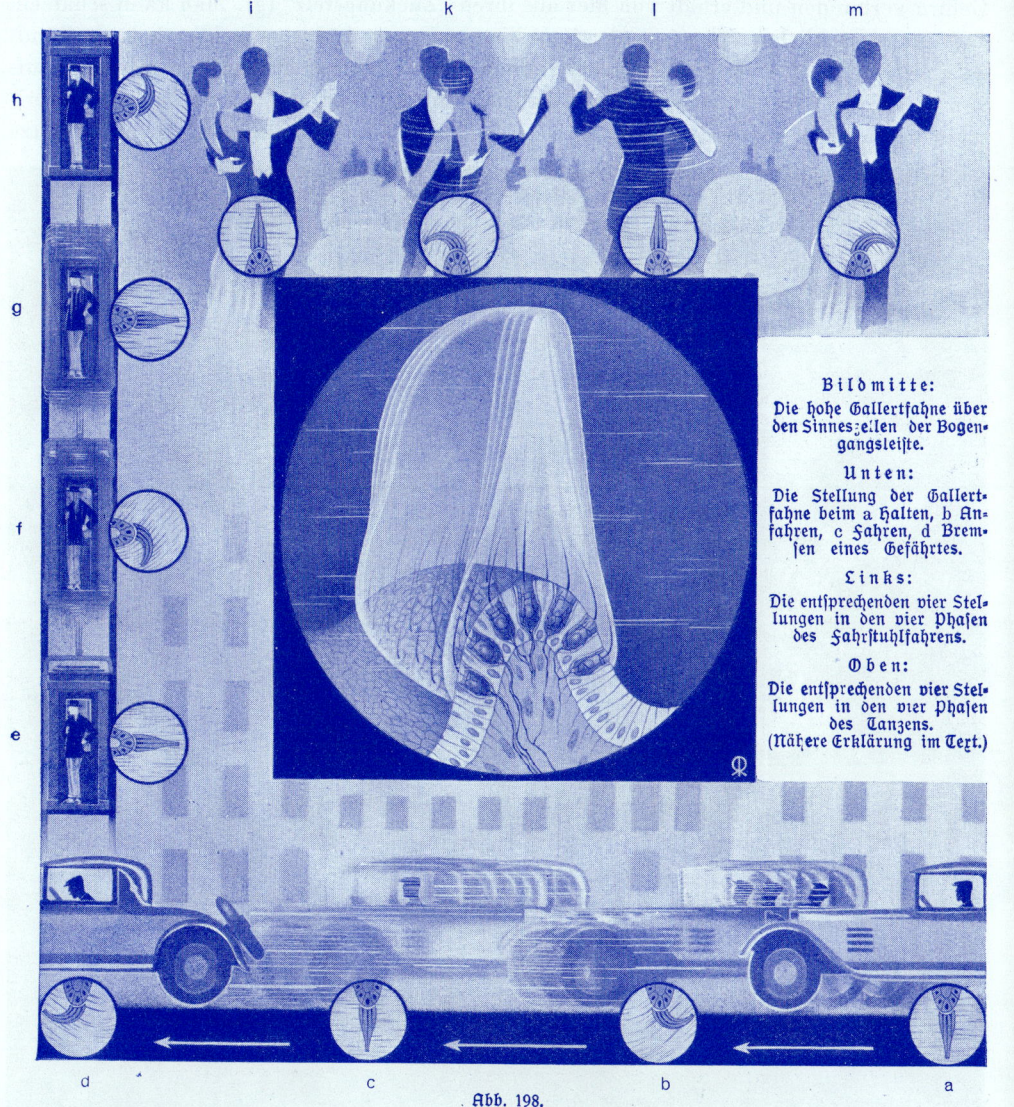

Bildmitte:
Die hohe Gallertfahne über den Sinneszellen der Bogengangsleiste.

Unten:
Die Stellung der Gallertfahne beim a Halten, b Anfahren, c Fahren, d Bremsen eines Gefährtes.

Links:
Die entsprechenden vier Stellungen in den vier Phasen des Fahrstuhlfahrens.

Oben:
Die entsprechenden vier Stellungen in den vier Phasen des Tanzens.
(Nähere Erklärung im Text.)

Abb. 198.

Tintenfisch gleitet von der Glaswand ab, und der Hund kann den Knochen nicht mehr zerbeißen. Raubt man einer Taube ein Labyrinth, so hält sie durch die Ungleichheit der Muskelspannung ihren Kopf schief. Entfernt man beide Labyrinthe, so kann man infolge der Halsmuskelschwäche ihren Kopf durch ein 20 g=Gewicht in jeder beliebigen Lage fixieren (Abb. 197). In Rußland beobachtet man vereinzelt Pferde, die ihren Kopf nicht nach Pferdeart senken, sondern erhoben halten, sogenannte „Sterngucker=Gäule". Wahrscheinlich leiden diese Tiere an einer Abnormität ihres statischen Apparates. Ein Opfer der Labyrinthdegeneration ist die japanische Tanzmaus, die Körperreizungen mit raschen und bis zur Erschöpfung fortgesetzten Kreisbewegungen beantwortet, weil ihr Gleichgewichtsapparat anormal arbeitet; ebenso ist ihr Hörapparat, die Schnecke, sehr oft unent-

Nervenströme sendet. Jede Muskelfaser ist durch einen Leitungsdraht, den Nerven, mit dem Gehirn verbunden und erhält von hier aus ihren „Zuckungsreiz" (g). Man kann schätzen, dass im menschlichen Körper mehrere Millionen Nervendrähte ausschliesslich als Zündleitungen zwischen Gehirn und Muskeln laufen und sich hier in Milliarden von Enden auflösen. Jede Leitung endet an der Muskelfaser mit einer breiten Elektrode, der motorischen Endplatte (Abb. 131, Bildmitte). Die Indianer von Guayana bestreichen die Spitze

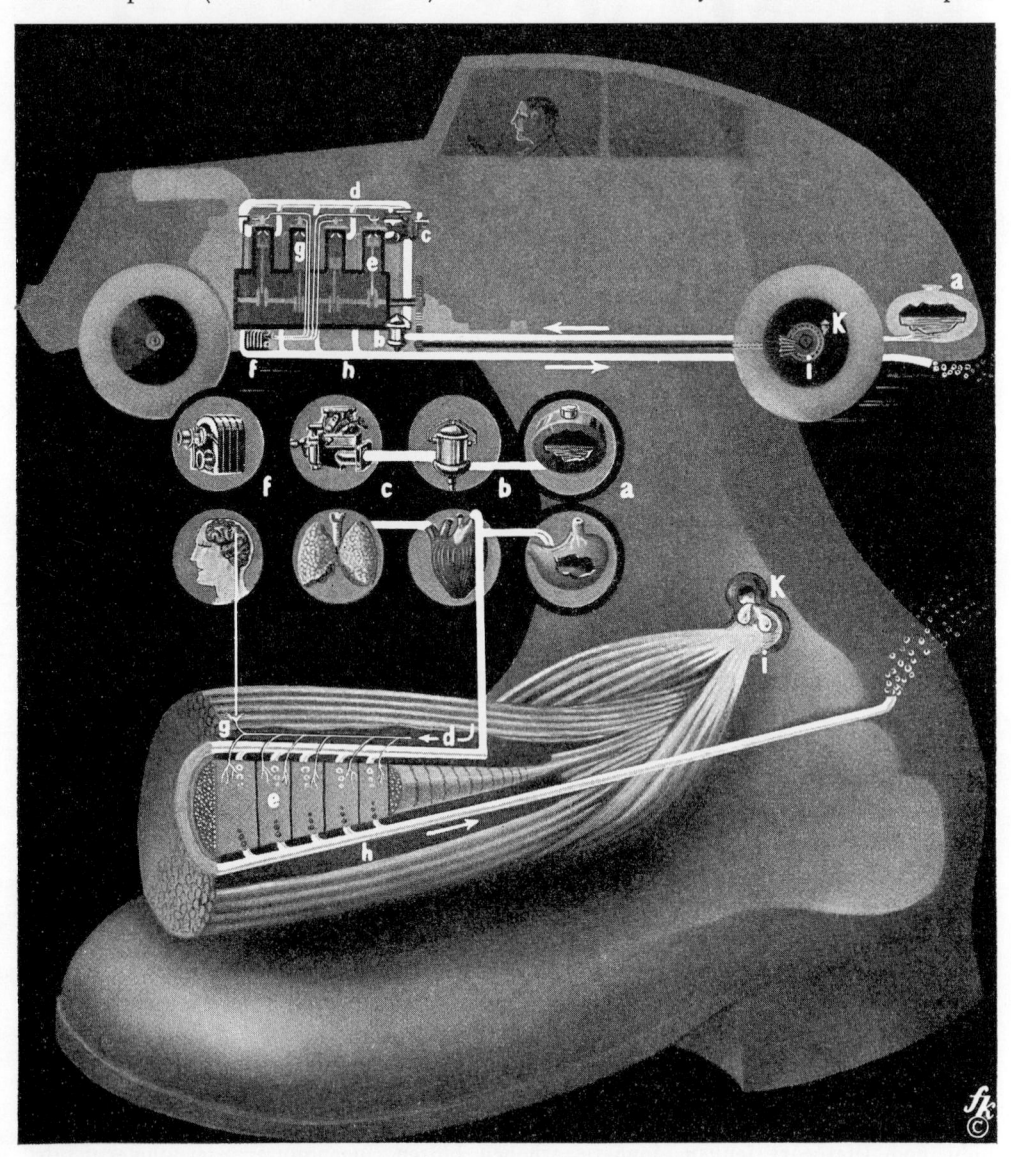

Abb. 130 Muskelfaser und Automotor zeigen weitgehende Aehnlichkeit in der Konstruktion. a) Benzintank und Magen. b) Benzinpumpe und Herz. c) Vergaser und Lunge. d) Saugrohr und Arterie. e) Zylinder und Fibrillenkasten. f) Zündmaschine und Gehirn. g) Zündkerze und motorische Endplatte. h) Auspuffrohr und Vene. i) Radgelenk und Knochengelenk. k) Schmierachse und Schleimbeutel. (Nähere Erklärung im Text.)

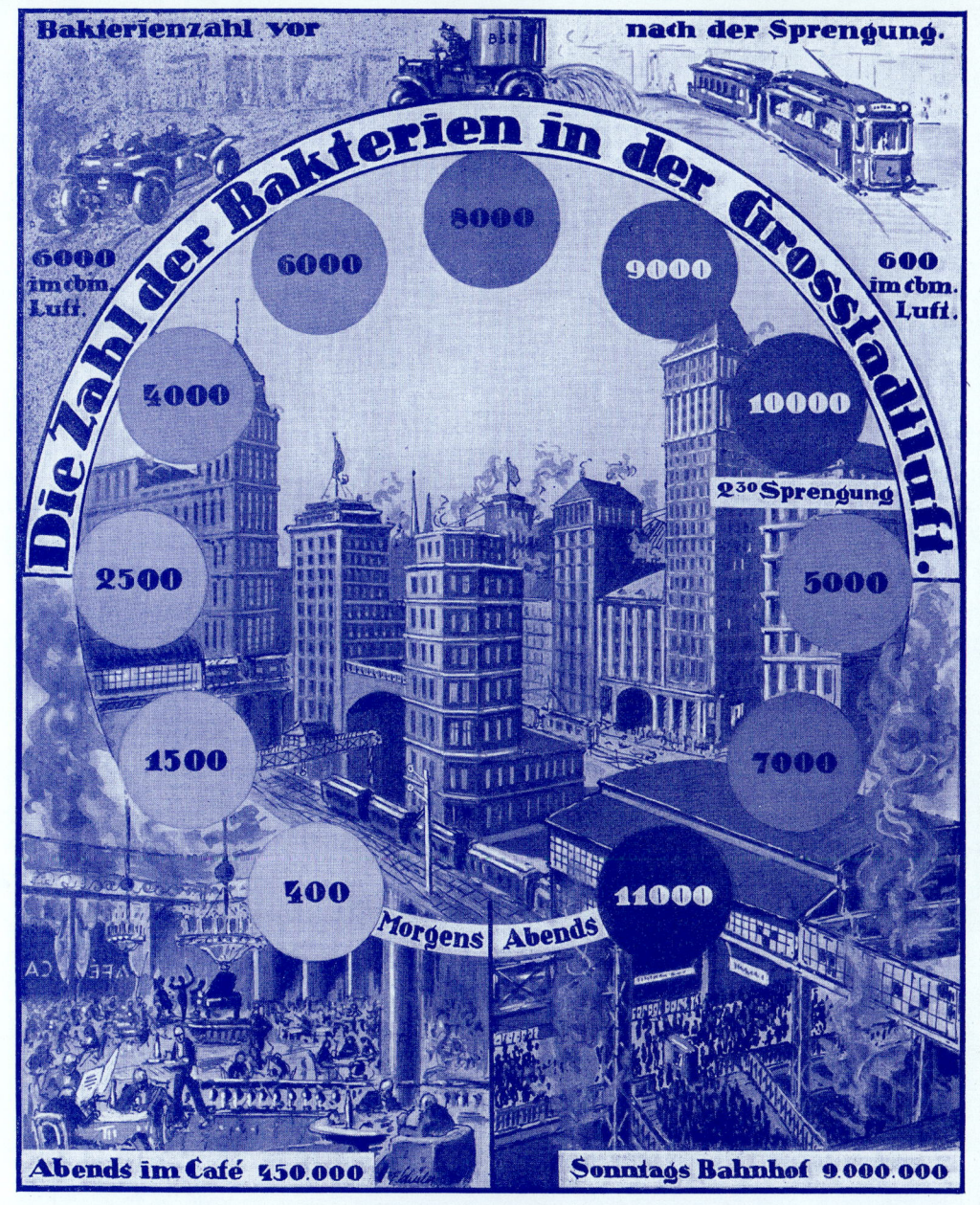

Abb. 50. Die Zahl der Bakterien in der Großstadtluft. Die in Zifferblattform angeordneten Kreise geben die Bakterienzahl im Kubikmeter Luft in den einzelnen Tagesstunden an. Man erkennt die außerordentliche Bedeutung der Straßensprengung für die Entstaubung und Entkeimung der Luft und die gesundheitlichen Gefahren aller großen Menschenanhäufungen.

des Restaurants, und auch hier nur durch solche fast unmittelbaren Verschleppungen, wie sie in Abb. 51 skizziert sind. Die überwiegende Mehrzahl von Krankheitsübertragungen erfolgt durch unmittelbaren Kontakt mit dem Kranken. Dies gilt auch von der Atem- und Lungenkrankheit par excellence, der Tuberkulose. Vereinzelt überall und allzeit,

Die hormonale Schwangerschafts-Bestimmung

die Nacht. Und vielleicht sitzt in einer Weltzentrale eine internationale Kommission von ersten Spezialisten der verschiedenen Fächer und steht den Aerzten in allen Ländern zur Begutachtung besonders wichtiger Krankheitsfälle zur Verfügung, ein medizinischer Weltrat, der die Kenntnisse und Fähigkeiten der besten und erfahrensten Aerzte der ganzen Menschheit dienstbar macht. Die Ferndiagnose wird eine neue Epoche der ärztlichen Arbeitsmethoden herbeiführen.

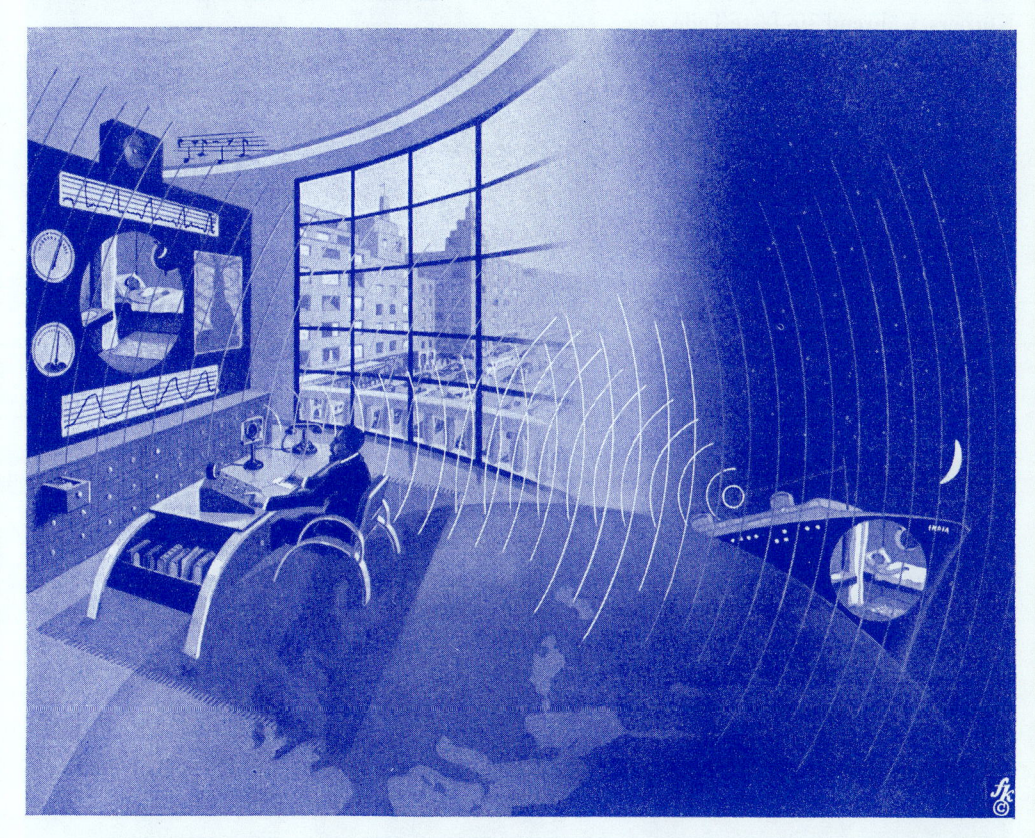

Abb. 175 Der Arzt der Zukunft
berät durch Radio und Fernseher seinen Patienten auf Schiff „India" in der Südsee.

Die Krankheiten des Herzens. Wer Bau und Funktion des Herzens verstanden hat, begreift auch leicht die Krankheiten des Herzens, die auf Abb. 176 halb schematisch zusammengestellt sind. Die Krankheiten des Herzens, von denen die Herzbeutel-Entzündung (a und b) schon beschrieben wurde, gruppieren sich in zwei Klassen: die allgemeinen Krankheiten des Herzens, die in jedem Alter, vor allem aber in der Jugend auftreten, und die spezifischen Alterserkrankungen.

Herzentzündung und Herzklappenfehler. Das Kind ist gegen Bakterien und Bakteriengifte viel empfindlicher als der Erwachsene, denn der Mensch erwirbt erst im Lauf des Lebens durch steten Kampf mit den Bakterien die notwendigen Abwehrkräfte. Dringen bei den Infektionskrankheiten des Kindesalters: Halsentzündung, Diphtherie, Scharlach, Gelenkrheumatismus Bazillen oder Toxine in die Blutbahn, so werden sie auch

dieser Schwingungen übersteigt jedes menschliche Begriffsvermögen: 300 Millionen mal 1 Billion in der Sekunde. Sie breiten sich mit der allgemeinen Aetherbewegungs-Geschwindigkeit von 300 000 km aus. Da sie einige tausend Male kürzer sind als die Lichtwellen, strahlen sie durch die Weichteile des menschlichen Körpers, während sie feste Teile, wie Knochen, Herz, Leber, nicht durchsetzen. Durchleuchtet man den Körper mit Röntgenstrahlen, so entsteht auf einer photographischen Platte hinter dem Körper ein Schattenbild der festen und von den Strahlen nicht durchsetzten Innenteile des Körpers, das Röntgenbild (Abb. 5).

Mit Hilfe der Röntgenstrahlen kann man ohne Oeffnung des Körpers die Knochen, die Gestalt des Herzens, verschluckte Münzen, ein-

Abb. 5 Die Entstehung der Röntgenstrahlen und ein erster Einblick in den Menschenkörper.

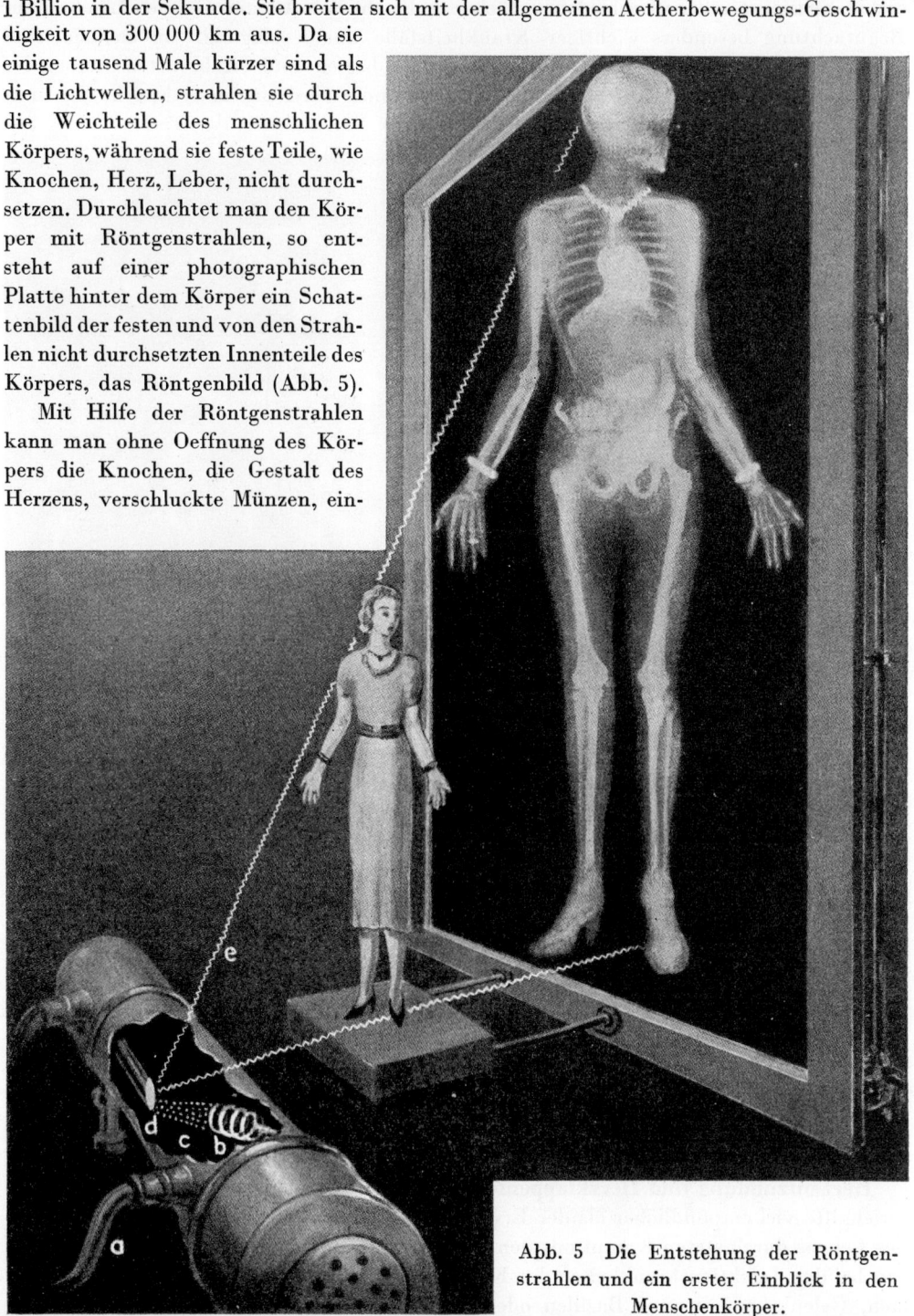

DAS ERSTE ODER PRIMÄR-STADIUM

BEGINN 2 WOCHEN NACH DER ANSTECKUNG

① **DER KUSS** EINER SYPHILITISCHEN FRAU ÜBERTRÄGT

② **SYPHILIS-ERREGER** 500 fache Vergrösserung IN EINEN

③ **HAUTRISS DER LIPPE** HIER ERSCHEINT CA 2 WOCHEN SPÄTER EIN

④ **SYPHILITISCHER PRIMÄR-AFFEKT** ALS HARTES GESCHWÜR

⑤ DURCH DIE **LYMPH-GEFÄSSE** WANDERN DIE ERREGER IN DIE

⑥ **LYMPH-DRÜSEN** (LYMPHDRÜSEN-SCHWELLUNG) UND DRINGEN DURCH DIESE IN DAS

⑦ **BLUT** HIER WIRD DIE SYPHILIS EINE BLUTKRANKHEIT

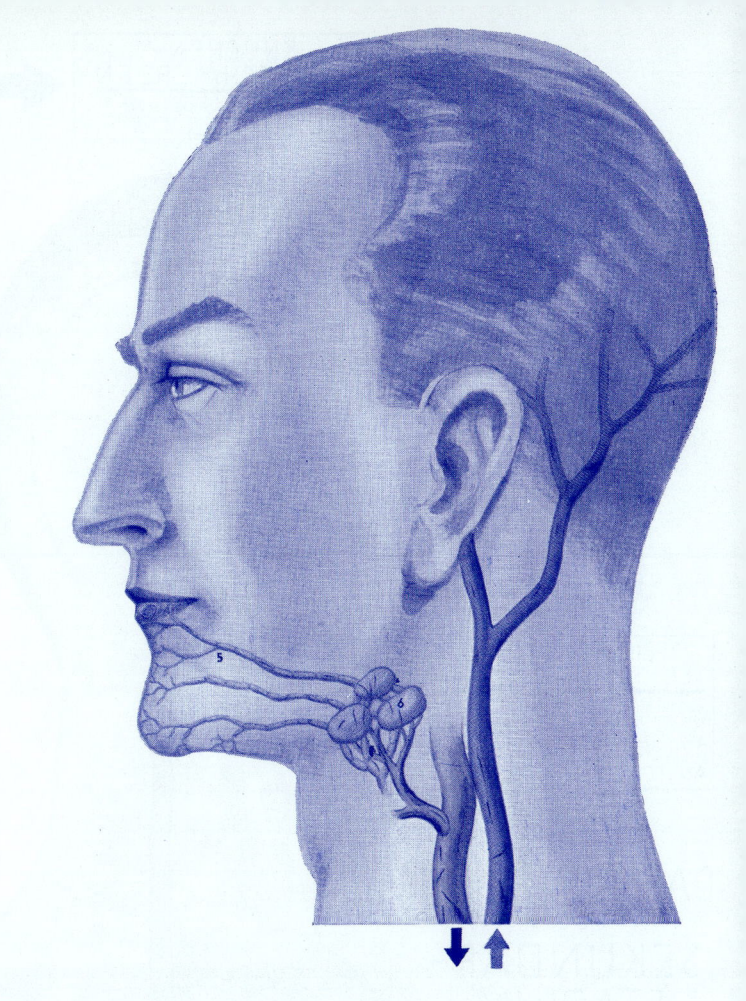

Eine amerikanische Frau

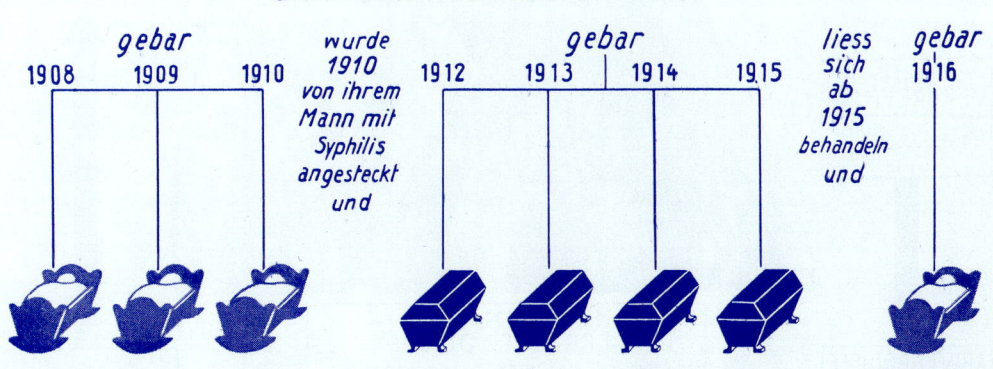

1908	1909	1910	wurde 1910 von ihrem Mann mit Syphilis angesteckt und	1912	1913	1914	1915	liess sich ab 1915 behandeln und	1916
gebar	gebar	gebar		gebar	gebar	gebar	gebar		gebar

je 1 gesundes Kind

je 1 totes Kind u. 1 nach 4 Monaten sterbendes Kind

1 gesundes und gesund gebliebenes Kind.

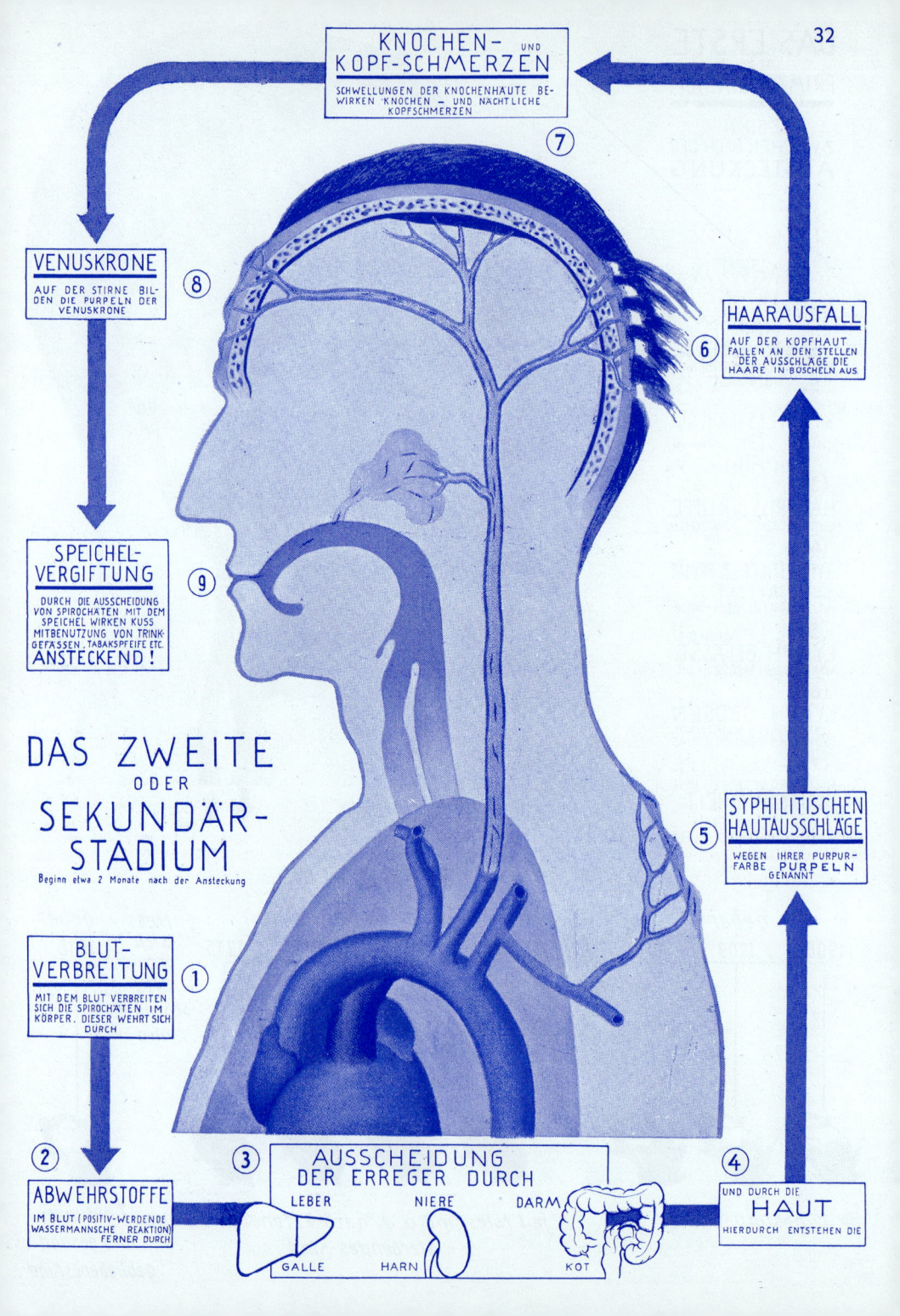

DAS ZWEITE ODER SEKUNDÄRSTADIUM
Beginn etwa 2 Monate nach der Ansteckung

① BLUTVERBREITUNG
MIT DEM BLUT VERBREITEN SICH DIE SPIROCHÄTEN IM KÖRPER. DIESER WEHRT SICH DURCH

② ABWEHRSTOFFE
IM BLUT (POSITIV-WERDENDE WASSERMANNSCHE REAKTION) FERNER DURCH

③ AUSSCHEIDUNG DER ERREGER DURCH
LEBER — NIERE — DARM
GALLE — HARN — KOT

④ UND DURCH DIE HAUT
HIERDURCH ENTSTEHEN DIE

⑤ SYPHILITISCHEN HAUTAUSSCHLÄGE
WEGEN IHRER PURPURFARBE **PURPELN** GENANNT

⑥ HAARAUSFALL
AUF DER KOPFHAUT FALLEN AN DEN STELLEN DER AUSSCHLÄGE DIE HAARE IN BÜSCHELN AUS

⑦ KNOCHEN- UND KOPF-SCHMERZEN
SCHWELLUNGEN DER KNOCHENHÄUTE BEWIRKEN KNOCHEN- UND NÄCHTLICHE KOPFSCHMERZEN

⑧ VENUSKRONE
AUF DER STIRNE BILDEN DIE PURPELN DER VENUSKRONE

⑨ SPEICHELVERGIFTUNG
DURCH DIE AUSSCHEIDUNG VON SPIROCHÄTEN MIT DEM SPEICHEL WIRKEN KUSS MITBENUTZUNG VON TRINKGEFÄSSEN, TABAKSPFEIFE ETC. **ANSTECKEND!**

Image Factories.
Infographics 1920–1945

Fritz Kahn,
Otto Neurath et al.

Edited by Helena Doudova,
Stephanie Jacobs & Patrick Rössler

Spector Books

Table of Contents

Fritz Kahn. Infographics — 1

Introduction — 37

The Age of the Eye—Fritz Kahn and Otto Neurath — 43
Bernd Stiegler

Imagination and (the) Imaginary — 49
Vilém Flusser

Image Factories. Infographic Concepts 1920–1945 — 57
Helena Doudova

Fritz Kahn, Otto Neurath. Infographics — 73

Fritz Kahn—A "Creative Director" of — 105
Artistic-scientific Illustration
Helena Doudova in conversation with Uta von Debschitz

The Isotype Work — 115
Otto Neurath

Isotype after 1945 — 125
Helena Doudova in conversation with Eric Kindel

Gender Relations — 129
Visual essay: Patrick Rössler

Biographies — 137

Otto Neurath. Infographics — 145

37 Introduction

In the course of the nineteenth century, increasingly complex social processes went hand in hand with an explosion in the volume of available information, facilitated by an increase in the speed of data processing. But by the turn of the twentieth century, a new globalized world view was emerging, creating new images and new conduits for information. Whether in the universal language of Esperanto, the art movement of modern primitivism or the pictogram as a building block for a global lingua franca, the complexity of social processes was juxtaposed with a quest for coherent systems and orientation, which also brought about innovation in art and design. The visual cipher—concise in form and colour, easily decodable and independent of language—gained traction, bringing an internationalized world of images in its wake.

The central theme of the exhibition *Image Factories. Infographics 1920–1945: Fritz Kahn, Otto Neurath et al.* is the acceleration in the field of visualization that occurred in the early twentieth century against the backdrop of a flood of information in the expanding media of the time—and two specific answers from the then newly established field of information graphics. Starting from two different traditions, the Austrian economist Otto Neurath, who became museum director in Leipzig in 1918, and the physician Fritz Kahn, who was born in Halle, developed their distinctive visual languages almost simultaneously, in each case based on a formal stylization of the human body. While Neurath's concept of the "Isotype" generated pictogram-like graphics as counting units for the quantification of social realities, Kahn's "Factories of the Human Body" employed mechanistically interpreted diagrams in which the human being was depicted as an "Industrial Palace" (the title of his most famous diagram).

This research and exhibition project on the history of information graphics therefore started from striking contrasts: on the one hand the operating principle of our body, illustrated in the detailed and evocative charts of Fritz Kahn's books, and on the other hand the functions of our global social order, as exemplified in Otto Neurath's Vienna Method of Visual Statistics. Both approaches to popular information graphics were developed in the 1920s, and both were intended to be understood across the globe within the context of a universal visual language. And yet there is a fundamental difference between the pictorial world of the human being as Kahn's "industrial palace" and this visual world as a unit of measurement in Neurath's early pictograms. With their various collaborators and illustrators, Kahn and Neurath defined positions that shape our visual socialization to this day. The exhibition itself and this publication are the first to make a comprehensive connection between these two different approaches.

The pictorial worlds open a new perspective on the human being—the human as an element of social organisms but at the same time the human as a cluster of biological processes. Both at the macro level (how does human coexistence work on a societal level?) and at the micro level (how does the human body with its individual organs work?) the general public has a growing need for information. Taken together, these pictorial worlds mark two alternative approaches to the visualization of scientific-statistical insights and thus each represents a contribution to the iconic turn of that era, with their pronounced interest in the internationalization of science and ways of imparting knowledge. In the context of the New Objectivity and the Bauhaus, a new "iconic" representation of the human being was created. The popular infographic—which was to become remarkably fashionable upon its rediscovery a hundred years later—was born.

In the ensuing period, both visual approaches became an international success story that continues to this day. The global appeal of Kahn's pictorial worlds, as well as that of the Isotype, can be attributed partly to the protagonists' own life stories and partly to the universality of their respective visual languages in different cultural contexts.

The careers of Otto Neurath and Fritz Kahn, both persecuted by the National Socialists because they were Jewish, were frequently interrupted owing to long periods in exile, as well as changes of professional direction. Throughout his life, Otto Neurath pursued his political vision of a new egalitarian world community, which he sought to promote by developing a universally comprehensible depiction of information. Having faced massive political persecution three times in his life, Neurath worked towards his International System of Typographic Picture Education (abbreviated as Isotype) in Austria, the Netherlands, and Britain, as his book *International Picture Language* (1936) demonstrates. As a standard work of reference for the idea of language-independent pictograms it retains its relevance to this day; to promote this idea, Neurath established the International Foundation for Visual Education as early as 1932, and directed the Museum for Social and Economic Affairs in Vienna, with satellites in Moscow, Prague, Amsterdam, and New York. Fritz Kahn, on emigrating from Germany, went first to Israel, then via Paris and Bordeaux, Spain, and Portugal to the USA, finally returning to Switzerland. Throughout this long exile he worked on his iconographic system, developing copyrighted visual metaphors that could be understood across cultures. The homunculi in his drawings illustrate the processes inside the human body in anthropomorphic form, and can therefore be regarded as avatars *avant la lettre*.

Neurath's motto "Words divide, pictures unite" condenses the particular international appeal of both concepts. Their simplified graphical representations have been especially recognized for their potential benefits in the instruction of less well-educated adults, as well as in schools and in furthering transnational communication. This is evidenced in various fields of application, from children's books to information campaigns in Nigeria, which have already been discussed in earlier publications and exhibitions. Fritz Kahn's body worlds succeeded in illuminating the basis of our existence in all nations and cultures—the human body—through visual metaphors in such a way that their operating principle was understood independently of culture. The exhibition "Fritz Kahn—Man Machine" in the Berlin Museum of Medical History (2010) presented the illustrations in the context of scientific specimens, which are used for educational purposes all over the world, and emphasized Kahn's principle of blending instruction, edification, and entertainment.

The "Image Factories" project examines how both bodies of work exist in harmony. They represent early educational attempts to produce material in an interculturally comprehensible and thus globally applicable form through visual condensation, in the face of the increasing complexity of information. But the dark side of this education impetus was that these simplifications of complex issues through memorable images and graphical abbreviations always ran the risk of stereotyping; they thus remain firmly of their time. This is another focus of the exhibition and this publication.

In the "century of the image," these pioneers—who are not known ever to have met—developed proposals for stemming the overwhelming tide of information at the beginning of the twentieth century. One hundred years later the diffusion of new information technologies (Internet, social media etc.) has turned this tide into a veritable flood. To this extent, critical engagement with Neurath's and Kahn's historical positions can also contribute to the current discussion about a new information economy.

Today this juxtaposition of the similarities and differences between micro and macro perspectives on the human being seems less nation-specific than ever but reflects global trends. It is, therefore, a stroke of luck that the project received a major funding contribution through the International Museum Fellowship program of the German Federal Cultural Foundation. With the help of this program, we were able to recruit Helena Doudova, an outstanding young academic and curator. She previously worked at the Museum of Books and Writing at the German National Library, where she could gain a deep insight into the structures and processes of a large cultural institution while also introducing new methods and an international perspective to the museum's collections. It is for this reason that our first thanks go to the

Federal Cultural Foundation, specifically to Marie Haff, for her trust and competent support of our project—and, of course, to "our" Fellow Helena Doudova for her months of intensive and profound research on the topic, numerous research trips, her work on the implementation of the exhibition and publication—and especially for always skilfully managing to maintain a balance between the possible and the feasible. Without her, neither this book nor the presentation at the Museum of Books and Writing on which it is based would have come into being. A central mission of this museum is the scholarly processing of its inventory and the cross-linking of its collections of historical media, assembled over more than 130 years, with today's academic and cultural discourse. We would also like to thank Julia Rinck for her overall coordination of the project, Barbara Schinko for supervising all conservation aspects with regard to the exhibits, Reinhard Meerwein and his collaborators from Tecton Berlin for the exhibition design, and above all the team at Spector Books—Jan Wenzel and Anne König, and especially Kay Bachmann for the layout of this publication: as the subject matter deals with the history of design this is of particular importance. Thanks also to the Friends of the German National Library for their generous support of this publication.

    We would like to express our sincere gratitude to lenders from all over the world: the Otto and Marie Neurath Isotype Collection at the University of Reading (Department of Typography and Graphic Communication) and the Austrian Museum of Society and Economy, Mr. Gerhard Halusa (Vienna), as well as the Arthur and Fritz Kahn Collection at the Leo Baeck Institute (New York) and the Zurich Central Library, which holds the estate of Fritz Kahn as part of the estate of Walter Robert Corti in its manuscript collection. Special thanks are due to Uta and Thilo von Debschitz (Berlin/Wiesbaden), who have been committed to commemorating Fritz Kahn and his work for many years. Their support, in the form of material and research, has been invaluable to the project from the start. For the presentation of the work of Otto Neurath, the contact with Eric Kindel, curator of the Otto and Marie Neurath Collection in Reading, and Laura Weill, the Collections Administration Assistant, as well as with Christopher Burke, expert in the graphic design of Otto Neurath and beyond, has been of vital importance; they made it possible for us to exhibit documents that are rarely seen. Furthermore, we thank Dror Kahn, the grandson of Fritz Kahn, for his willingness to take part in an interview in New York, which can be seen in the exhibition as well. We also thank the curator and architectural theorist Nader Vossoughian, who pointed us toward new associations and shared his experience with Neurath's body of work in another interview; also Günther Rechn and Wolfgang Trester for providing us with portrait photos of Roman Rechn and Ottomar Trester, two illustrators who worked for Kahn, and the Berlin State Archive, which contributed the portrait photo of

Fritz Schüler. We were further supported by Michael Simonson, archivist at the Leo Baeck Archive, New York; Philipp Paulsen from the German University in Cairo with information about the German Museum of Wartime Economy in Leipzig; and Henning Lederer, who allowed us to use his wonderful animation of Kahn's "Man as Industrial Palace." Finally, we would like to thank the University of Erfurt for its administrative support throughout the duration of the project—and for its readiness to assist this unconventional undertaking with practical involvement that was always prompt and flexible.

Collective projects such as this one hold promise for future collaboration between museums and universities, for the interlinking of conservation and research interests. Third-party funding has enabled the project to open up a fresh perspective on historical material.

Stephanie Jacobs & Patrick Rössler
September 2017

43 The Age of the Eye —Fritz Kahn and Otto Neurath

Bernd Stiegler

In 1930, Otto Neurath surmised, not without good reason, that "one day our age may well be called the Age of the Eye."[1] And it did not take decades for this to happen; the age he was talking about was already constantly describing itself as a visual, optical, and pictorial age. It wasn't so much the human being but above all the eye that was continually on the go, that was confronted with the demands of life in a modern metropolis and the realm of acceleration and speed, that transformed itself, last but not least, into the technical eye of photography and film. All the talk was of the "photo eye" (Roh and Tschichold) or the "cinema eye" (Vertov), but what was really meant was that the technical apparatus would replace the human eye, in order to be able to focus on it and to change it, to regenerate and to train it.

László Moholy-Nagy summarized this adventurous life of the eye in the modern age in a striking image: "Example: you are traveling by tram and look out of a window. A car is following. The car's windows are also transparent. Through them, you can see a shop, which again has transparent windows. In it, there are people, buyers, and sellers. Another person opens the door. Pedestrians walk past. The traffic policeman stops a cyclist. All of this is registered in a single instant because the window panes are transparent and everything happens in the line of sight."[2]

Writing this text in German, the author deliberately dispensed with the obligatory capitalization of nouns in order to make perception easier for the eye; this shows how much he cared about it. In the Age of the Eye, everyday life was no placid comfort zone, but a hotbed of challenges and shifting impressions.

The acceleration of technology and media went hand in hand with social acceleration, and the volatility of impressions was matched by the volatility of societal bonds. As an astute observer of his time, Robert Musil noted that images materialize at the moment when the bond vanishes. In the interwar period images paradoxically become a catalyst for acceleration and deceleration, for disintegration

[1] Otto Neurath, "Das Sachbild," in *Die Form*, 5(2), 1930, pp. 29–36, and 6(6), 1931, pp. 219–25, here pp. 153–71, 154.
[2] László Moholy-Nagy, "fotografie ist lichtgestaltung" [Photography is designing with light], in Krisztina Passuth, *Moholy-Nagy* (Weingarten, 1986), pp. 319–22.

and bonding, all at the same time. On the one hand, it is precisely the frames of film, but also of illustrated magazines and books, that embraced rhythm, acceleration, and stimulation, pushing them to their limits through editing and montage. On the other hand, the realm of technical images is described as a neutral training ground, where the daily routine of acceleration could be explored without risk of death. It is self-evident that this sensory training would be linked to explicit programs and content. If the eye had to be instructed in the new and different ways it needed to see in *Modern Times*, it was, above all, images that were to take on this task.

Fritz Kahn and Otto Neurath each tried, individually and in his own way, to shape the Age of the Eye—and both succeeded in a different way. While Kahn was above all trying to create a "total artwork," as he called the monumental five-volume project *The Life of Man*, Neurath was concerned with the systematic organization of a new, universally comprehensible visual language and, beyond that, a new society.[3] And while Kahn explored the human body concurrently as a wonderland and an industrial palace, Neurath wanted to set about "systematically framing the entire order of life" with the help of his images.[4] One looked at the human body in order to discover inside an authentic social and even industrial order, while the other emphasized the formation of a new social body which would have to be constructed purposefully. Yet the National Socialist rhetoric of the "national body" was alien to both of them. For Kahn, as for Neurath, construction and technology rule, and their images are also constructed purposefully and systematically. Kahn is primarily looking for pictorial metaphors—in particular, visual descriptions of physiological processes which he draws from modern life, whereas Neurath seeks a new visual language that can be applied universally and internationally. Their respective visual logic is thus different: the illustrations in Kahn's *magnum opus* are often reminiscent of the cross-sections of tenement houses which were common in nineteenth-century journals, with the difference that it is not social classes that are depicted, but the divided responsibilities within the process. We have arrived right inside industrialized modernity. Humans should realize, in other words, that they have long been functioning just like a machine, unwittingly and in all likelihood inadvertently. This is demonstrated to them in pictures which show bodily processes comic-like as stories of modern life.

In a short text published in 1926 in the popular daily *Berliner Illustrirte Zeitung*, Kahn outlined the agenda of the "Book of Man," as he called it.[5] Right at the beginning, a quote from world champion boxer Gene Tunney supplies

---

3   Fritz Kahn, *Das Leben des Menschen. Eine volkstümliche Anatomie, Biologie, Physiologie und Entwicklungsgeschichte des Menschen* [The Life of Man. A popular anatomy, biology, physiology and biogenesis], vol. I (Stuttgart, 1926), p. 1 (Foreword).

4   Otto Neurath, *Gesellschaft und Wirtschaft* [Society and Economy], Bildstatistisches Mappenwerk des Gesellschafts- und Wirtschaftsmuseums in Wien (Leipzig, 1930), p. 144.

5   Fritz Kahn, "Es ist ein Wunder, daß wir länger als zwei Minuten leben. Der Mensch—die komplizierteste Maschine!" [It's a miracle that we survive longer than two minutes. Man—the most complex of all machines!], in *Berliner Illustrirte Zeitung*, October 31, 1926, pp. 1467f.; also in Thilo von Debschitz, *Fritz Kahn. Man Machine* (Vienna/New York, 2009), pp. 345f.

the metaphor: "The human body is the most powerful and at the same time the most resistant machine that can be imagined."[6] The human is thus by no means inferior to technology, but its extraordinary organic fundamental principles can only be described through metaphors if its formidable performance is to become at all clear. Yet this talk of performance also underlines that the real subject here is work. Work is the basis on which the comparison between the body and the machine is made. Kahn demonstrates that the organism is constantly working, even when people are not aware of it: the body is work and when we look inside it, we behold the modern world with its rules, its regulations and, its achievements. But this world is ultimately nothing but an image that makes it possible to capture the wonder of the human body in the first place. According to Kahn, the world itself is "unrecognizable"; we see "only the image of the world and the concept the human mind has of the world, but never the world itself."[7] The body is a projection of modern industrial society, for which, however, the same is true in turn. Kahn's descent into the human body is reminiscent of Jules Verne's *Journey to the Center of the Earth*, which does not lead to pulsating magma nor to the metal at the earth's core, but to the earliest history of humankind, except that we now remain squarely in the present. The impressive host of images weaves a dense web of comparisons that for the most part refer to industrialized modernity: bodily functions are switchboards in the process of functional differentiation and the division of labor in the industrial age. While the primordial sea still lurks in the depths of the body, it has long been technically tamed. "In the human body the salty torrent murmurs on, that once surged all around it," but it has been channeled, organized, and harnessed, not least in the pictures.[8] And these pictures reveal a body and a society, no matter which human being has been chosen as an example. Each body corresponds to the modern world. The diagram "Man as Industrial Palace: Attempts at a Technical Representation of the Most Important Life Processes," which was appended to the work and was also sold on its own, is a wonderful showcase of the metaphor made manifest in the image.

    We are not contemplating a factory floor here, but a palace, which for all its rationality elicits wonderment and presents the cells of the various workshops room by room. The explanatory text accompanying a folded chart opens with an explanation of the special form of visualization: "Since most life processes are chemical processes of invisible character, they can't be illustrated directly. For this reason, there may well be numerous depictions of the anatomical structure of the human body, but no pictorial representation of the life processes within. The chart "Man as Industrial Palace" is an attempt to portray the most important life processes—which as stated above can never be observed—in the form of familiar

---

[6] von Debschitz, *Fritz Kahn*, op. cit., p. 345.
[7] Fritz Kahn, *Das Leben des Menschen* [The Life of Man], vol. I, pp. 124 and 129.
[8] Ibid., pp. 45f.

technical processes, in order to produce an overall picture of the inner life of the human body." Architectural metaphors hold sway and the body is technically reconstructed as a universal industrial plant: Kahn speaks of floors and headquarters, of departments and gateways. Reason is the "supervisory board," volition is "a kind of directorate," the mind is the "factory manager." In line with the theory of organ projection, the sensory organs correspond to technical apparatus such as radio and camera.

Neurath, who was close philosophically to the Vienna Circle but politically to Marxism, would probably not have been unfamiliar with a constructivist approach such as Kahn's. But he perceives it in a completely different way; he does not assign the construction a descriptive function but one of politics and pedagogy. His new visual language, which he first called the "Viennese Method of Image Statistics" (1926), and later Isotype (1935), reacts to the much-invoked economy of attention and attempts to make complex social contexts visually representable and easy to understand, while at the same time taking account of the exigencies of the technical age. He suggested that in view of a mechanized modernity a "Renaissance of the hieroglyphs"[9] could be observed, i.e. a return of pictorial language. If the resource of attention was growing ever scarcer and the pace of life kept accelerating, this language would be able to educate and inform much more quickly than conventional writing systems. It should, therefore, be consciously utilized and marshaled in the sense of a new literacy campaign. For this purpose, a "pictorial pedagogy"[10] was to be developed, intended to illustrate complex social processes and simultaneously be comprehensible as an international language beyond boundaries of class and countries. "Words divide, images connect"[11] is a recurring formula of Neurath, used to summarize the mission of pictorial pedagogics in the technical age. What he was aiming for was nothing less than a literacy campaign for the political education of humankind as a whole: "Visual statistics don't just concern schools but beyond that the education of all of humankind."[12] Neurath's campaign for the promotion of literacy was understood as political education and pedagogical instruction. The images become elementary symbols that were able to represent facts and processes and at the same time guide humankind out of the Gutenberg galaxy into the realm of technology. The visions of technology doubled up as social utopias.

Children were expected to learn this new visual writing system at a young age and thus understand the new order of the world. They were meant to cut out shapes and to understand them, in a very concrete and practical way, as ciphers of the world. They had to enter the flat new world and master it technically. They were to sit at the drawing board and cut out shapes of the present and of

---

9 Otto Neurath, "Bildstatistik nach Wiener Methode" [Visual statistics according to the Viennese Method], in *Die Volksschule*, 27(12), 1931, pp. 569–79, in Neurath, *Gesammelte bildpädagogische Schriften* (Rudolf Haller and Robin Kinross, eds) (Vienna, 1991), pp. 180–91; this metaphor is found in many of Neurath's texts. Cf. e.g. ibid., pp. 192 and 197.
10 Ibid., p. 189.
11 Ibid., p. 190. This phrase can also be found on pp. 205 and 208. It is one of the constants in Neurath's theory.
12 Neurath, "Bildstatistik nach Wiener Methode," p. 191.

the future. For this purpose, Neurath developed a new type of children's book which was meant to implement visual literacy in a very concrete manner.[13] Neurath's texts were printed in a wide range of publications ranging from specialist philosophical journals, to journals of the avant-garde and gazettes of the city of Vienna, to educational writing. The intention, however, remained the same: a new visual language for a new era, which at the same time was understood as political education.

In Kahn's work, the body was transformed into an industrial palace, in order to depict the social body with a single stroke. For Neurath, society becomes a "giant enterprise," which contains the body of the individual:[14] "Is it not as if a new spirit had entered the technicians who with ever-growing urgency demanded uniformity, standardization, specialization, who demanded ever more urgently that the work, the factory, basically all that can be technically mastered be designed according to general principles, should be organized as efficiently as possible, as rationally as possible?"[15] This system of industrial standardization then forms the basis of the new society along with the prerequisite "statistical hieroglyphs" to which Neurath devotes an entire chapter.[16] The "education through the eye"[17] is also "social enlightenment" and "it is primarily museums and exhibitions, pictures and films that are suitable in the century of the eye" when one considers the scope of their application.[18] The proximity of perception and experience thus plays a decisive role in the new visual writing system.

Otto Neurath often mentions that it is his intention to bring Comenius's *Orbis Pictus* from 1658 into the present.[19] The visible world in pictures—that is his mission. He is concerned with the facts—and as social reality, these are to be captured mainly in statistical terms. Facts are of a general rather than a specific nature. And as such, they are objects of general societal interest. This is social technology à la Neurath: the proliferation of visual literacy in the age of technical constructability. It is also Neurath's understanding of constructivism: "Authentic pictorial writing recognizes a sword and a table but not being."[20] In his view social existence can only be mediated via statistics, via forms of "sociological graphics,"[21] which for their own part convey certain facts about society. It is an example of visual, political, and social construction; in other words, of social technology. Political-social existence determines the visual-statistical consciousness. And both are subject to political change. So are pictures—and what is more, they are a means of social transformation. This is Neurath's model for spreading visual literacy in the technical age.

---

13 C.f. Neurath, "Die bunte Welt. Mengenbilder für die Jugend" [The multicolored world. Quantitative images for young people] (Vienna, 1929).
14 "Soziale Aufklärung nach Wiener Methode" [Social education according to the Viennese Method], in *Mitteilungen der Gemeinde Wien*, No. 100, 1933, pp. 25–33, in *Gesammelte bildpädagogische Schriften*, op. cit., pp. 231–39, p. 236.
15 Ibid., p. 239.
16 Ibid., pp. 295–301.
17 Neurath, "Internationale Bildsprache" [International Picture Language] (London, 1936), in *Gesammelte bildpädagogische Schriften*, op. cit., pp. 355–98, p. 361.
18 "Soziale Aufklärung nach Wiener Methode," op. cit., p. 234.
19 Cf. e.g. Neurath, *Gesellschaft und Wirtschaft*, op. cit., where he speaks of the "beginning of a new '*Orbis Pictus*'."
20 Ibid., p. 269.
21 "Das Sachbild," op. cit., p. 159.

49 Imagination and (the) Imaginary

Vilém Flusser

An inaugural lecture for the Theo Gerber exhibition on June 3, 1977, at Galerie Influx, Marseille

Editor's note:
The following, hitherto unpublished lecture was originally written in German, and the manuscript was discovered in the Flusser Archive at the University of the Arts Berlin by Helena Doudova, the co-editor of the present volume. In our opinion, Flusser's reflections on the relationship between reality and its visual representation lend a new perspective to the positions of Otto Neurath and Fritz Kahn. Flusser's particular linguistic style, which can also be explained by the time when this text was written, has only been slightly smoothed out with respect to grammar and orthography. However, in order to adapt Flusser's argument for our context, some minor changes had to be made to the original; these have been indicated as appropriate in the footnotes. In particular, whenever Flusser, in the context of his lecture, speaks of the "images surrounding us", the expression has been substituted "exhibited images". We thank Miguel Flusser for giving his permission to publish this text here for the first time.

The exhibited images challenge our imagination and in doing so call into question our ability to imagine. That is, into a question which is also raised in other contexts. For example, it is the question raised in May 1968 by the call "All power to the imagination!" and that emerges again and again when there is talk about the world becoming less and less imaginable. The question is: "What conditions are necessary to provoke images in us, and how do these images operate?"[1] The call of May 1968 raises this question because it implies that the current rulers are incapable of creating for themselves images of the given situation, and therefore of other possible situations. The claim that the

---

1 The source text includes an additional reference to the works of Theo Gerber which is irrelevant to us here: "The paintings surrounding us here pose this question, because they are neither figurative (offering images), nor abstract (prohibiting the making of images), but because they offer themselves to the making of images by the observer."

world is getting less and less imaginable raises this question because it claims that scientific discourse, technological progress, social change etc. no longer allow for the creation of images of the world that had previously been possible. If we consider these three questions, we realize that all three affirm imagination: the exhibited images want to provoke it, the 1968 call wants to install it, and the claim of the advancing unimaginability of the world mourns this circumstance. This is surprising because the concept of "the imaginary" actually has a pejorative connotation, namely that of the unreal, and the concept of the imagination is related to the concept of madness. Strictly speaking, therefore, it is unreality and madness that are in question in our current surroundings, and it is to this that I want to direct your attention.

It goes without saying that the question can be avoided if we claim that images function dialectically: they bring forth reality (they "mediate"), yet they also obscure the real (they "alienate"). We can use them like maps to orient ourselves in reality, or lose ourselves in them as in Hollywood movies. And we can say that the exhibited images, just like the call of 1968 and the claim that the world is unimaginable, affirm not the alienating but the mediating aspect of the imaginary—namely that here, imagination is not regarded as a symptom of the loss of reality, but its opposite: as the ability to capture the real. What we seem to be dealing with is therefore not a romantic approval of imagination as madness, but the advocacy of imagination as de-alienation. But such an evasion of the question is insufficient, because the question is not only how the imaginary world operates, but also, and above all, what conditions are necessary to create an imaginary world. The question here is not only how maps, films, and paintings function, but above all how the position from which maps, films, and paintings can be produced is reached—that is, the position outside and opposite reality, from which imagination takes place. Despite all attempts at evasion, it is unreality and madness, namely "existence" in the literal sense of "standing outside of," that are being called into question.

If we formulate the question of imagination as one of a standpoint toward the world, we realize that we are dealing with a question of distance. In order to be able to make an image of something, one has to be able to step back from that something. Yet if one steps back too far, one loses sight of it and making an image is just as impossible as when one stands too close. Hence we could attempt the following answer to the question raised here: "In order to be able to imagine, one has to have established an optimal distance from the world, neither too small nor too great. And from this distance images can be made, which either remediate or obscure the world left behind." On the basis of such a tentative answer we could come to the following diagnosis: we are in danger of becoming so mad that we are no longer able to imagine anything. This is what the claim that the world had become unimaginable was mourning, which was precisely what the call of 1968 was in revolt against.[2] In other words, we are in danger of becoming so mad that we are unable to imagine anything, let alone grasp reality.[3]

Such a diagnosis, however, cannot be regarded as satisfying. On the one hand, a superficial view of our surroundings proves that, as never before, we have we dived into an imaginary world, a world of billboards, magazines, TV programs, and shop window displays, so that there can be no truth in the claim that we are incapable of having images. Hence it's not that we have distanced ourselves too far from the world, but our images, maps, films, and paintings have become too numerous and too good to be truly perceived. The imaginary world has been so well perfected that every other world, the "real" one for example, becomes obsolete: this imaginary world itself has become "real". On the other hand, some of us still have enough distance from this imaginary world to realize that it is "imaginary" after all.

What we realize is that the world surrounding us is imaginary not because we compare it with a real one, but because we know how and why it is made. We "demythify" the imaginary world not by recourse to an underlying reality, but by recourse to an overlying intention. The provisional diagnosis, according to which our weakening imagination can be traced back to being too distant from the real world, therefore cannot really be upheld. And yet it cannot be denied that the provisional response to the question raised here is moving in the right direction, namely that of increasing distance. It just has to be rephrased.

To imagine means to see something with the "inner" eye, to create an image of it. The image created in this way then presents the seen; it represents and symbolizes it. Thus to imagine means to symbolize, according to a specific, two-dimensional code. The symbols of imagination are two-dimensional because they are visual. What happens during imagination can be described roughly as follows: one steps back from something, creates a "mental" image of it (reducing it to two dimensions), and then allows for this reduction to take the place of what was originally left behind. This mental two-dimensional symbol can be projected back as map, painting, photograph, or geometrical model, etc., in turn materializing the imaginary world. The advantage of this world is that it reduces the four-dimensional world and hence facilitates orientation. The disadvantage is that the imaginary world is poorer than the one it symbolizes, and that it brings with it the risk of obscuring the symbolized world rather than signifying it. We can currently assess these advantages and disadvantages because we are in an imaginary world that is becoming ever more compact and perfect.

2 The source text includes an additional reference to the works of Theo Gerber which is irrelevant to us: "( ) and against which Gerber positions the paintings surrounding us."

3 The source text includes an additional reference to the works of Theo Gerber which is irrelevant to us: "It is in light of this danger that Gerber paints: he doesn't try to lead us back to reality, but to a position from which we can imagine something again."

Imagination, however, is not the only code we use to symbolize. There are many others, but among them is one with a particularly important role, the concept of grasping. The graspable conceptual symbols are tactile, just as the imaginary ones are visual; one grasps with the "mental" hand and imagines with the "mental" eye. Therefore the code of grasping uses "punctual" (e.g. alphabetical, logical, chemical) symbols, and these punctiform symbols, with which the symbolization is scanned, sampled, "read," can be ordered in a linear way (such as through texts or equations). We can therefore say that the imaginary world, the world of photography and painting, is two-dimensional, whereas the conceptual world, that of books and lectures, is linear.

Now we could assume that we are closer to what is symbolized when grasping than when imagining, because the hand touches the object more closely than the eye. In fact, however, the hand can only feel the surface, which means we can only grasp what has already become clear—that is, superficial—thanks to imagination. Conception follows imagination and cannot exist without it, because the conceptual code is a reduction of the two-dimensional code to one dimension. When we grasp, we read images, concepts signify parts of images and it becomes clear that the graspable conceptual world directly signifies the imaginary world, and therefore only indirectly the real one. The real world is structurally inaccessible to conception, and "reality" is consequently a false term, actually meaning "metaphysical."

That we have distanced ourselves further from the world by grasping it than through the imagination becomes clear from individual as well as human history: children imagine before they grasp and the magico-mythical, scenic, imaginative being of pre-history precedes the philosophico-prophetic, procedural, conceptual being of history in the stricter sense. But it is not enough to say that we first distance ourselves from the world in order to imagine it (banishment from paradise) and then step back from the imaginary world in order to grasp it (demythifying through historical consciousness). Rather, what begins during this double withdrawal from the world is a dialectical feedback between imagination and conception, the complexity of which defies any description. We do grasp original images, yet we continue to imagine graspable terminologies, and then grasp imaginary terminologies, in an infinite reduction toward an abyss that has long been called "progress." To put it in a more concrete way: originally, linear texts describe images of scenes (cuneiform texts, for example, describe images on tablets), but then images illustrate linear texts (for example in medieval bible manuscripts) and then texts explain images illustrating texts (for example textual explanations of drawn atomic models). But it is clear that with each of these steps away from the world a new level is reached. Only when we are aware of this can we attempt to rephrase the initially attempted provisional answer to the question of the conditions and functions of imagination.

We could simplify and say that the Lascaux cows are imaginary symbols of concrete experiences, that the cows in medieval paintings are imaginary symbols of concepts like "Birth of Christ," and that in realist painting, cows are imaginary symbols of zoological concepts which try to grasp imaginary aspects of concrete experiences. In this succession, the painter of Lascaux would be behind the hunter, the medieval painter behind the theological explainer of the painter of Lascaux and the realist painter behind the scientific explainer of the medieval painter. But such a simplification of progress as a progressive loss of reality toward an ever more bottomless imagination does not encompass the actual complexity of the situation. For although the cow painters of Lascaux, the Middle Ages and the nineteenth century do move on different levels of imagination, this difference is small compared with the levels on which a composer tries to imagine a score, a physicist a neutrino, an economist an economic model, or a philosopher the structure of a new thought. Only when we consider all these currently and ubiquitously overlapping levels of imagination, and how they break through different conceptual levels, do we begin to sense the scope of the problem posed here.

That is because at this point we begin to understand that "imagination" today doesn't just mean creating images of something, but breaking through existing images, because they obscure what one wants to create an image of. This means that, at present, imagination is iconoclastic. And furthermore, we begin to understand that these days "Imagination" actually doesn't just mean illustrating texts but going beyond their linearity (for instance, stepping beyond the equation of the neutrino through a model of the neutrino). It means that, at present, imagination is over-conceptual. In short, at present imagination is a revolutionary stance, because it has to attempt to break through the world surrounding us and to raise the world of texts that program us, away from its uni-dimensionality. And this imagination, as demanded of us by the present, can hardly be imagined in its inner contradiction (because it has to be iconoclastic) and in its outer contradiction (because it has to abolish and retain conception within itself), because it is so contradictory and has to move on such a high level.

Let's return to the three questions with which we began. When we claim that the world is becoming increasingly unimaginable, then we mean that it becomes increasingly hard to summon the energy for the imagination that is currently demanded. First, because the concepts of scientific discourse move on a level that imagination has not yet reached. (Which means that the world becomes ungraspable, too, because in order to grasp it, science must imagine it.) Second, because the perfection and the omnipresence of the imaginary world surrounding us make it harder and harder for us to create and retain an image of the world hiding behind it. (Which means that this world also becomes incapable of being experienced, because we experience the imaginary world instead.) And third, because we are programmed by texts that are intended to prevent any revolutionary imagination but to provoke instead the kind of harmless imagination of "science fiction" or "industrial design." (Which means that the level of imagination is currently below the level of conception and has in fact been programmed this way.)

In short, when we claim that the world is becoming increasingly unimaginable, we mean that we no longer possess any revolutionary imagination.

So the 1968 call "All power to the Imagination!" doesn't just mean any old imagination, such as the gentle, polite kind of fashion designers or formal poets, or the efficient kind of engineers and media programmers; it means the sort of imagination that would be capable of breaking the images obscuring our social reality. That means images such as national state, bourgeois family, division of labor, or discursive school. That is, an imagination that would be capable of imagining a situation without national state, bourgeois family, division of labor, or discursive school, and so on, and of creating for itself an image of what lies beyond the destruction of these images. That is why the call "All power to the Imagination!" is only revolutionary when we can say which imagination we are dealing with. The call becomes reactionary when we trivialize the concept of imagination, sweetening and diluting it, which is what has actually happened.[4]

We can divide the world into three ontological levels: one to be experienced, one to be imagined and one to be grasped. These three levels have become muddled. Because of this, the world cannot be experienced, or imagined, or grasped. This means that it has become unreal, which in turn means that we are in the process of literally becoming mad. One form of therapy against this danger is the attempt to provoke ourselves into an imagination that exists at the very level where our madness—that is, our distance from the world—is located. This means an imagination at the level of contemporary science and technology, of current mass culture and of programming with cybernetic apparatus. The exhibited images have to be viewed as just such an attempt. They aim to provide us with some conditions for making our own images, to enable us to orient ourselves in a world that is concealed by frozen images and concepts, in order to experience, imagine, and grasp this world. The exhibited images are training

---

[4] The paragraph refers to Theo Gerber: "The images surrounding us here are to be understood solely as an invitation to a very specific imagination. They negate figurative painting because it is part of the imaginary world that is intended to stifle every true revolution in us with frozen images. They also negate so-called conceptual art because it downgrades imagination to an illustration of linear texts. Ultimately they negate so-called hyperrealist art, because it does not—as it perhaps alleges it does—break through our imaginary surroundings by over-emphasizing them, but because it becomes part of them itself, as it were. What the exhibited images are trying to do is to open up parameters for our imagination. It's up to us on which level we attempt to imagine something, whether on the harmless levels of what has been handed down, or on the level that is currently demanded, of which we have spoken. It's up to us whether we see phalluses when viewing the paintings, or fields of purely intentional relations. Perhaps we are dealing with a reinterpretation of the word 'surrealism': to make concepts real, in other words capable of being experienced, through imagination?"

grounds and playgrounds for the imagination, and in this sense they are experimental answers to the question raised at the beginning: "What conditions are necessary to provoke images in us, and how do these images operate?"

57 Image Factories: Infographic Concepts 1920–1945

Helena Doudova

In 1919, as director of the German Economic Museum in Leipzig, Otto Neurath described three phases necessary for the development of modern society: machine technique, work and factory technique, and social technique ("Gesellschaftstechnik").[1] Otto Neurath was guided by Logical Positivism, and his view of the machine age was connected with a vision of emancipation and objectivity freed from ideology. As a co-founder of the Vienna Circle, he sought to reconcile science and philosophy in a rational and "objective" image, the "Sachbild". In contrast, Fritz Kahn´s vision of the modern world was motivated by pleasure, closely linked to the pleasure of seeing and to the pleasure of the form, speed and, technical level that Western society had achieved. Fritz Kahn invited his readers to see the modern world through modern eyes—to be scientized but also to be seduced—to dive into the images, to step into the industrial body, just as they would test-drive a new car. "Image Factories" is a blueprint for the modernist projection of modern man and modern woman in the infographic concepts of Otto Neurath and Fritz Kahn. Contrary to the usual perception, these concepts had a particular stylistic coherence based on a shared modernist scientific worldview, on technical progress, rationalization, and standardization. "Image Factories" unveils the iconography of infographic visualizations in its depictions of factories, workers, modern working environments, and communication media. It was a style that focused on the micro level of the modern body and the macro level of modern society. It was intentionally international and global—its precondition was the "universal" comprehensibility of the image, as opposed to the spoken or written language.

"Image Factories" looks behind the scenes of the scientific objectivity of infographics by analyzing the apparatus of image creation, editing, and display. The visualizations followed scientific concepts of explanation and illustration—legitimized by the rhetoric of the scientific objectivity of "social facts," the transformation of sociological data into visual charts (Neurath), and popular explanation of new medical and technological discoveries and

[1] Otto Neurath, *Technik und Wirtschaftsordnung* (Leipzig, 1919), p. 5.

medical knowledge (Kahn). On the other hand, both authors were well aware of the power of imagery and visual argumentation. They deliberately organized studios and created teams to keep up with the visualization strategies of their time, and in order to reach broad audiences they employed most of the common contemporary mass-reproduction techniques of print and display in the media of posters, books, magazines, exhibitions, or films.

Particular attention is paid in "Image Factories" to the collaborative efforts of these teams, even if the collaborative structures of Fritz Kahn and Otto Neurath differed quite considerably. It is a little-known fact that Fritz Kahn worked as a "creative director" alongside his employment in a neurological clinic in Berlin. He presumably intended to devote himself fully to the field of infographic visualization, establishing a graphic studio for popular scientific illustration and advertising graphics. He carefully selected first-class modernist illustrators—Fritz Schüler, Ottomar Trester, and Roman Rechn—to help him design the countless images that illustrated his major works on the human body. In a similar way, Otto Neurath set up a team with Marie Neurath and Gerd Arntz at the Gesellschafts- und Wirtschaftsmuseum (Social and Economic Museum—GWM) in Vienna in order to develop a unique method of visual statistical re-presentation and visual argumentation. Cooperation took the form of a mutual process of exchange and design, which could be termed the "Denkkollektiv" or "thought collective."[2] This lasted throughout the period of the GWM (1925–34) in Vienna, and was continued in the International Foundation for Visual Education (1934–40) in the Netherlands, and the Isotype Institute in England (1942–71).

The political turbulence of the period 1933/34–45 created a peculiar "stateless status" in the lives of Kahn, Neurath, and their colleagues, all of whom shared experiences of forced exile, internment and repeated moves from one country to another. Although their migration brought about a broad internationalization of their knowledge, it also created uncertainties, especially in terms of the legal conditions of copyright and of the repeated reproduction and circulation of their work. Kahn was faced with an extreme case of plagiarism, being deprived of the authorship of his work due to his Jewish origins.[3] The Neuraths experienced similar problems after they were forced to flee from Holland to England in dramatic circumstances in 1940, leaving everything behind.[4] Both cases deserve to be researched further within the framework of exile studies, especially in relation to the legal consequences of exile for the oeuvre of emigrants.

[2] Ludwig Fleck, *Entstehung und Entwicklung einer wissenschaftlichen Tatsache. Einführung in die Lehre vom Denkstil und Denkkollektiv* (Basel, 1935), p. 46.

[3] See the detailed description in the interview with Uta von Debschitz in this publication, as well as in Uta von Debschitz, Thilo von Debschitz, *Fritz Kahn—Man Machine* (Vienna, 2009), p. 31; Uta von Debschitz, Thilo von Debschitz, *Fritz Kahn* (Cologne, 2013), p. 21; Miriam Eilers, "Fritz Kahns ‚Das Leben des Menschen'. Zur Produktion und Transkription eines populären Werks," in *Zeitschrift für Geschichte der Wissenschaften, Technik und Medizin*, 23, 2015, pp. 1–31.

[4] Marie Neurath describes the extremely difficult situation after the war in Marie Neurath, "An was ich mich erinnere," unpublished typescript, Vienna Circle Foundation, 370/L.15, p. 83; see also Matthew Eve, "Isotype in trouble, 1946–1948," in *Modern Typography in Britain: graphic design, politics and society* (Typographic Papers 8) (London, 2009), pp. 131–34.

"Image Factories" is a comparative study in the visual culture of the 1920s and 1930s. It draws upon the methodology of visual studies and media history—comparative analysis, image theory, theories of visualization in infographics, media-historical analysis of the techniques of image/infographics production, reproduction and distribution, and of intermedial exchange. With reference to Ludwig Fleck's term "Denkstil" (thought style), infographics and popular-science illustrations are seen as an an expression of the forms of questioning and knowledge that become established in any particular period of time. From a more specifically art-historical viewpoint, the general psychological and mental conception would remain confined to the question of a work's formal appearance.[5] But the image should rather be seen as a complex interplay between visuality, apparatus, institutional discourse, physical bodies, and numbers. The image is reinvented through the practice of seeing, as a post-linguistic and post-semiotic practice, rendered even more urgent by the ubiquitous flow of image representations.[6] Infographics as a specific form of imagery, related to diagrammatics, is based on a combination of text and image. In terms of the classification of infographics, the LATCH system (L-Location, A-Alphabet, T-Time, C-Category, and H-Hierarchy) propounded by Richard Saul Wurman is informative.[7]

1. Fritz Kahn's "Man-Machines" in *Das Leben des Menschen* (1922–31)

What a surprise the poster "Der Mensch als Industriepalast" [Man as Industrial Palace] must have given to subscribers of the fourth volume of the medical book *Das Leben des Menschen* [The Life of Man] when it arrived as a supplement. Fritz Kahn's five-volume *magnum opus* was a popular-scientific introduction to the workings of the human body, written and published between 1922 and 1931. It was a bestseller, with a print-run of 131,000 copies,[8] and was also one of the German National Library's most requested works according to its visitor statistics for 1930.[9] The book was first available as a subscription edition from the Franckh/Kosmos publishing house in Stuttgart.

"Der Mensch als Industriepalast" was the epitome of the man-machine metaphor, a significant feature of Kahn's infographics. Ernst Kapp's theory of "organic projection" stated that technical inventions mirrored the functional principles of nature, and mechanical tools and instruments

5 "Bildbeschreibungen. Eine Stilgeschichte technischer Bilder? Interview w. Horst Bredekamp," in *Das Technische Bild* (Berlin, 2008), p. 37.
6 W.J.T. Mitchell, *Bildtheorie* (Frankfurt am Main, 2008), p. 108.
7 Sandra Rendgen/Julius Wiedeman (eds), *Information Graphics* (Cologne, 2012).
8 Statement on the total circulation of DLdM, vols 1–5, by Franckh´sche Verlagshandlung, file of Fritz Kahn´s restitution claims, Staatsarchiv Ludwigsburg, FL300/33I Bü13824, p. 147, information from UvD.
9 Newspaper cutting, Leo Baeck Institute, AR–A 1024/3534, Scrapbook I–X.
10 "Cornelius Borck," in U. and T. von Debschitz, *Fritz Kahn—Man Machine*, op. cit., p. 10; Ernst Kapp, *Grundlinien einer Philosophie der Technik* (Braunschweig, 1877), p. 42.

were understood as extensions of bodily organs.[10] Moreover, the notion of "biotechnics" was presented in the book *Das Leben der Pflanze* [The Life of Plants] by Raoul Heinrich Francé, published by Kosmos in 1921. Francé extended the metaphor of technical functionality to the functionality of form, understanding the cell as "a technical form of life."[11]

The style of Fritz Kahn's illustrations was taken from American infographic design, whose particular aesthetics were oriented toward "low," everyday imagery and advertising graphics. Symptomatic of the new approach was a diagram published in 1917 in the children's encyclopedia "Pictured Knowledge." It portrayed the human head as a "Look into Headquarters." using the metaphor of a house and an office, with separate rooms for the different directory functions (centre for speech, memory files, etc.), accompanied by architectural elements like stairs, curtains, chimneys, and so on. Kahn's natural affinity to the United States could be traced back to his early years, as at the age of six he had travelled to New York with his father on an ocean liner.[12] He was also the author of three texts in the book *Wunder in Uns* [Wonders Inside Us].[13] This book reproduced the "Look into Headquarters" and signified a "pictorial turn" in popular-scientific publications in Germany between 1900 and 1920.[14]

Fritz Kahn's engagement went far beyond the role of author of popular-scientific books. His role can be best described as that of a "creative director"—an impresario of popular-scientific illustration. In his apartment in Berlin he set up an artistic studio and a workshop to check the illustrations and to keep an eye on the production of visualizations. He perceived books as multilayered compendia of information, including quotes by philosophers and scientists, as well as poems, music, and images.[15] Kahn was skilled in drafting book concepts and in researching visual material. For most ambitious illustrations and charts he would commission illustrators. "[Fritz Kahn] as a sharp analyst in his critique ... forced us to never-ending intellectual activity. It was not the drawing of one illustration that would take weeks, but the constant conceptualization of new ideas for a single problem."[16] After emigrating from Germany in 1933 Kahn strove to reestablish his practice, continuing his work as founder of Studio Hayad, which could look back at "twenty years of experience in one of the most acclaimed European workshops for artistic and scientific graphics."[17]

Fritz Kahn selected three Berlin artists who suited the passion of his time for technology and modernity. These artists—Fritz Schüler, Ottomar Trester and Roman Rechn—came from the artistic field of "Neues Bauen"

---

[11] Raoul Heinrich Francé, *Das Leben der Pflanze* (Stuttgart, 1921), p. 13.
[12] See boarding pass for *S. S. Augusta Victoria*, December 12, 1895, travel line New York—Plymouth—Cherbourg—Hamburg in the names Fred Kahn and Mrs. Kahn and infant, Archive ZB Zurich, Estate Corti, Fritz Kahn, Box-1.
[13] Reprint of "Head as headquarters" in Hanns Günther, *Wunder in uns* (Zurich, 1921), Plate XII.
[14] For details see interview with Uta von Debschitz in this publication, and Michael Sappol, *Body Modern. Fritz Kahn, Scientific Illustration, and the Homuncular Subject* (Minneapolis: University of Minnesota Press, 2017), pp. 29–47.
[15] The documentation of the original material for DLdM was lost in the Second World War. A number of insights into Kahn's work are provided by the scrapbooks and the unpublished manuscript of the "Natural History of Palestine" in the Leo Baeck Archive, New York. For a precise description of the book-production process, see Eilers, "Fritz Kahns ‚Das Leben des Menschen,'" op. cit.
[16] Letter from Roman Rechn to Franckh publishing house. Staff file Fritz Kahn, envelope V, Archive of Kosmos, Stuttgart. Information by UvD.
[17] Self-description of Studio Hayad, February 13, 1934 (New York: Leo Baeck Institute), OS 43/X, 252–53. The translation was provided by UvD.

[New Building] and "Neue Sachlichkeit" [New Objectivity] and translated medical illustrations into modernist visuality and iconography. They belonged to the second generation of Kahn's illustrators, active between 1924 and 1933.[18] Fritz Schüler drew "Der Mensch als Industriepalast" (1926).[19] His mode of artistic expression was strongly influenced by architecture and modern technology, especially by the motif of electricity and wire-transmission, which was related to his engagement with the German electric industry. As an architect and exhibition designer he cooperated with Mies van der Rohe on the Pavilion of the German Electricity Industry at the International Exposition in Barcelona in 1929.[20] He designed large collaged panoramic photo-prints portraying electricity production and distribution in Germany. In 1934 he became the leading exhibition architect for the state energy provider Reichs-Elektrowerke (EWAG). Roman Rechn studied architecture and consciously positioned himself within the modernist avant-garde. In his unsuccessful application to the Bauhaus, we read: "As the tree and the sky are elements of creativity, so are the house and the machine. Not away from civilization, but penetrating it, reviving it, giving it new design and form."[21] Most importantly, he authored the collaged book jackets for the second edition of the series *Das Leben des Menschen*. Ottomar Trester, with his diagrammatic approach, was by far the most represented illustrator in *Das Leben des Menschen*. He cooperated with Kahn from 1924 to 1931, but his association with the Jewish author meant that later on he gained virtually no commissions.[22]

Infographic visualizations of the modern body

Fritz Kahn constructed his books around the functionality of the modern body; it became a hybrid between a human and a machine. However, Kahn's images, settings and scenes tell a broader story—that of the subconscious dimensions of the modern world—of circulation, mobility, rationality, and the division of labour in modernity.

Kahn's infographic strategies depicted the mechanics, cognition, nutrition, and reproduction of the modern body, in the spirit of Kapp. Mechanistic metaphors of the body dealt with the basic functions—the circulation of blood and air. Most symptomatic was the heart as an engine, with breathing as a hoist or an elevator. An illustration with the title "Die Leistung des Herzens als Pumpe" provided an analogy of the "heart as the most powerful machine of the world." Vessels of different sizes were compared to indicate how many liters a heart pumped in one

18 See the detailed biographical overviews in this publication by Uta von Debschitz.
19 The work is not signed.
20 Mathias Horstmann, "Miesianische Welten, eine Rezension zur Ausstellung Mies van der Rohe: Die Collagen aus dem MoMA in Ludwigforum Aachen," in: *ARCH+* (online), http://www.archplus.net/home/news/7,1-13499,1,0.html, accessed 25.07.2017; information from UvD.
21 Application to the Bauhaus Weimar, Thüringisches Hauptstadtarchiv Weimar, Staatliches Bauhaus Weimar Nr. 161, Bl. 216–20. The document was provided by UvD.
22 Interview with Wolfgang Trester, the nephew of Ottomar Trester, by UvD.

second—0,1l (a laboratory glass); in one minute—6l (6 glass bottles); in one year—a grain elevator, etc. In 70 years the heart pumped a volume of 250 million liters, shown in the form of a gasometer.[23] The sensory system was construed as a sophisticated means of communication and transmission, the bodily nerves epitomized in electric transmission wires. The modern working office environment found its expression in the analogy of the head-as-headquarters, as telephone switchboard rooms and their operators. Nutrition's most important function was to convert food into energy—measured by caloric intake and output, broken down into digestion cycles. Food was burnt in the gastrointestinal tract in a similar way to the coal in the furnace of a steam locomotive. A variety of infographic explanatory tools was presented—graphs, circular diagrams (such as one of meal-times), timelines, and comparisons of proportion. To enhance the diagrams pictorially, the illustrators developed very elaborate formal strategies for the spatial organization of motifs in the image frames, as well as particular artistic montage techniques.

The graphic projection of the modern body was highly schematic. It most frequently appeared as an outline, as the black profile of a male torso, or as a cutaway section of a human body (as in medical atlases). Sometimes a frontal outline was used, interestingly sexless, even when female bodies were depicted. Occasionally illustrations zoomed in on sections of the body to show certain organs more clearly and to enable a better understanding of its functions. Since Fritz Schüler and Roman Rechn were trained architects, they may well have been attracted to the architectonic visualization of different sections of a house as an analogy to these cut-away sections of a human body. As in architecture, the different service systems were marked with different colors—breathing with blue, heart and blood circulation with red, digestion with yellow, etc.

The images often used montage to create visual analogies. In two picture frames, the construction of the human bone was directly juxtaposed with that of the Eiffel Tower, and the movement of a crying woman's eyelids with that of a car's windshield wiper. These juxtapositions were realized visually either as two independent sections of a picture frame, or as different picture planes, overlapping each other to create a multilayered impression. One of Roman Rechn's montages combined two planes, comparing the performance of a projector with human vision. In "Die Übereinstimmung zwischen Autotypie und Netzhautbild" [The Correspondence between Autotypy and Retina], a portrait of Nefertiti was transmitted and broken down into dots. The autotypy (print) reproduces a raster of such dots, while the retina creates a more elaborate grid of cells (→ p. 10).

[23] Fritz Kahn, *Das Leben des Menschen II* (Stuttgart, 1924), p. 278.

Humans as "viewing machines"—film and comic

For Fritz Kahn and his illustrators the human brain was a viewing machine, cognition being formed by the projections of concepts. They developed very sophisticated design strategies to seduce the viewer. These often related to filmic equipment and film techniques, and can be described by means of film terminology—sequence, storyboard, scene, or setting. The analogy of the film industry is productive in two ways: through reading of the image in numbered sequences and through the way the portrayal of devices used in motion pictures stimulates a sense of contemporaneity.

One significant example is a cross-section of the human head. Entitled "Der Sehakt" [The Act of Viewing], it illustrates what happens in a man's head when he sees a key—the process of cognition, seeing, conceptualizing and abstraction of the object—the key is a "word-image" [Wortbild]. The object seen through the lens of the eye is transmitted to film, transported to the "optical centre of cognition" and beamed onto a projection wall in the centre of memory. There the key is matched with an already pre-existing idea of the key. This word-image is then typed on a piano-like device into written form, coded and wire-transferred by nerves to the motor centre—the vocal cords which enable the pronunciation of the word key. It is worth noting that this scheme was redrawn in different versions—in Kahn's later books it was modified and the object, the key, was substituted by a car.[24] In "Der Sehakt" (→ p. 79), viewers read a storyboard and followed a numbered sequence of picture frames with a written commentary, which enabled them to understand the process of cognition of the key. The setting of the internal picture frames may have recalled the setting in cinemas, consisting of projectors, reels of film, and projection screens. It included a piano, as silent films were accompanied by music. The spoken word, key, appeared in a comic-like speech bubble.

The scenes for the illustrations were constructed around particular modern settings—either macro-scenes of the modern metropolis or micro-scenes of the human body (the workers performed orders in bodily interiors). Often the scenes sketched mini-stories, plot-moments, which stimulated the curiosity of the viewer and raised questions (like a woman ringing a bell at a presumably unknown man's door, or a man carefully monitoring the arrival or departure of a particular train in a railway station). In another artistically beautiful scene by Fritz Schüler a car driver became an object of scientific analysis. A street scene depicted a car driver on a busy tram crossing. All aspects of the modern metropolis were included as objects a–d: a–plane, b–clock tower, c–car in front of the driver and d–speedometer on the car's dashboard. A cutaway,

---

24 Fritz Kahn, "Es ist ein Wunder, dass wir länger als zwei Minuten Leben," *Berliner Illustrirte Zeitung*, 1926, p. 1468; *Das Leben des Menschen*, vol. IV, 1929, chart 8; *Der Mensch, gesund und krank*, vol. II, 1940, pp. 204–05.

zooming in to the driver's eye, revealed the upside-down projection of objects a–c within the driver's field of vision and object d (speedometer) outside it (located quite surrealistically outside the man's head).

Special effects were developed in the process of sequencing. One of the key qualities of infographics is to try to explain facts by means of diagrams or sequences. Kahn would very often mark the imagery with explanatory numbers or letters that required the viewer to read the image step by step and frame by frame, as was the case for the image of "Bratenduft" [smell of roast] or "Sehakt." Sometimes arrows directed the viewer's attention toward the correct reading of the image. Occasionally, the visualization would become a motion-sequence, a phasing diagram of the movement of a car, a dancing couple or an elevator, analyzing the motion-sensoric function of the semicircular canals in the ear [Der Mechanismus der Bogengangfunktion]. Real comic sequences were introduced, like "Ein daktyloskopischer Kriminalroman" [A Dactyloscopic Detective Novel], or "Die Nikotinprobe" [The Nicotine Test].

2. Isotype and "Bildstatistik" by Otto Neurath, Marie Neurath, and Gerd Arntz

Isotype (International System Of Typographic Picture Education) was a communication system that aimed to "turn the statements of science into pictures."[25] The name was invented by Marie Neurath when the team received a commission for the book "International Picture Language."[26] The system derived directly from the "Vienna Method of Pictorial Statistics" [Wiener Methode der Bildstatistik], developed at the Viennese Gesellschafts- und Wirtschaftsmuseum (GWM). Isotype and "Bildstatistik" found broad application in books, exhibitions and posters from 1924 until the official dissolution of the Isotype Institute in England in 1971.

In an age of overproduction of images by magazines, motion pictures and advertisements, Otto Neurath considered it all the more necessary to develop visual literacy. At school, visual aids conveyed important arguments in a simple way, explaining social facts like the basic history of nations or the distribution of goods through "teaching-pictures" as guides to a deeper knowledge and to science. As a proponent of visual argumentation Neurath would distinguish between networks and chain arguments. A picture as a network argument could present correlations that pointed in various directions on a single page. In writing and reading statements follow each other in a linear chain, and the correlations have to be remembered.[27] Isotype reduced and standardized things

25 Otto Neurath, *International Picture Language. The First Rules of Isotype* (London, 1936), p. 8.
26 Marie Neurath / Robin Kinross, *The Transformer: Principles of Making Isotype Charts* (London, 2009), p. 47.
27 H.E. Coppen, "Discussion on visual education with Dr. Neurath," 1943, typescript Vienna Circle Foundation Archive, 414/S.20, p. 3. In the interview Neurath also mentions the "Pictures in 'Life', illustrating the Physiology text of Dr. Kahn," p. 5.

in order to achieve visual clarity and a clear-cut shape, condensed in Neurath's famous notion of the three views in looking at an infographic chart.[28] For Neurath, writing a visual language like Isotype or hieroglyphics was difficult, but "reading" it very simple.[29] Isotype had to adhere to strict rules, Neurath would assert, and Isotype specialists had to be trained and educated. Creating the Isotype charts essentially required an attitude of logical empiricism.[30] Although Isotype was based on Basic English, it was not intended as a sign-for-sign picture language or as a substitute for a written language. At the same time, Neurath recognized similarities to picture scripts like Chinese or hieroglyphics.[31]

Isotype and "Bildstatistik" owed much to the style of "Neue Sachlichkeit." Otto Neurath was directly connected to the Bauhaus, especially to its second director Hannes Meyer. They articulated a common vision of a modern way of life which drew upon the same scientific and machine-centred images.[32] Neurath devoted considerable energy to defining the "Sachbild" in graphic visualization: "Maybe the most unique achievement would be when … an artistically strong originality is paired with a typical universality and evidence, …"[33] He demanded the highest artistic standards and skills of the graphic designers, and called for a convincing style, unique in its graphic expression. At the same time the artists were asked to forgo their personal signature and the cutting-edge artistic individuality, needed in the field of advertising, and to adopt a new working method with a restrained visual style. Such pictograms would then become the hallmark and code of modern industrial society, coherent with Ernst Mach's search for beauty in the simplicity of description.[34]

The "Bildstatistik" method was crystallized in the team of the GWM, consisting of the director, two transformers, two graphic designers and skilled technicians, who worked on the cutting, coloring and printing of the charts. Later, due to war and emigration, Neurath founded new institutes—the International Foundation for Visual Education in Holland and, together with Marie Neurath, the Isotype Institute in England. Transformation—"information design" in contemporary terminology—translated expert knowledge into infographics, distinguished the essential facts, and created visual drafts for the diagrams. The transformers, headed by Marie Neurath, instructed the artists and graphic designers and also directed the production of the final charts.[35] An archive for visual education held photographs of object-related images, documentation of professions, of workers' postures and of different aspects

---

[28] For his charts Neurath developed a system of three views: "At the first look you see the most important points, at the second, the less important points, at the third, the details, at the fourth, nothing more—if you see more, the teaching picture is bad." Otto Neurath, *International Picture Language: The First Rules of Isotype* (London, 1936), p. 27.

[29] Coppen, "Discussion on visual education with Dr. Neurath," op. cit., p. 3.

[30] Christopher Burke, *The Linguistic Status of Isotype*, in Richard Heinrich/Elisabeth Nemeth/David Wagner, *Image and Imaging in Philosophy, Science and the Arts*, vol. II (Heusenstamm 2011), p. 46.

[31] Ibid., pp. 39–40.

[32] Peter Galison, "Aufbau/Bauhaus: Logical Positivism and Architectural Modernism," in *Critical Inquiry*, 4/1990, p. 749.

[33] "Vielleicht aber läge eine solche Spitzenleistung so, dass sie mit künstlerisch starker Eigenwilligkeit doch auch eine typenhafte Allgemeingültigkeit und Selbstverständlichkeit verbinden würde." Otto Neurath, "Das Sachbild," in *Die Form*, 2/1930, p. 38.

[34] Friedlich Stalder, "Otto Neurath (1882–1945)—Zu Leben und Werk in seiner Zeit," in *Arbeiterbildung in der Zwischenkriegszeit. Otto Neurath und sein Gesellschafts- und Wirtschaftsmuseum in Wien 1925–1934. Politische Grafik von Gerd Arntz und den Konstruktivisten* (Vienna, 1982), p. 8.

[35] For more detailed information on transformation see Neurath/Kinross, *The Transformer*, op. cit.

of social-democratic Vienna. The graphic department developed pictograms (originally called "Signatures") in cooperation with other members of the team. The graphic preparation of the charts was the responsibility primarily of Gerd Arntz, whom Neurath invited to Vienna after they had met in Düsseldorf in 1926, and also the Swiss graphic designer Erwin Bernath. With Arntz, the final technique of Isotype became established around 1929 as lino-cuts, colored and printed. The pictograms were gathered in "picture dictionaries," a visual thesaurus—standardized sheets of paper, entitled "Man," "Woman," etc., with variations in form and color for use in different compositions. The entire workshop compiled the charts, which were drawn, cut out, printed and montaged on large sheets of paper into visual statistics.

Gesellschaft und Wirtschaft—
a global projection of modernity

Otto Neurath and his team—Marie Neurath and Gerd Arntz—were key in creating a democratic and emancipatory vision of the modern world. The atlas *Gesellschaft und Wirtschaft* [Society and Economy] (1931), commissioned by the Bibliographic Institute in Leipzig, and the book *Modern Man in the Making* (1939) provided the most concise idea of modern society shaped by "Gesellschaftstechnik" [technological developments]. As an astute sociologist, Neurath defined the most important sociological trends toward modernity in the diagram "Silhouettes": the average life expectancy of the female population, the suicide rate, rates of literacy and the number of radio-sets.[36]

Gesellschaft und Wirtschaft, the GWM's most advanced work, spelled out a whole repertoire of infographic visualization, but also revealed the ideological basis of modernism.

A set of 100 charts provided a global overview, "a colorful image of human civilization today and its development." This most comprehensive atlas was the product of a year's collaboration in the extended interdisciplinary team of the GWM (1929–30). Neurath commissioned Arntz as a full-time employee, and invited graphic designers Peter Alma and Augustin Tschinkel to assist him. A broad network of specialists (experts in statistics, medicine, engineering, history, etc.) was built up as an advisory board.[37] Karl Peucker, the renowned cartographer famous for his plastic use of colors [Farbenplastik], redrew the maps [Kartogramme] according to the Eckert projection of 1906, which depicted the actual surface of the Earth more precisely than the Mercator projection, which made Europe appear larger than in reality.[38] The arrangement of the pictograms in charts along the vertical or hori-

---

36 Otto Neurath, *Modern Man in the Making* (New York, 1939), p. 61.
37 Neurath/Kinross, *The Transformer*, op. cit., pp. 27–44.
38 *Gesellschaft und Wirtschaft. Bildstatistisches Elementarwerk*, Leipzig, 1930, p. 103; Christopher Burke/Eric Kindel/Sue Walker, *Isotype. Design and Contexts, 1925–1971* (London, 2013), pp. 191–92.

zontal axis, or in a spatial arrangement on a map, was guided by sets of rules of transformation described in detail by Otto and Marie Neurath. The most important rule concerned the horizontal reading of the icons, which allowed for a comparison of quantities, absolute volumes and changes over time. Further rules applied to proportional comparisons and the use of colors.[39]

Chart no. 96, "Völkergruppen der Erde" [Ethnic Groups of the World] showed the proportional division of ethnic groups across the globe. Each was assigned a color—white for Europeans and their successors, brown for the populations of the Orient and India, yellow for "Mongolians" (Japanese and Chinese). "Negroes and Mulattoes" were portrayed as black, and finally "American Indians" were red. In this division, some exceptions were acknowledged. For instance, Jews and the "civilized" populations of Central and South American republics were counted as white. Neurath associated the "civilized" world with the whites, in contrast to the "primitive" rest of the world. Moreover, the ethnic groups showed the iconographic time-specificity of the pictograms. A hat, as a symbol of Western man, was automatically extended to all ethnic (color) groups of the Earth. The white groups were characterized by a middle-class hat, the yellow groups by a straw hat and the brown groups by a turban.

The most advanced charts of the atlas combined proportional comparisons with timelines and locations. For example, in chart no. 57, "Entwicklung der Eisenbahnen" [Development of the Railroads], a timeline to the left showed the technological development of trains in pictures from 1825 to 1926. A "tree" diagram to the right indicated the growth of the total railroad network from 1851 to 1926 and showed the proportions of the distribution of railroads globally, with the USA and Europe accounting for 60.4 percent of railroads in 1926. (The railroad icon was in the form of a square that enabled proportional comparison.) A map of the world above this axis showed the spread of the transcontinental railroads. In Neurath's classification the USA and Europe were among the most developed compact areas of the modern economy, with advanced machine techniques, as opposed to the areas of "all-culture-nations" [Allkulturvölker] or "primitive" economies (like some indigenous tribes, and others).[40]

Certain aspects of the projection of the modern world in the atlas are problematic by today's standards. The atlas was definitely a product of its time, depicting the story of white Western man as logically re-presenting humankind's highest phase of development. A typological classification based on color (possibly analogical to the division by race) would be perceived as impossible to defend nowadays, since ethnographic research and societal convention assert that humankind is too diverse and too mixed to be able to

[39] Neurath/Kinross, *The Transformer*, op. cit., pp. 14, 19.
[40] *Gesellschaft und Wirtschaft*, op. cit., p. 104.

be divided into such simplified categories. Nor would the fact that the share of the female population remained unaddressed withstand contemporary feminist critique.

Modern man in crisis— Berlin exhibitions 1929–32

The Berlin series was a unique set on the modern lifestyle planned for a Berlin museum branch of the GWM. Otto Neurath became acquainted with Carl Herz, the social-democratic mayor of Berlin-Kreuzberg, and was asked to prepare a permanent Berlin exhibition similar to the visual statistics displayed in Vienna's Town Hall. With the support of Herz, Neurath initially opened the exhibition "Wien im Bild" [Vienna in the Picture], which ran from March 9 to 31, 1929 at the "Gesundheitshaus am Urban" in Kreuzberg, the "proletarian district in the south of Berlin."[41] This exhibition showed the first charts of Berlin—population statistics and social stratification.[42] The permanent exhibition then displayed the full range of Bildstatistik's analytical abilities, in its most developed phase around 1930. Marie Neurath later recalled anxiously updating the statistics of the election results in different German federal states with the shadow of the NSDAP rising to power.[43] Another central chart displayed the unemployment rate in Berlin, with a dramatic increase between 1930 and 1932. It was to become a symbol of the turbulent developments to come.

About 50 stunning charts with socio-economic data addressed the broadest variety of modern issues related to demographics, the economy and lifestyle—like the consumption of meat, the development of food cooperatives, the number of municipal libraries and public baths, the number of Berlin apartments with electric light or bath, etc.[44] These charts originated in two periods; the first set was produced in 1928–29 for the exhibition "Wien im Bild." The later charts originated between mid-1931 and summer 1932. Some of the designs were drawn twice, enabling a comparison of the museum's changing approaches to visualization. In earlier pictograms, the human figure included more details of clothing and the outline of the human face (see the charts for "Eheschliessungen" [Marriages], or "Entwicklung der deutschen Gewerkschaften" [Development of German Labor Unions]). Later, the pictograms of men and women had a stronger modular and serial appearance, and the figures became more schematic and compact. This modularity enabled technical innovation in pictogram

---

41 Carl Herz, "Wien im Bild," in "Die Kunstgemeinde Mitteilungsblatt der Kunstgemeinde des Bezirks Kreuzberg," 4/1929, p. 26.
42 "Die Ausstellung ‚Wien in Bild' in den Räumen des Gesundheitshauses Kreuzberg, Am Urban, 10–11", in "Die Kunstgemeinde Mitteilungsblatt der Kunstgemeinde des Bezirks Kreuzberg," 4/1929, p. 27. The reference was kindly provided by Dr. Dietlinde Peters.
43 The exhibition display presumably did not last long. Marie Neurath remembered she visited the Kreuzberg museum once in 1932 on her way to visit her parents. On the train, with a sign of hope, she began to update the losses of the NSDAP in the election of November 1932. One finished chart from the original set shows the results of the German federal election of July 1932. The political turbulence which brought Adolf Hitler to power also overturned the mayor of Kreuzberg, Carl Herz—as early as March 1933, as a leading SPD politician of Jewish origin, he was fired from office and publicly mistreated by the Nazi Sturmabteilung (SA). Neurath, "An was ich mich erinnere," op. cit., p. 48.
44 See Otto and Marie Isotype Collection Reading, T-charts, IC, 5/13.

design—"marking off."[45] Neurath pushed for the convention of clustering pictograms into groups of five or ten to present "easily countable groups of objects" (see the "Arbeitslosigkeit" [Unemployment] chart, → p. 152).

Intermedia practices—
"Rondom Rembrandt" and diagrammatic film

Both *Bildstatistik* and Isotype introduced early intermedial practices, allowing experimentation with different formats without prioritizing one over another. The exhibition "Rondom Rembrandt" ("Around Rembrandt") and the "diagrammatic" films were two examples of this approach. One addressed the confrontation between infographic schemes and the paintings of Rembrandt, the other combined the Isotype method with animated film. In each medium Neurath saw a special value for visual pedagogy.[46]

At its best, "Rondom Rembrandt," conspicuous for its visualization of Rembrandt's paintings in infographic form, promoted the pedagogical practice of Isotype. Commissioned by De Bijenkorf in Holland in 1938, it was a particularly successful exhibition seen by 10,000 visitors in that company's department stores in Amsterdam, Rotterdam and The Hague. It portrayed Rembrandt in his historical and social background and inserted reproductions of his paintings in the infographic frame—in timelines, sequences of self-portraits, a comparison of the motifs of Rembrandt and Rubens, etc. The analytical powers of the Isotype method were here developed to their fullest extent, employing the art-historical procedures of comparative viewing or iconographic analysis. As such, the Isotype approach proved itself well qualified to serve the educational purposes of art history. At the same time it highlighted the difference between an explanatory, diagrammatical tool and a free work of art like Rembrandt's paintings, distinguished precisely by their uniqueness and authenticity, and opening up questions about the value of reproduction and originality, and the accessibility of knowledge in general.

Animated film as a cross-medium between diagram and (documentary) film could be compared to the pioneering Walt Disney animation films.[47] The Neuraths became scriptwriters and storyboard illustrators, co-directing films proposed by Paul Rotha, an English documentary filmmaker. Film experiments had already begun in Vienna at the GWM and peaked during the Second World War as educational films for the British Ministry of Information. These appeared either as animated sequences ("Blood Transfusion," "Total War in Britain") or as fully animated films ("A Few Ounces a

---

[45] A term by Robin Kinross. For a more detailed description of pictogram design, see "The graphic formation of Isotype 1920–1940," in Christopher Burke / Eric Kindel / Sue Walker, *Isotype. Design and Contexts, 1925–1971* (London, 2013), pp. 107–85.

[46] Otto Neurath, "Von Hieroglyphen zu Isotypen," in Rudolf Haller / Robin Kinross (eds), *Otto Neurath: Gesammelte bildpädagogische Schriften* (Vienna, 1991), p. 644.

[47] For detailed information see Christopher Burke, "Animated Isotype on film," in Burke / Kindel / Walker, *Isotype. Design and Contexts, 1925–1971*, pp. 367–89.

Day"). Neurath saw the strength of diagrammatic film as its potential for displaying arguments, whereas realistic films could only use verbal argumentation. Generally, the limitation of film as a medium was its inability to present visual comparisons, because its pace was too quick. It also included a lot of irrelevant visual material, which complicated the message. Diagrammatic films, on the other hand, enabled the visualization of processes of growth, motion, and circulation.[48]

Conclusion

This essay has described in detail the crucial characteristics of infographic concepts, the visual style and the most significant works by Fritz Kahn and Otto Neurath and their teams. The common denominator of this style was modernity, even though the strategies varied. Fritz Kahn stood closer to the notion of popular-scientific illustration and advertising graphics originating in the United States, while Neurath, as a Logical Positivist, promoted a reduced, standardized visual language. Both were eager to be inspired by and to experiment with the most advanced media of their time, including film and comics. Infographic projections portrayed a particular form of Western modernity, embodied in the technological progress of the 1920s and 1930s. A number of different aspects of this projection—the unreflective embracing of machines or the belief in scientific objectivity—can be regarded critically. At the same time, however, Fritz Kahn and Otto Neurath witnessed a decisive and radical change, the advent of the information society. They spelled out the first rules and techniques of infographic visualization, and they became role models for a great number of twentieth-century artists, information designers, and visual and media theorists. As such their contribution remains valued, appreciated, and fruitful for contemporary discourse.

48 Coppen, "Discussion on visual education with Dr. Neurath," p. 4.

Fritz Kahn, Otto Neurath. Infographics 1920–1945

73 World powers. In *Gesellschaft und Wirtschaft. Bildstatistisches Elementarwerk*, Leipzig, 1930, pl. 23

74 The cycle of power and substance. In Fritz Kahn, *Das Leben des Menschen*, vol. III, Stuttgart, 1926, pl. 26

75 Respiration. In Fritz Kahn, *Das Leben des Menschen*, vol. III, Stuttgart, 1926, pl. 7

76 Slavery in the 15 southern states of the U.S.A. In *Gesellschaft und Wirtschaft. Bildstatistisches Elementarwerk*, Leipzig, 1930, pl. 78

77 Merchant navies of the world. In *Gesellschaft und Wirtschaft. Bildstatistisches Elementarwerk*, Leipzig 1930, pl. 55

78 Camera and human eye. In Fritz Kahn, *Der Mensch, gesund und krank*, vol. II, Zurich 1939, p. 308

78 Visual system in technology and nature. In Fritz Kahn, *Das Leben des Menschen*, vol. V, Stuttgart, 1931, p. 10

79 The act of seeing. In Fritz Kahn, *Das Leben des Menschen*, vol. IV, Stuttgart, 1929, pl. 8

80 Import trade to Western and Central Europe. In *Gesellschaft und Wirtschaft. Bildstatistisches Elementarwerk*, Leipzig, 1930, pl. 32

81 Development of coal and oil production from 1870. In *Gesellschaft und Wirtschaft. Bildstatistisches Elementarwerk*, Leipzig, 1930, pl. 47

82 The heart's work rate. In Fritz Kahn, *Der Mensch, gesund und krank*, vol. I, Zurich, 1939, p. 193

83 Man and machine. In Fritz Kahn, *Der Mensch, gesund und krank*, vol. I, Zurich, 1939, p. 2

84 Development of the railways. In *Gesellschaft und Wirtschaft. Bildstatistisches Elementarwerk*, Leipzig, 1930, pl. 57

85 Monopoly-like production of non-European countries. In *Gesellschaft und Wirtschaft. Bildstatistisches Elementarwerk*, Leipzig, 1930, pl. 59

86 The perception of light. In Fritz Kahn, *Das Leben des Menschen*, vol. IV, Stuttgart, 1929, pl. 22

87 Sensory pathways. In Fritz Kahn, *Das Leben des Menschen*, vol. IV, Stuttgart, 1929, pl. 7

88 Strength of armies in the modern era. In *Gesellschaft und Wirtschaft. Bildstatistisches Elementarwerk*, Leipzig, 1930, pl. 26

89 Osteogenesis—bone building struggle. In Fritz Kahn, *Das Leben des Menschen*, vol. II, Stuttgart 1925, pl. 6

90 New York. In *Gesellschaft und Wirtschaft. Bildstatistisches Elementarwerk*, Leipzig, 1930, pl. 71

91 Density of occupancy in big cities. In *Gesellschaft und Wirtschaft. Bildstatistisches Elementarwerk*, Leipzig, 1930, pl. 72

92 Sunbath! In Fritz Kahn: *Der Mensch, gesund und krank*, vol. II, Zurich, 1939, p. 253

93 The erection. In Fritz Kahn, *Unser Geschlechtsleben*, Zurich, 1937, pl. 6

94 Migration flow in important countries 1920–27. In *Gesellschaft und Wirtschaft. Bildstatistisches Elementarwerk*, Leipzig, 1930, pl. 74

95 Infant mortality and income. In *Gesellschaft und Wirtschaft. Bildstatistisches Elementarwerk*, Leipzig, 1930, pl. 92

96 Internal structure of bone. In Fritz Kahn, *Der Mensch, gesund und krank*, vol. I, Zurich, 1939, p. 69

97 Walking man as a pendulum machine. In Fritz Kahn, *Der Mensch, gesund und krank*, vol. I, Zurich, 1939, p. 175

98 Big city living per 25 persons. In *Gesellschaft und Wirtschaft. Bildstatistisches Elementarwerk*, Leipzig, 1930, pl. 67

99 Working population according to economic branches around 1920. In *Gesellschaft und Wirtschaft. Bildstatistisches Elementarwerk*, Leipzig 1930, pl. 76

100 Oral digestion. In Fritz Kahn, *Das Leben des Menschen*, vol. III, Stuttgart, 1926, p. 101

101 Taste. In Fritz Kahn, *Der Mensch, gesund und krank*, vol. I, Zurich, 1939, p. 275

102 Strikes and lockouts. In *Gesellschaft und Wirtschaft. Bildstatistisches Elementarwerk*, Leipzig, 1930, p. 88

103 Machinery exports before the war and today. In *Gesellschaft und Wirtschaft. Bildstatistisches Elementarwerk*, Leipzig, 1930, pl. 60

104 Homo technicus. In Fritz Kahn, *Das Buch der Natur*, vol. II, Zurich, 1952, p. 471

Mächte der Erde

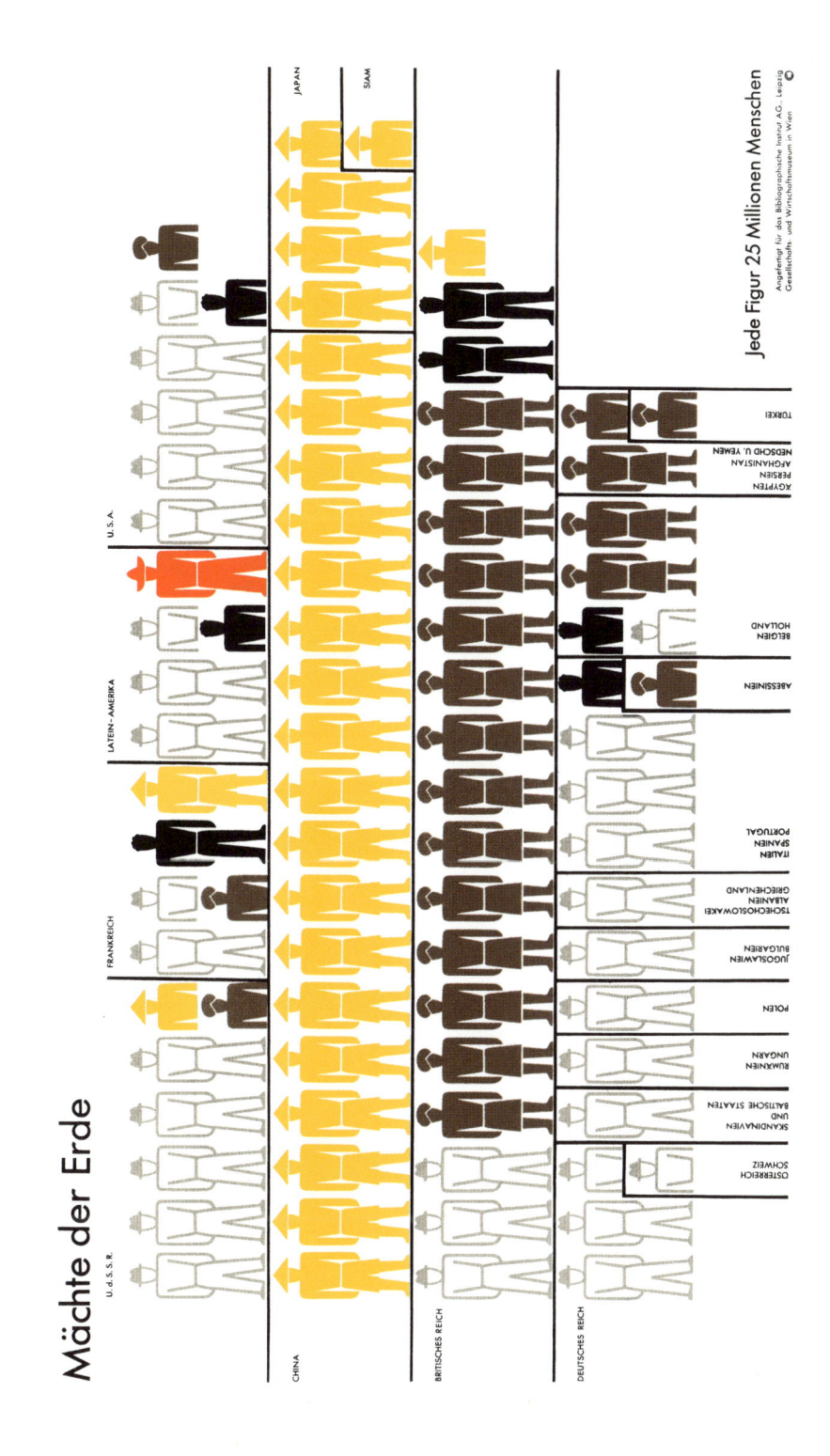

Jede Figur 25 Millionen Menschen

Der Kreislauf von Kraft und Stoff

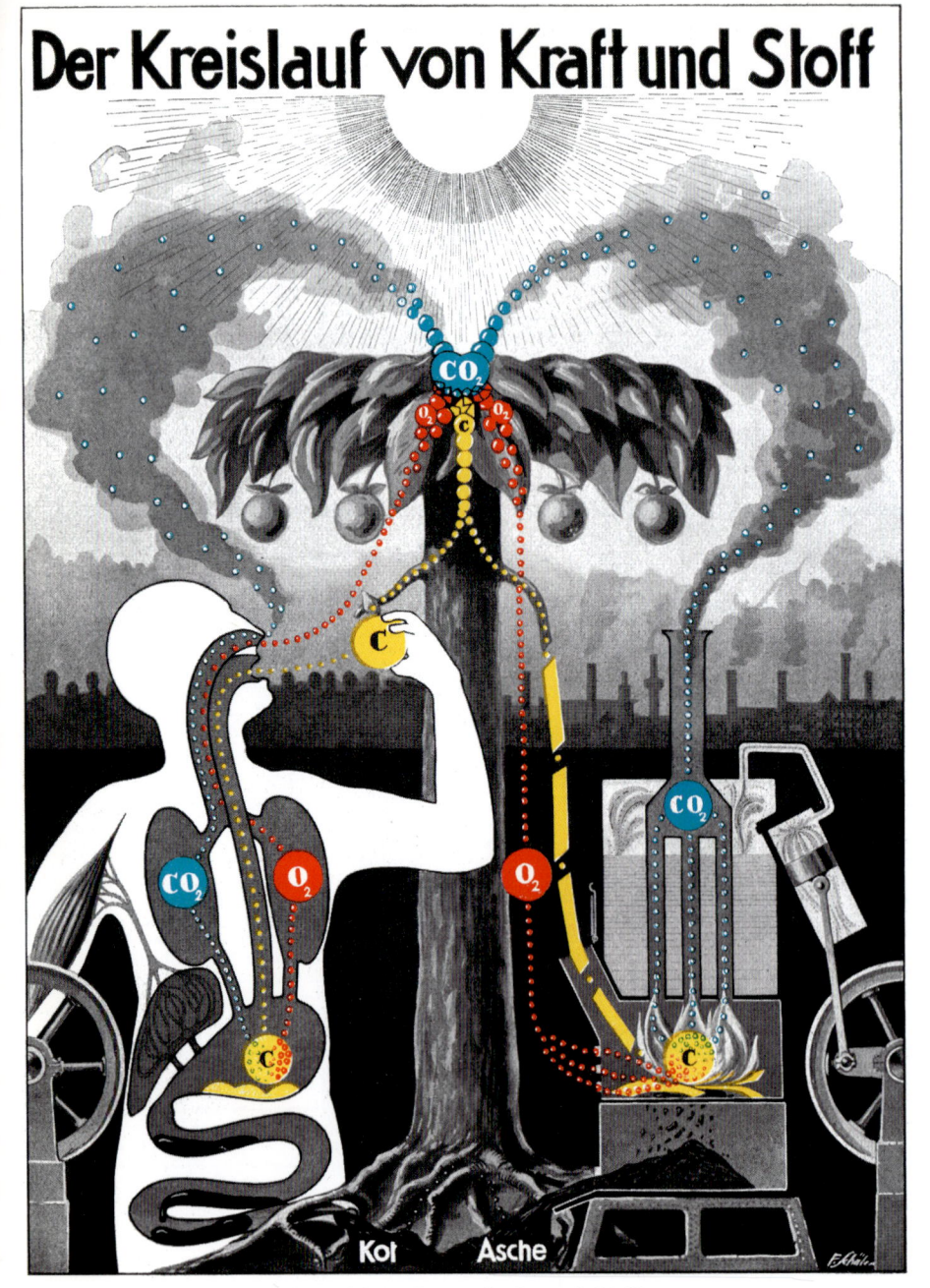

Der Kreislauf von Kraft und Stoff.

Die von Mensch und Maschine ausgehauchte Kohlensäure CO_2 (blau), zusammengesetzt aus Kohlenstoff C und Sauerstoff O_2, spaltet die Pflanze unter Verwendung von Sonnenwärme in Kohlenstoff C (gelb) und Sauerstoff O_2 (rot). Aus dem Kohlenstoff baut die Pflanze Holz und Früchte, den Sauerstoff hauchen die Blätter aus. Der Kohlenstoff wandert als Holz und Kohle in die Maschine, als Frucht in den Menschen und vereinigt sich hier mit dem zu gleicher Zeit eingeatmeten Sauerstoff unter Befreiung der in ihm gebundenen Sonnenwärme, die nun als Verbrennungswärme

Tafel XII

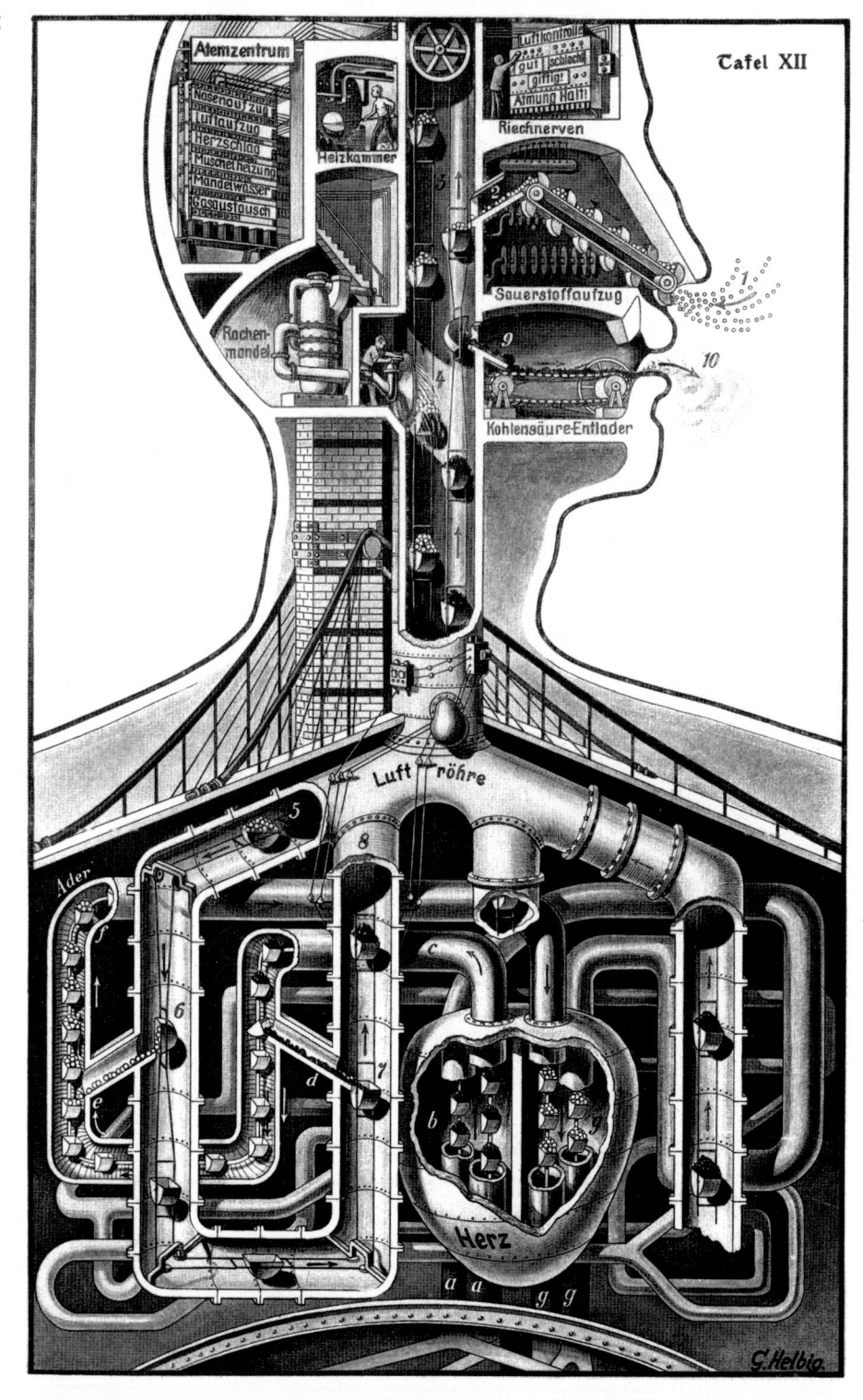

Negersklaverei in den 15 Südstaaten der U.S.A.

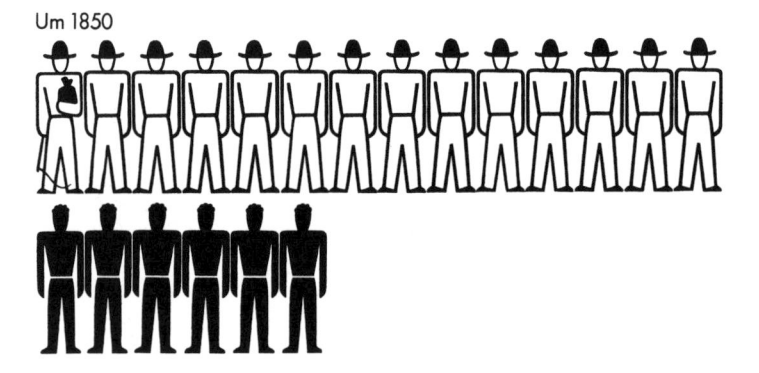

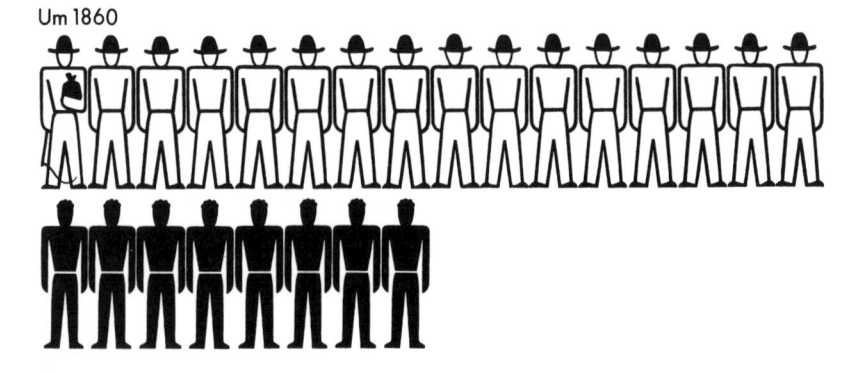

Um 1760

Um 1850

Um 1860

Weisse Bevölkerung (mit Peitsche Sklavenhalter)
Negersklaven

Jede Figur 500 000 Menschen

Angefertigt für das Bibliographische Institut AG., Leipzig
Gesellschafts- und Wirtschaftsmuseum in Wien

Handelsmarinen der Erde

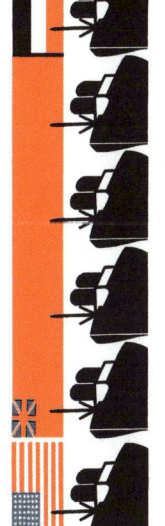

1850

1900

1913

1929

Jedes Schiff 5 Millionen Bruttoregistertonnen

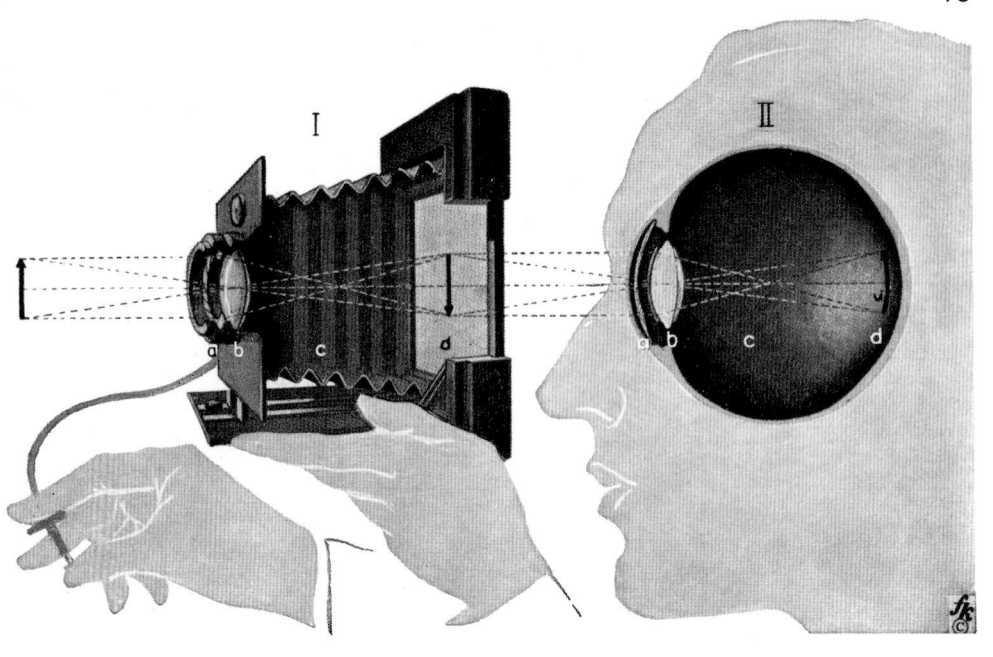

Photoapparat und **Menschenauge**
zeigen eine erstaunliche Aehnlichkeit in der Konstruktion.

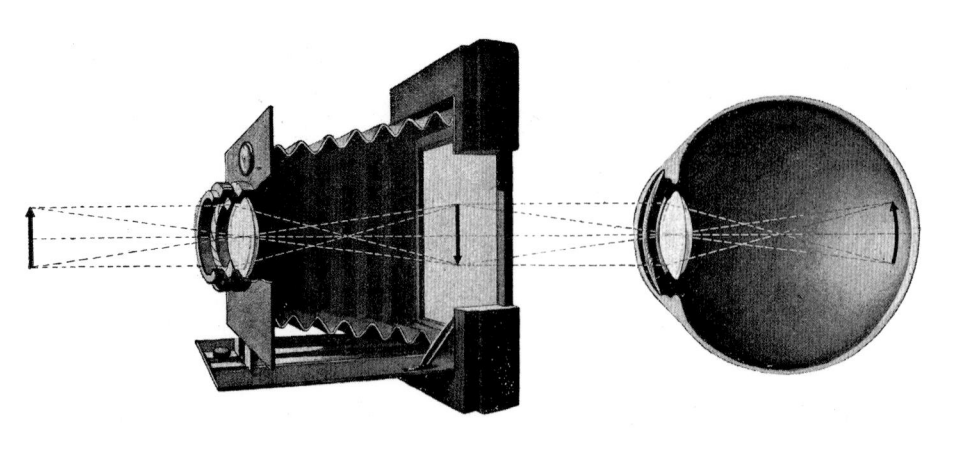

Blende	Linse	schwarz-tapezierte Camera-obscura	Mattscheibe (Lichtempf. Platte)	Blende	Linse	schwarz-tapezierte Camera-obscura	Netzhaut (Lichtempf. Platte)
a	b	c	d	a	b	c	d

Abb. 9. Die Übereinstimmung des Sehapparats in Technik und Natur.

Photographischer Apparat und Auge stimmen in ihrer Konstruktion wie zwei Schwestergebilde überein. Erblicken wir auf der Mattscheibe eines photographischen Apparats ein Bild, so durchlaufen die Lichtstrahlen zweimal einen Apparat gleicher Konstruktion, zweimal eine Blende a, eine Linse b, einen dunkel tapezierten Camera obscura-Raum c, eine lichtempfindliche Platte d.

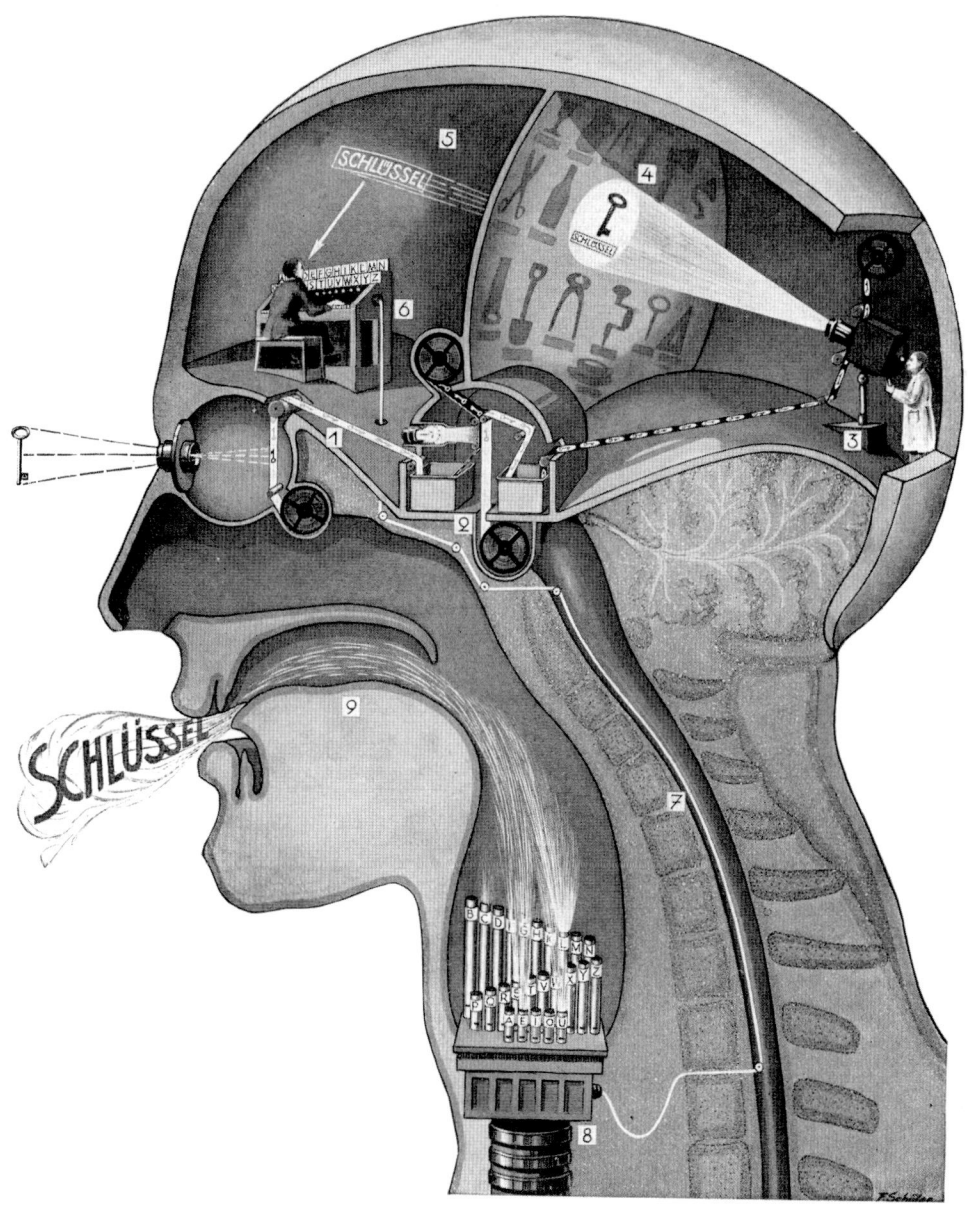

Der Sehakt

Das Bild des Schlüssels gelangt durch das Linsensystem des Auges auf die lichtempfindliche Netzhaut des Augenhintergrundes und belichtet diese. Das Lichtbild wird durch den Sehnerven (1) ins Gehirn zum Sehhügel (2) geleitet. Hier wird das Bild entwickelt, wahrgenommen, und auf eine zweite Nervenleitung übertragen, die Sehstrahlung, die das Lichtbild ins Hinterhirn zum optischen Bewußtseinszentrum (3) leitet. Dieses projiziert das Bild auf das Erinnerungszentrum (4), in dem unsere Erinnerungsbilder als dunkle Erinnerungen eingetragen sind. Das Bewußtseinszentrum sucht hier das kongruente Erinnerungsbild und findet es als Schlüssel, worauf die Bewußtseinszelle den Schlüssel als bekannt wiedererkennt. Mit dem Aufleuchten des Erinnerungsbildes (4) taucht automatisch auch das Wortbild „Schlüssel" im optischen Sprachzentrum (5) in uns auf. Wollen wir den Gegenstand mit Namen nennen, so setzen wir von hier aus über das motorische Sprachzentrum (6) hinweg das Wortbild Schlüssel durch die Nervenleitung (7) um in die entsprechenden Bewegungen des Kehlapparates (8) und formen die hier entstehenden Töne mit Hilfe des Mundes (9) zum Klang: Schlüssel.

Einfuhrhandel nach West- und Mitteleuropa

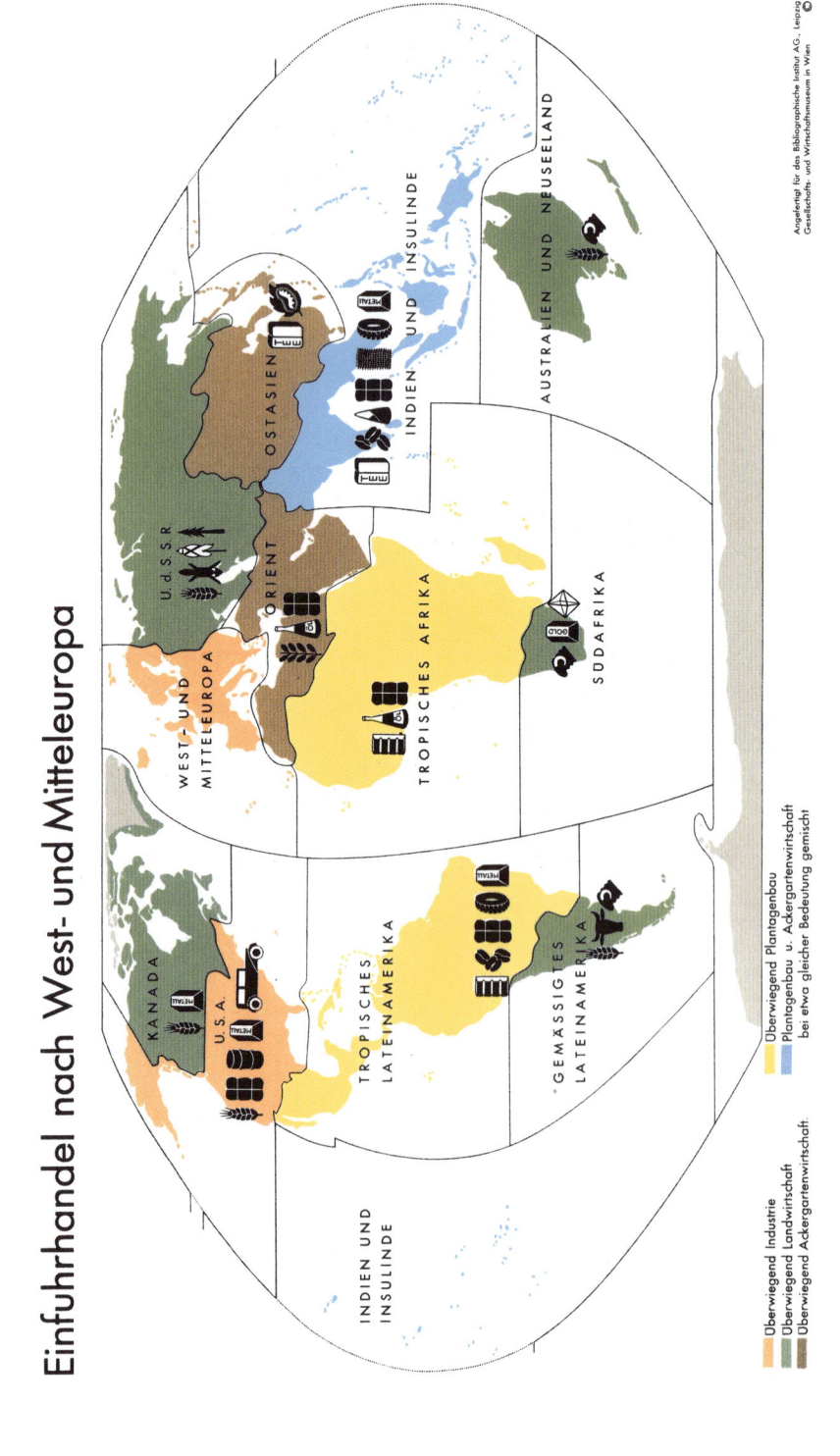

Entwicklung der Kohle- und Erdölproduktion seit 1870

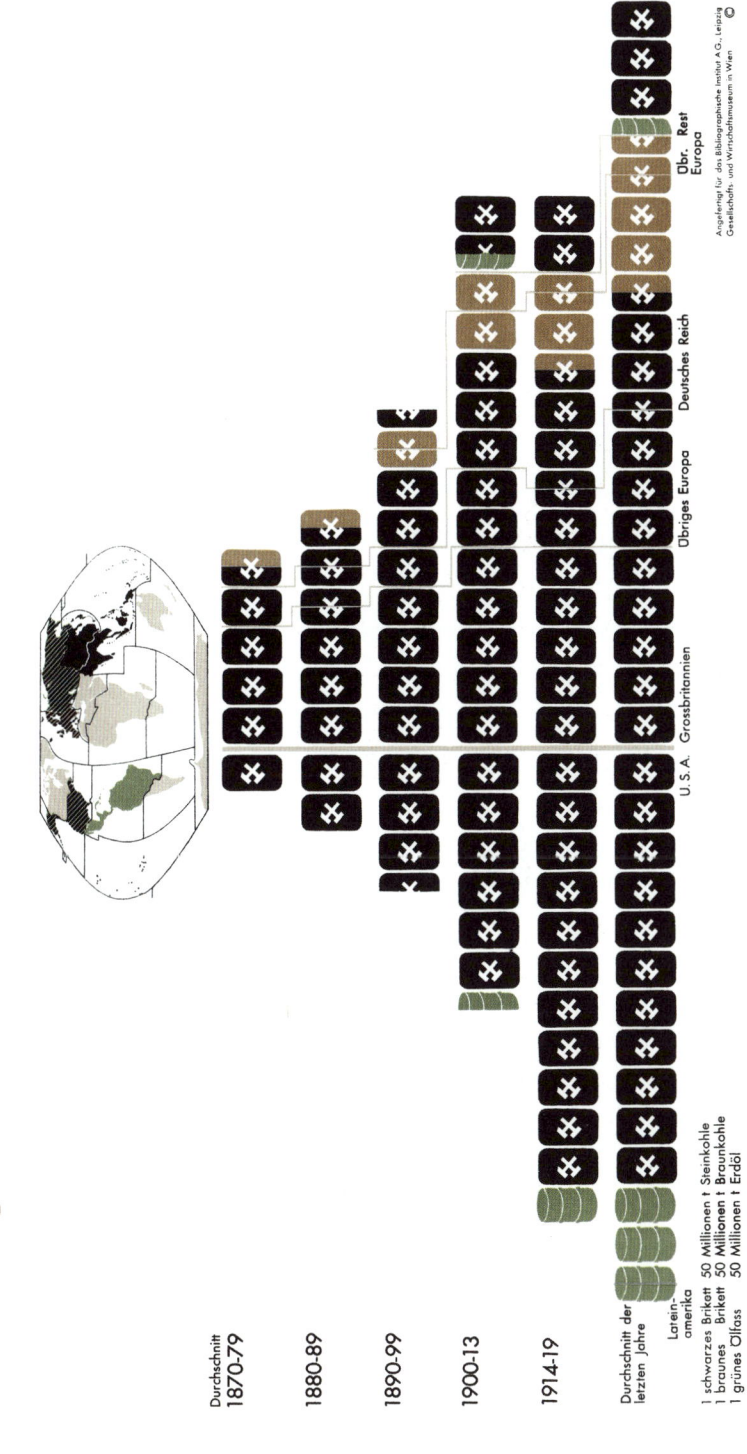

Durchschnitt
1870-79

1880-89

1890-99

1900-13

1914-19

Durchschnitt der
letzten Jahre

Latein-
amerika | U.S.A. | Grossbritannien | Übriges Europa | Deutsches Reich | Übr. Rest
Europa

1 schwarzes Brikett 50 Millionen t Steinkohle
1 braunes Brikett 50 Millionen t Braunkohle
1 grünes Ölfass 50 Millionen t Erdöl

Angefertigt für das Bibliographische Institut A.G., Leipzig
Gesellschafts- und Wirtschaftsmuseum in Wien

Abb. 170 Die Arbeitsleistung des Herzens.
Das Herz treibt einen Fahrstuhl in 40 Minuten 5 Stockwerke hoch. Es füllt im Lauf des Tages 3 Tankautos mit 10 000 Liter Blut und pumpt in 70 Jahren 250 Millionen Liter Blut, die den Rauminhalt eines Wolkenkratzers ausfüllen.

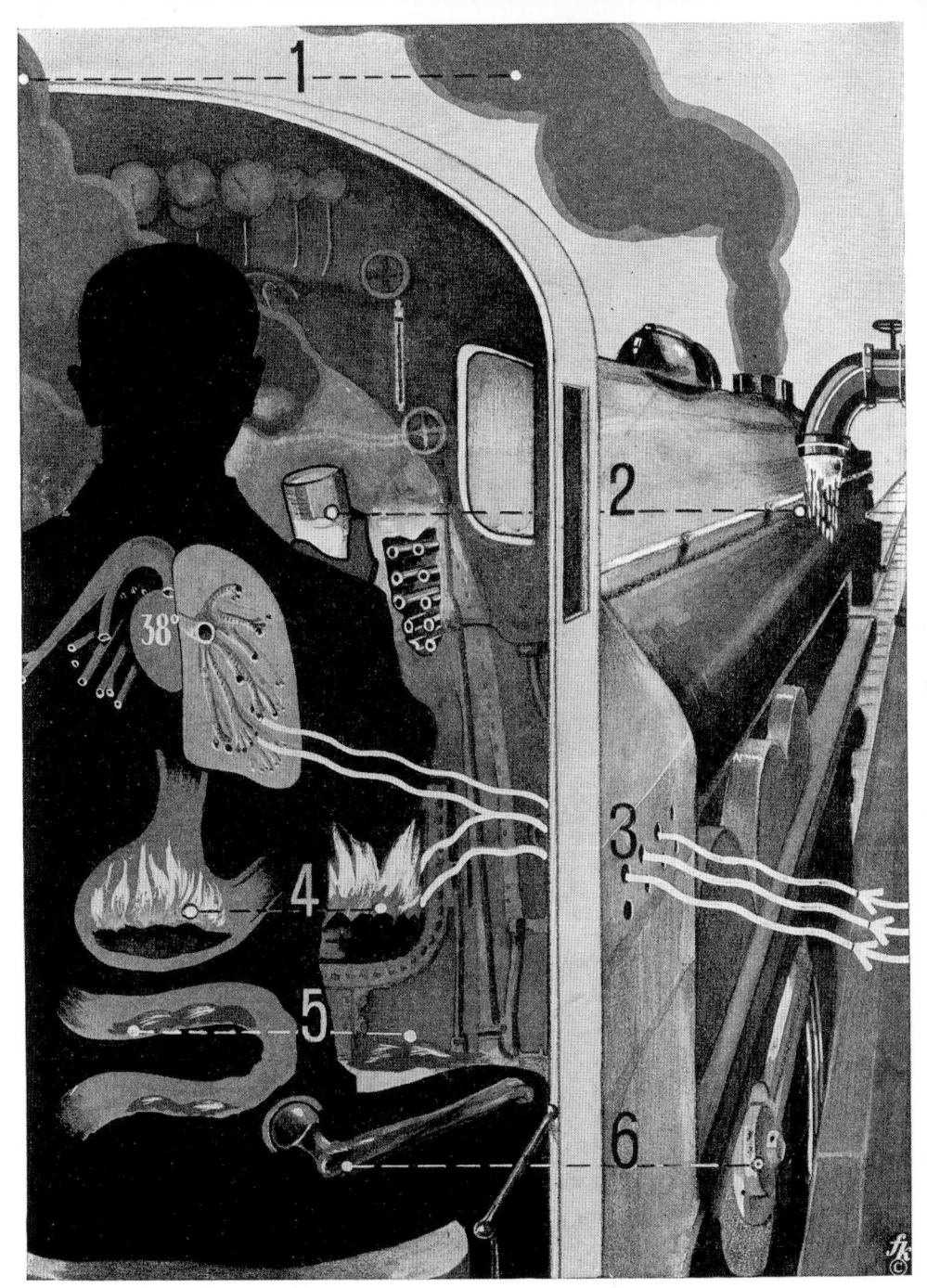

Mensch und Maschine nehmen als Betriebsmaterial kohlenstoffhaltige Pflanzenprodukte auf (4), verbrennen sie durch Zufuhr von Luft (3), benützen die gewonnene Wärme und atmen die entstehende Kohlensäure aus (1). Die Wärme wird durch eine in Röhren kreisende Flüssigkeit (2) verbreitet und zur Bewegung von Hebeln und Gelenken verwertet (6).
Die unverbrennbaren Rückstände werden als Asche oder Kot ausgeschieden (5).

Entwicklung der Eisenbahnen

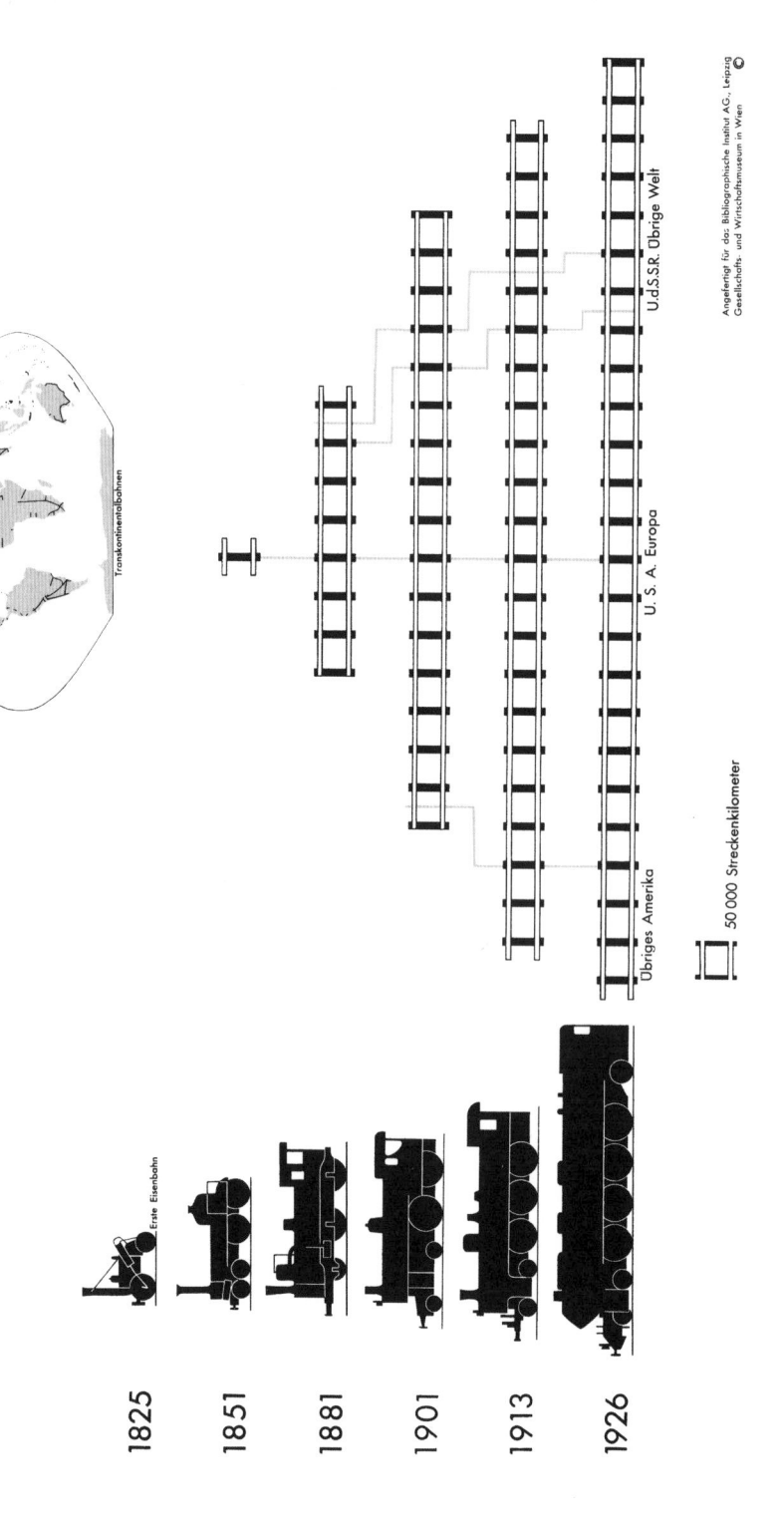

Transkontinentalbahnen

Übriges Amerika | U. S. A. Europa | U.d.S.S.R. Übrige Welt

50 000 Streckenkilometer

1825 Erste Eisenbahn
1851
1881
1901
1913
1926

Angefertigt für das Bibliographische Institut AG., Leipzig
Gesellschafts- und Wirtschaftsmuseum in Wien

Monopolartige Produktionen aussereuropäischer Länder

U.S.A.
Kupfer — Weltkupferkartell

Schwefel

Automobile — Ford, General Motors

Kinofilme

Erdöl — Standard Oil Konzern — in U.S.A. Royal Dutch & Shell Konzern

Mais

Baumwolle

BRASILIEN
Kaffee

CHILE
Chilisalpeter

JAPAN
Kampfer

Seide

Dunkelrot: Produktion innerhalb des Landes unter eigener Kontrolle
Hellrot: Produktion unter Kontrolle des Monopollandes in anderen Ländern
Grau: Sonstige Produktion

Jede Signatur 10 Prozent der Weltproduktion

Angefertigt für das Bibliographische Institut AG., Leipzig
Gesellschafts- und Wirtschaftsmuseum in Wien

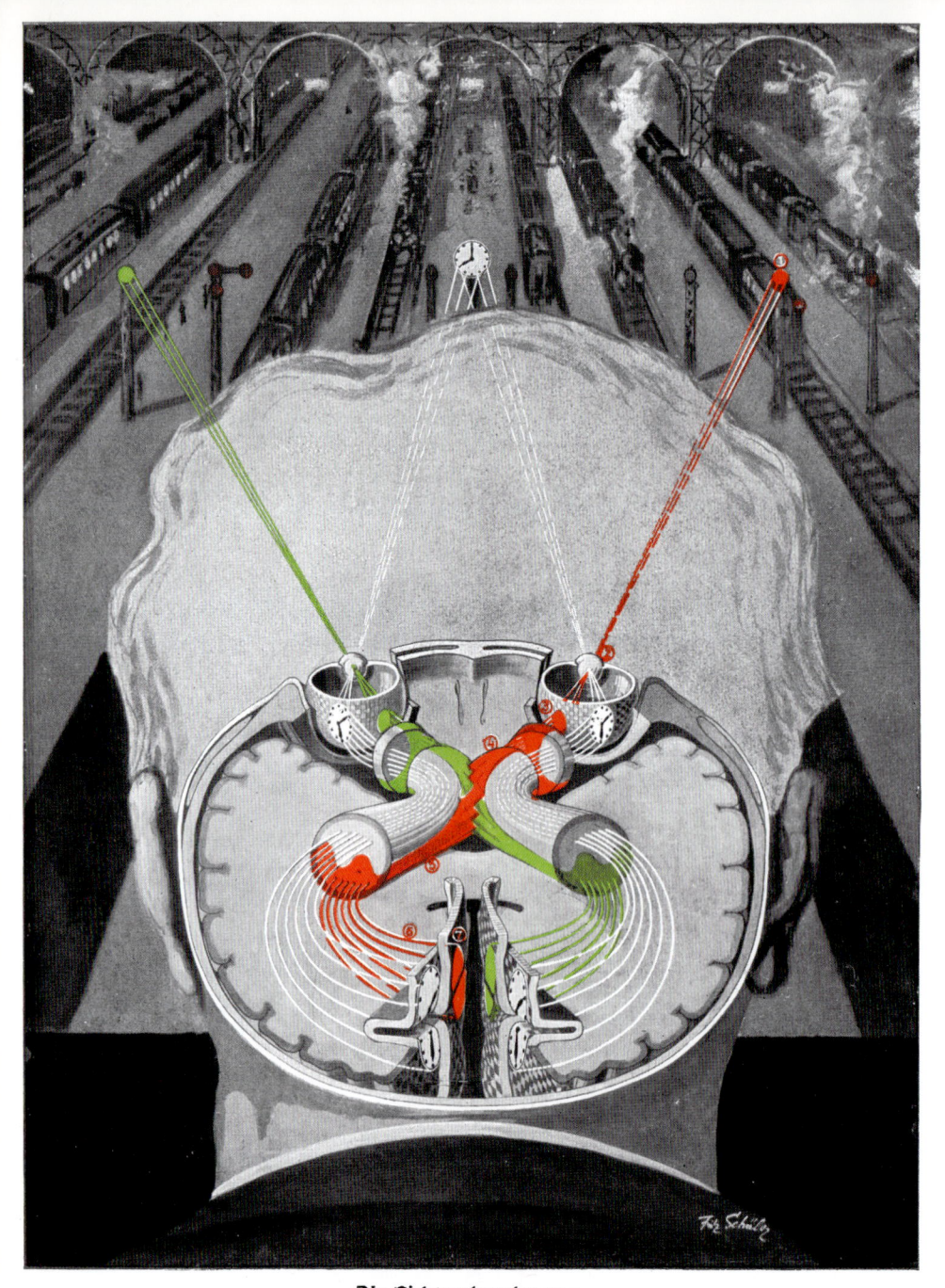

Die Lichtwahrnehmung

Das Bild der Außenwelt (1) wird von der Linse des Auges (2) gesammelt und (umgekehrt) auf die Netz=
haut des Augenhintergrundes (3) geworfen. Von hier wandert die Nervenerregung durch den Sehnerven (4)
ins Gehirn. Die Sehnerven der beiden Augen treffen sich in der Mittellinie und tauschen hier den inneren
Teil ihrer Fasern aus. Durch diese „Sehnervenkreuzung" wandern die Nervenfasern und mit ihnen die
optischen Eindrücke der inneren Hälfte des linken Auges (grün) auf die rechte Hirnhälfte hinüber und die

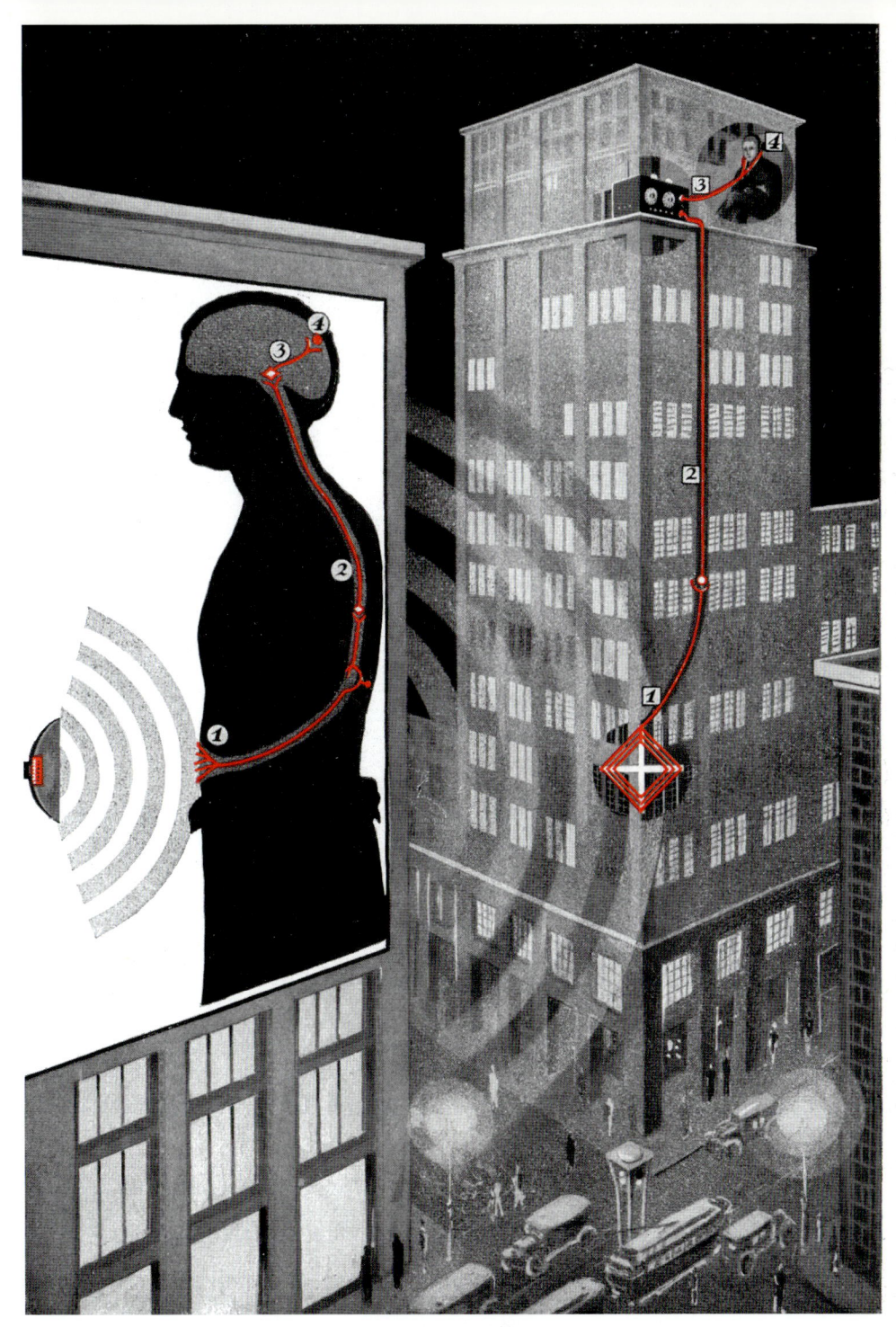

Die Empfindungsbahn

Heeresstärken in der Neuzeit

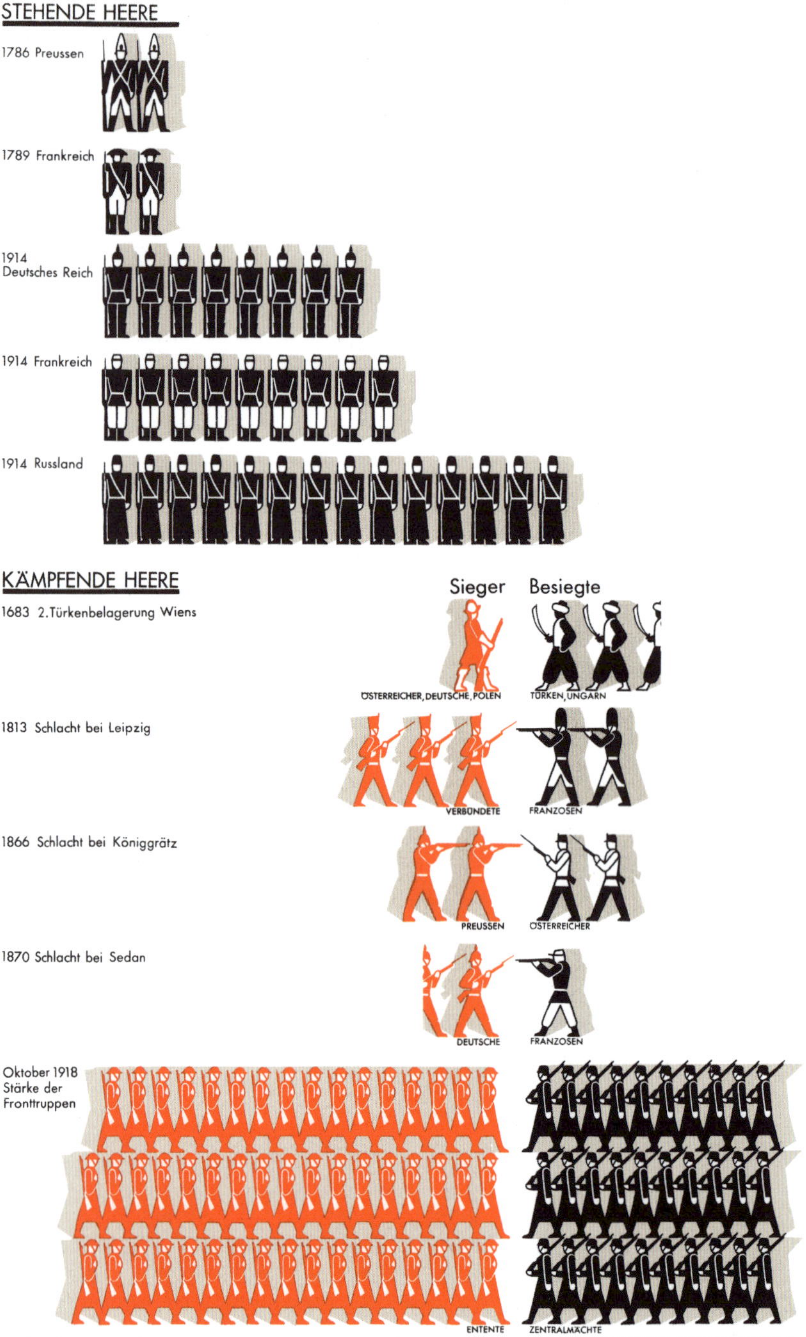

STEHENDE HEERE

1786 Preussen

1789 Frankreich

1914 Deutsches Reich

1914 Frankreich

1914 Russland

KÄMPFENDE HEERE

	Sieger	Besiegte
1683 2.Türkenbelagerung Wiens	ÖSTERREICHER, DEUTSCHE, POLEN	TÜRKEN, UNGARN
1813 Schlacht bei Leipzig	VERBÜNDETE	FRANZOSEN
1866 Schlacht bei Königgrätz	PREUSSEN	ÖSTERREICHER
1870 Schlacht bei Sedan	DEUTSCHE	FRANZOSEN
Oktober 1918 Stärke der Fronttruppen	ENTENTE	ZENTRALMÄCHTE

Jede Figur mit Grau 100 000 Soldaten

Angefertigt für das Bibliographische Institut A.G., Leipzig
Gesellschafts- und Wirtschaftsmuseum in Wien

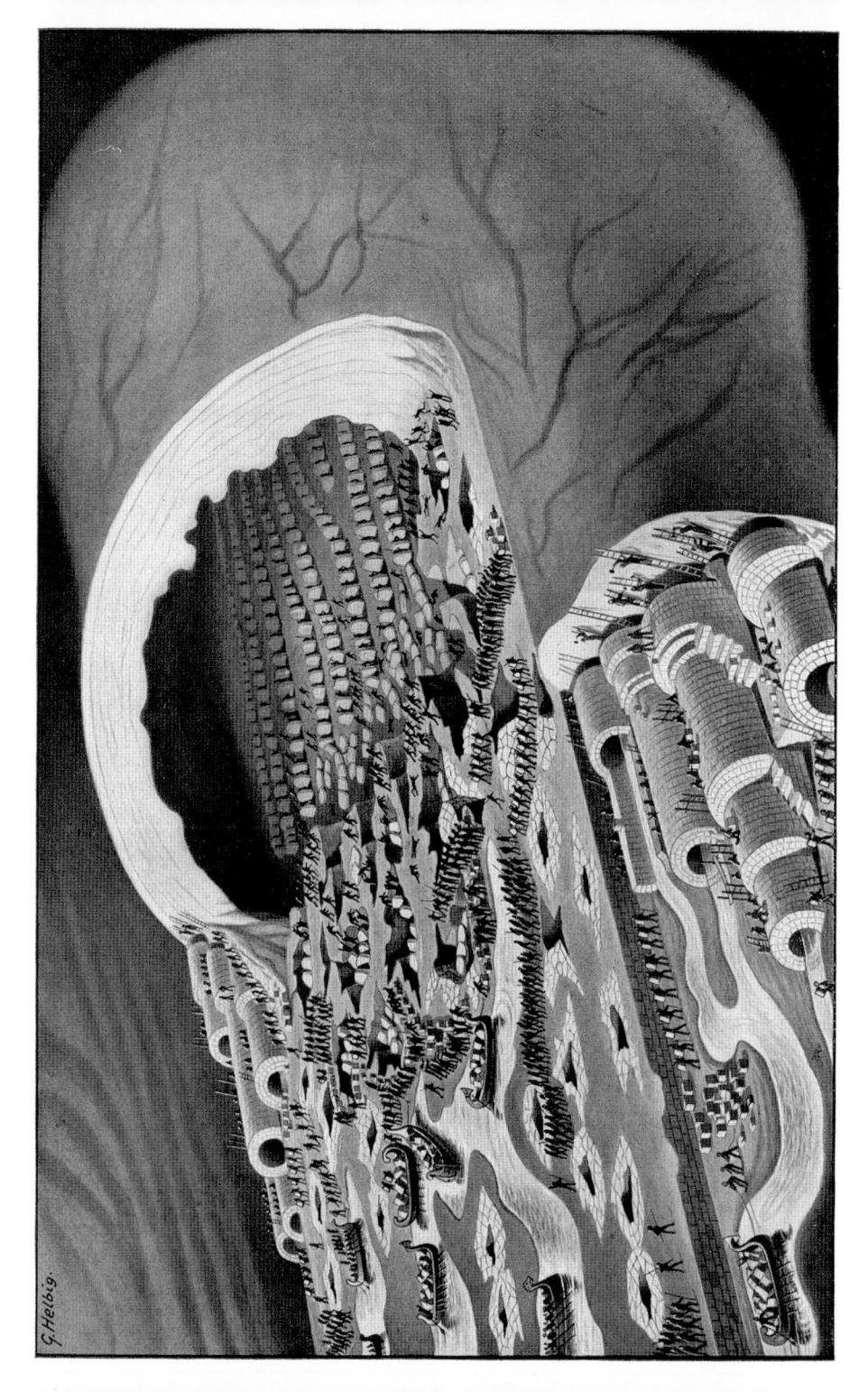

Der zur Verknöcherung führende Kampf des Knochens gegen den Knorpel.

New York

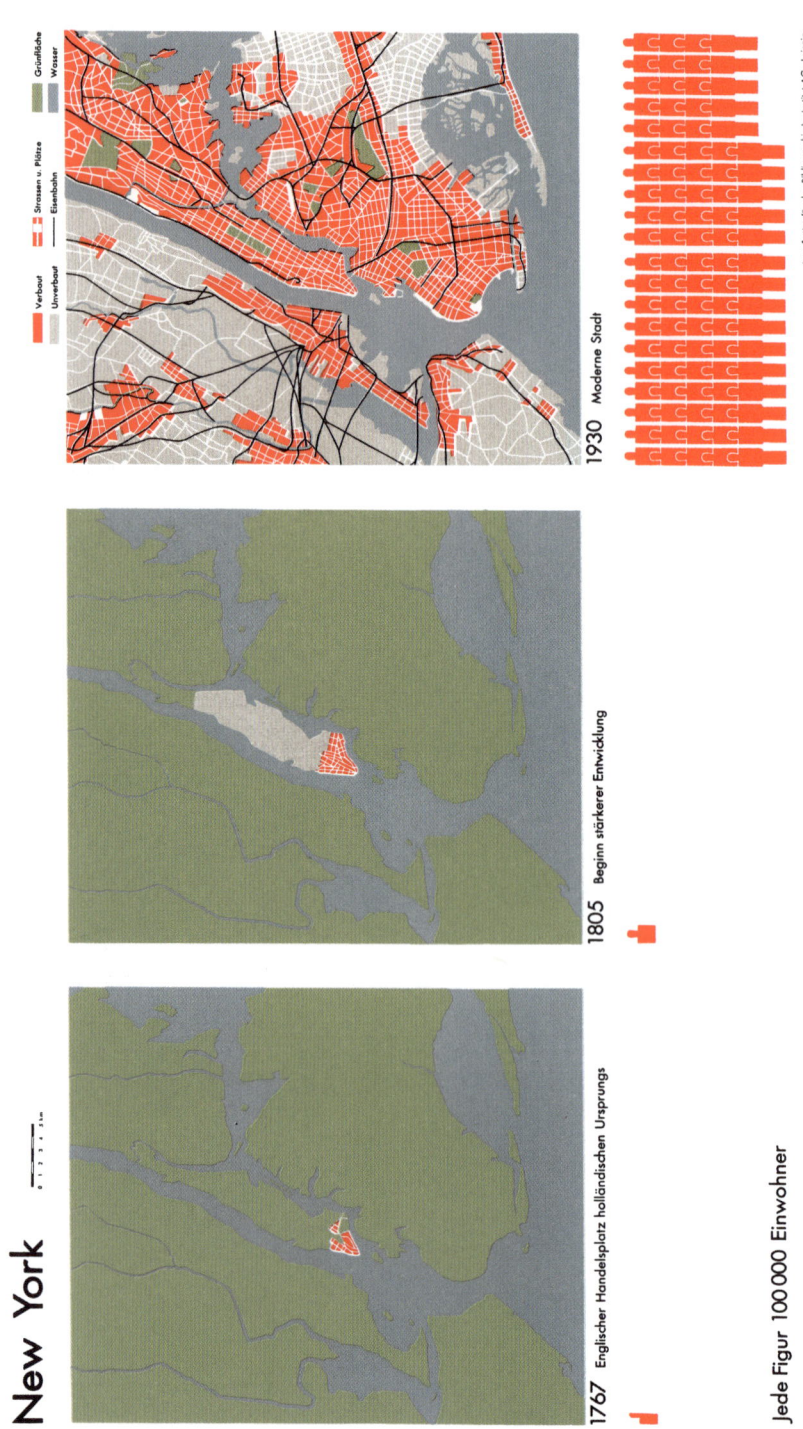

Verbaut | **Grünfläche** | **Strassen u. Plätze** | **Wasser** | **Eisenbahn**
Unverbaut

1767 Englischer Handelsplatz holländischen Ursprungs

1805 Beginn stärkerer Entwicklung

1930 Moderne Stadt

Jede Figur 100 000 Einwohner

Angefertigt für das Bibliographische Institut AG, Leipzig
Gesellschafts- und Wirtschaftsmuseum in Wien

Wohndichte in Großstädten

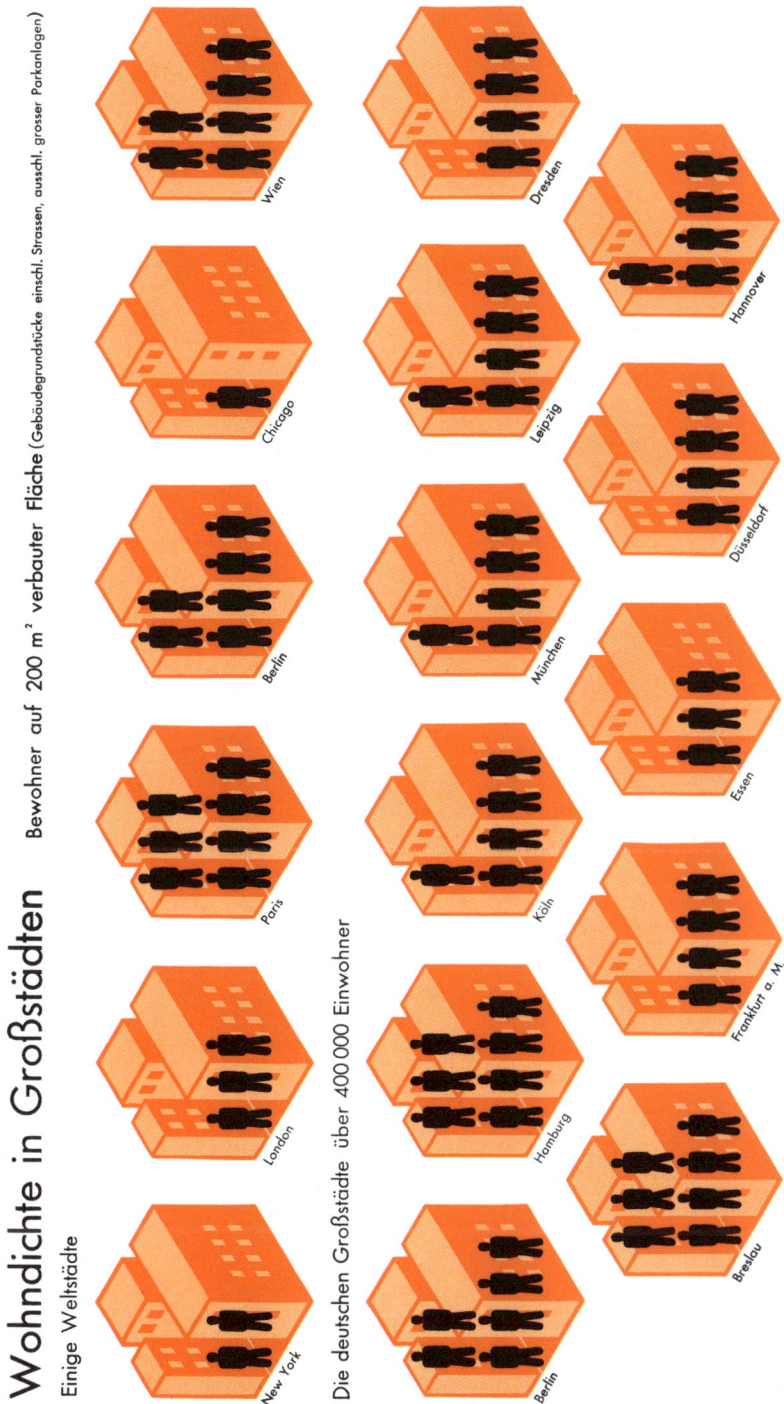

Bewohner auf 200 m² verbauter Fläche (Gebäudegrundstücke einschl. Strassen, ausschl. grosser Parkanlagen)

Einige Weltstädte

New York, London, Paris, Berlin, Chicago, Wien

Die deutschen Großstädte über 400 000 Einwohner

Berlin, Hamburg, Köln, München, Leipzig, Dresden, Hannover, Düsseldorf, Essen, Frankfurt a. M., Breslau

Anordnung der Städte nach ihrer Grösse. Anfang 1929

Angefertigt für das Bibliographische Institut AG., Leipzig Gesellschafts- und Wirtschaftsmuseum in Wien

Sonnenbad!

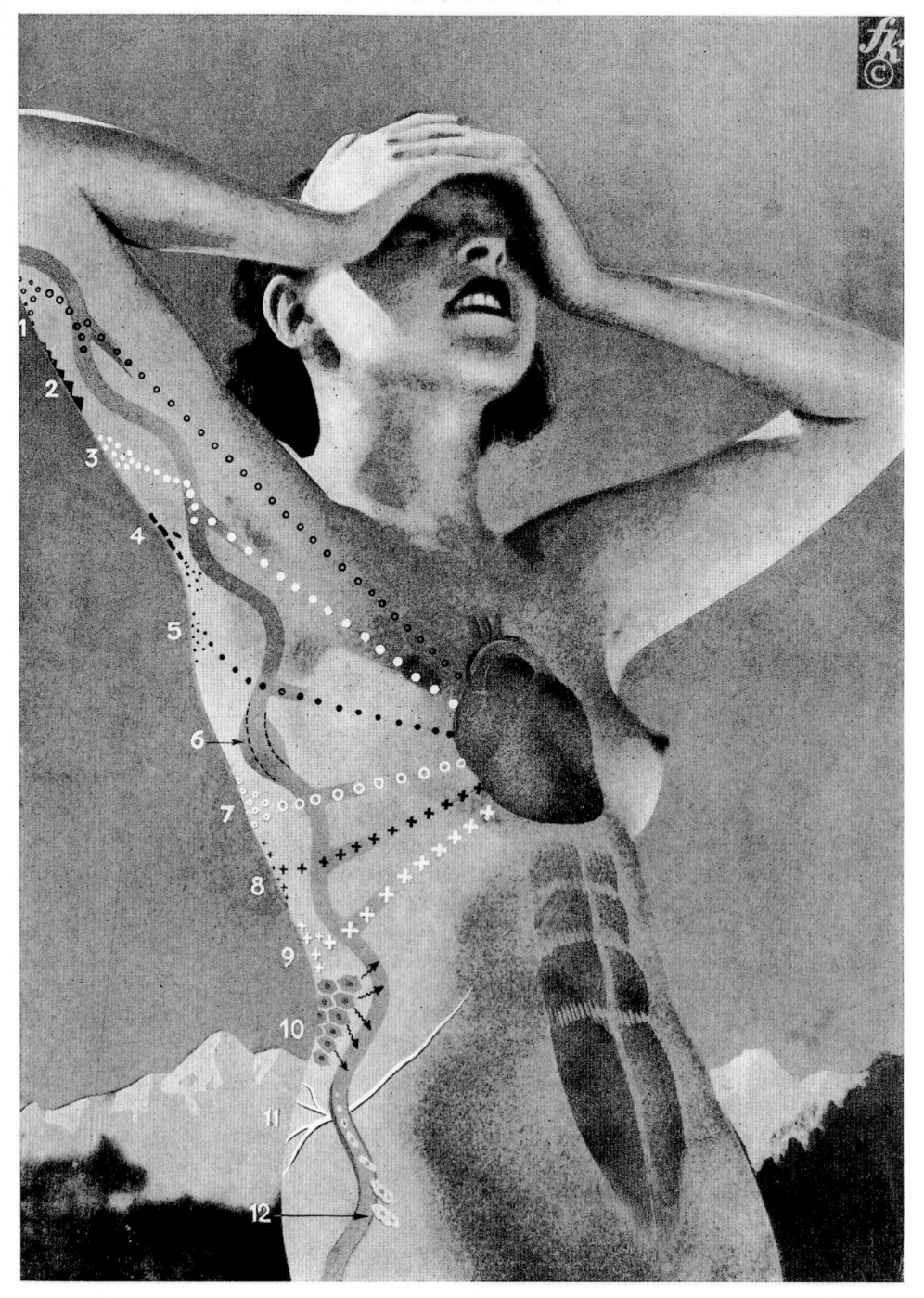

Die zwölf bis heute bekannten Wirkungen des Sonnenlichts auf die Haut.

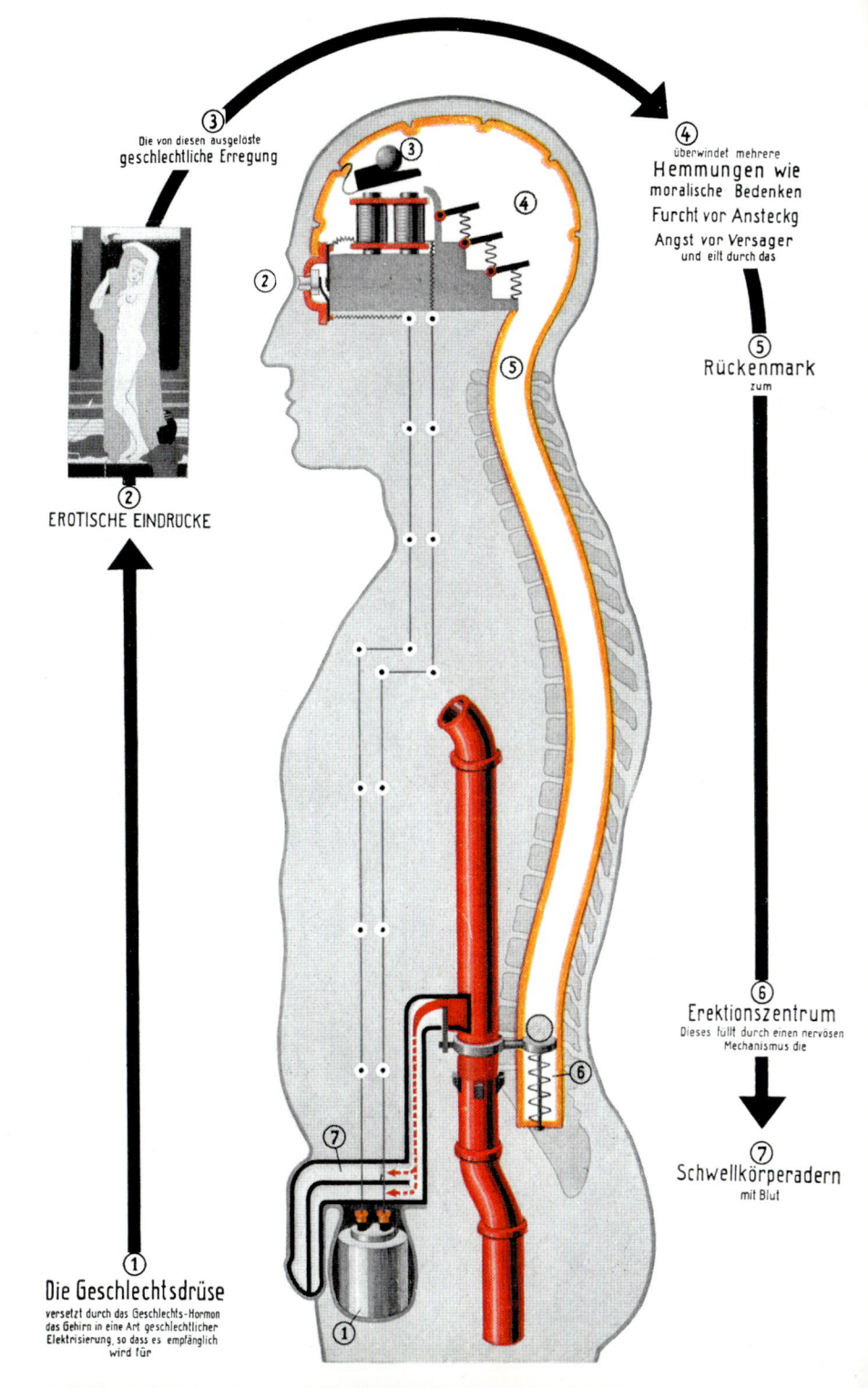

① **Die Geschlechtsdrüse**
versetzt durch das Geschlechts-Hormon das Gehirn in eine Art geschlechtlicher Elektrisierung, so dass es empfänglich wird für

② EROTISCHE EINDRÜCKE

③ Die von diesen ausgelöste geschlechtliche Erregung

④ überwindet mehrere **Hemmungen wie** moralische Bedenken, Furcht vor Ansteckg, Angst vor Versager und eilt durch das

⑤ Rückenmark zum

⑥ Erektionszentrum
Dieses füllt durch einen nervösen Mechanismus die

⑦ Schwellkörperadern mit Blut

Wanderbewegung wichtiger Länder 1920-27

Europa — Einwanderungsüberschuss

Grossbritannien und Irland

Frankreich

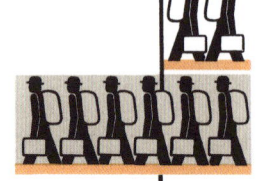

Italien

Deutsches Reich

Amerika

U.S.A.

Argentinien

Jede Figur auf weissem Untergrund 250 000 Auswanderer — über Land
Jede Figur auf grauem Untergrund 250 000 Einwanderer — über See

Angefertigt für das Bibliographische Institut AG., Leipzig
Gesellschafts- und Wirtschaftsmuseum in Wien

Säuglingsterblichkeit und Einkommen

U.S.A.	
GROSSBRITANNIEN	
KANADA	
AUSTRALIEN und NEUSEELAND	
ARGENTINIEN	
DEUTSCHES REICH	
SÜDAFRIKA	
SPANIEN	
BRASILIEN	
JAPAN	
RUMÄNIEN	
U.d.S.S.R.	
ÄGYPTEN	
BRITISCH-INDIEN oder CHINA	
FRANZ.-WESTAFRIKA	

Jeder Kreis 100 Mark Jahreseinkommen auf einen Einwohner (1929)

Jeder Sarg ein Todesfall im 1. Lebensjahr auf 10 Geburten

Angefertigt für das Bibliographische Institut AG., Leipzig
Gesellschafts- und Wirtschaftsmuseum in Wien

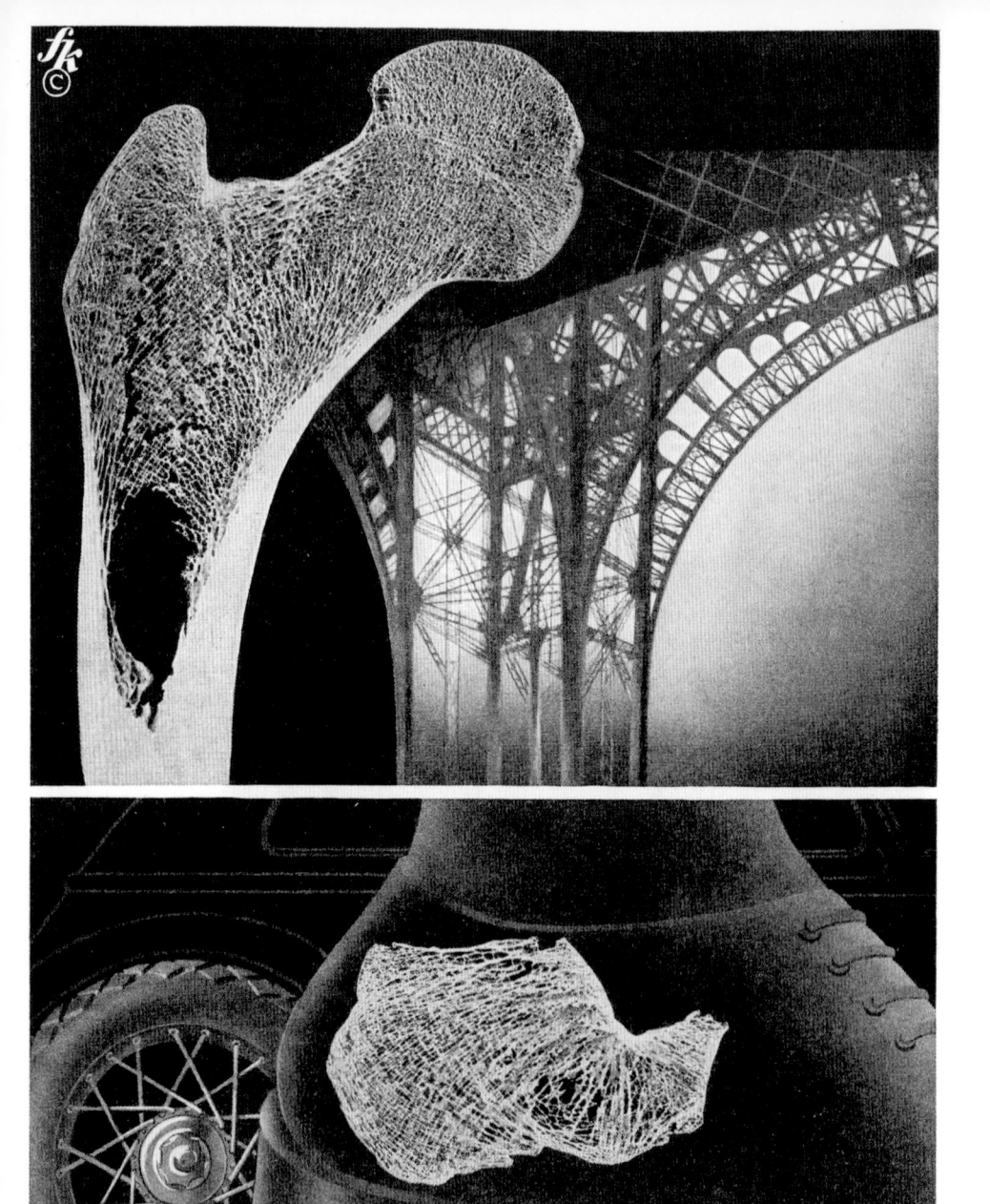

Abb. 67 Die Innenstruktur des Knochens.

Druck der Atmosphäre

Anziehungskraft des Erdballs

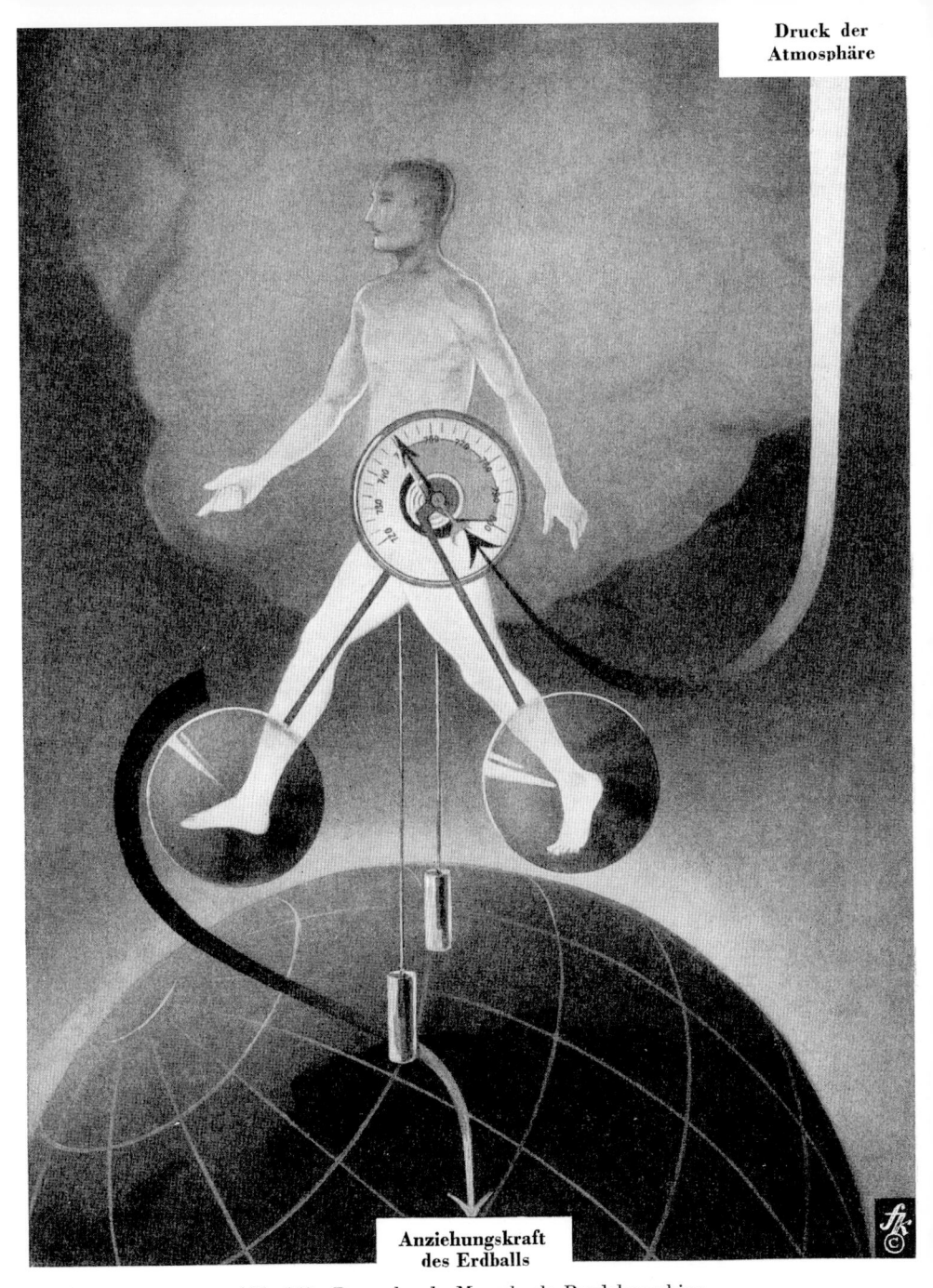

Abb. 153 Der gehende Mensch als Pendelmaschine.
Der gehende Mensch nutzt zwei Naturkräfte aus: Der Luftdruck presst den Oberschenkel in das luftleere Hüftgelenk, sodass er fast gewichtslos in diesem hängt. Das durch Muskelzug hochgeschwungene Bein wird von der Anziehungskraft der Erde als schwingendes Pendel angezogen. Nur die Mithilfe dieser beiden Naturkräfte ermöglicht und erklärt die erstaunlichen Marschleistungen des Menschen.

Großstädter unter je 25 Personen

Europa 1930

Grossbritannien und Irland

Frankreich

Italien

Deutsches Reich

Österreich

U. d. S. S. R.

Amerika 1930

U. S. A.

Argentinien

Asien 1930

Indien

China

Australien 1930

Römisches Reich um Chr. Geb.

Mittelamerikan. Altkulturbereich 13. Jahrhdt.

Großstadt: von 100 000 Einwohnern aufwärts
Rot: Großstädter

Angefertigt für das Bibliographische Institut A.G., Leipzig
Gesellschafts- und Wirtschaftsmuseum in Wien

Erwerbstätige nach Wirtschaftsgruppen um 1920

U.S.A.

GROSSBRITANNIEN

FRANKREICH

ITALIEN

DEUTSCHES REICH

U.d.S.S.R.

JAPAN

Jede Reihe 20 Millionen Erwerbstätige
Jede Figur ca. 2 Millionen Erwerbstätige

Die Erwerbstätigen sind auf 20 Millionen abgerundet,
die Wirtschaftsgruppen auf 5 Prozent

Grün: Land- und Forstwirtschaft, Fischerei
Rot: Industrie, Bergbau, Gewerbe
Blau: Handel und Verkehr
Braun: Rest

Angefertigt für das Bibliographische Institut AG., Leipzig
Gesellschafts- und Wirtschaftsmuseum in Wien

100

101

bitter sauer süss schmerzend heiss ätzend flüssig

Nasales Schmecken

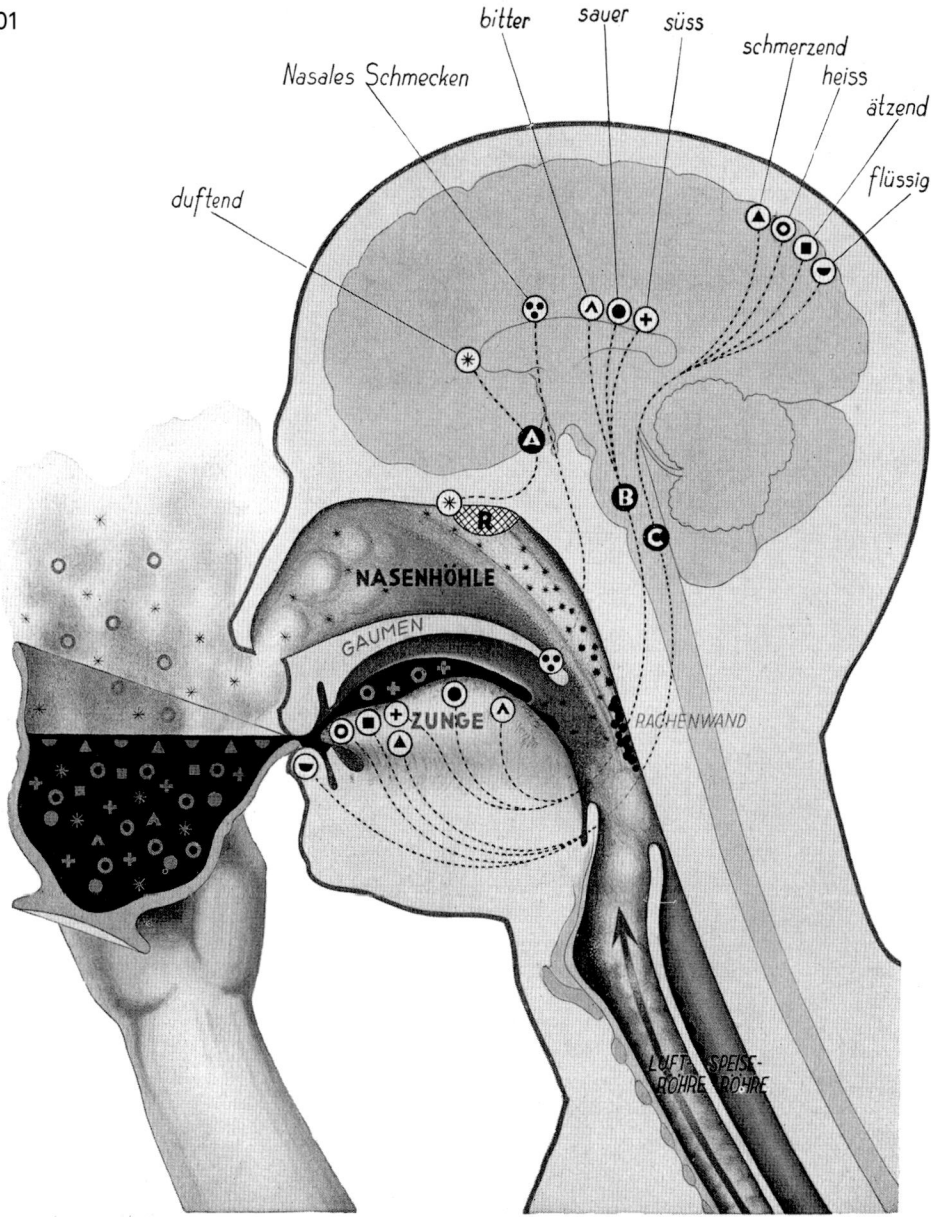

duftend

NASENHÖHLE
GAUMEN
ZUNGE
RACHENWAND
LUFTRÖHRE SPEISERÖHRE

- **Ⓐ GERUCH**
- **Ⓑ GESCHMACK**
- **Ⓒ HAUTSINNESERREGUNG**
- **❋ RIECHFELD**

- ⊖ Berührung
- ■ Ätzung
- ⊙ Hitze
- ▲ Schmerz
- ✷ Aroma

- ⊕ Süssgeschmack
- ● Sauergeschmack
- ▲ Bittergeschmack
- ☢ Nasales Schmecken

Das Schmecken
dargestellt am Genuß von Kaffee. (Erklärung im Text S. 274.)

Streiks und Aussperrungen

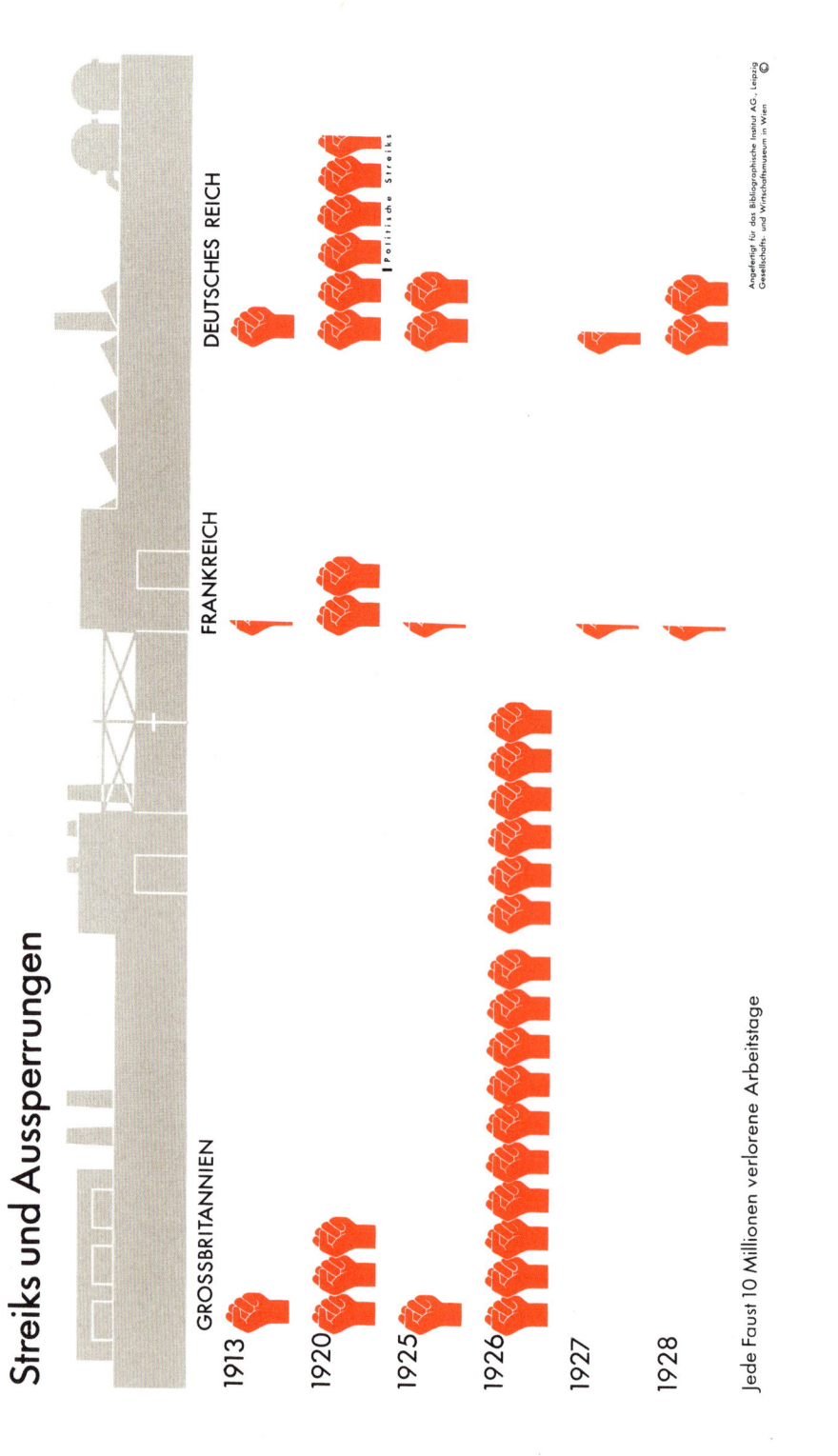

GROSSBRITANNIEN

FRANKREICH

DEUTSCHES REICH

Politische Streiks

1913
1920
1925
1926
1927
1928

Jede Faust 10 Millionen verlorene Arbeitstage

Angefertigt für das Bibliographische Institut AG, Leipzig
Gesellschafts- und Wirtschaftsmuseum in Wien

Maschinenausfuhr vor dem Krieg und jetzt

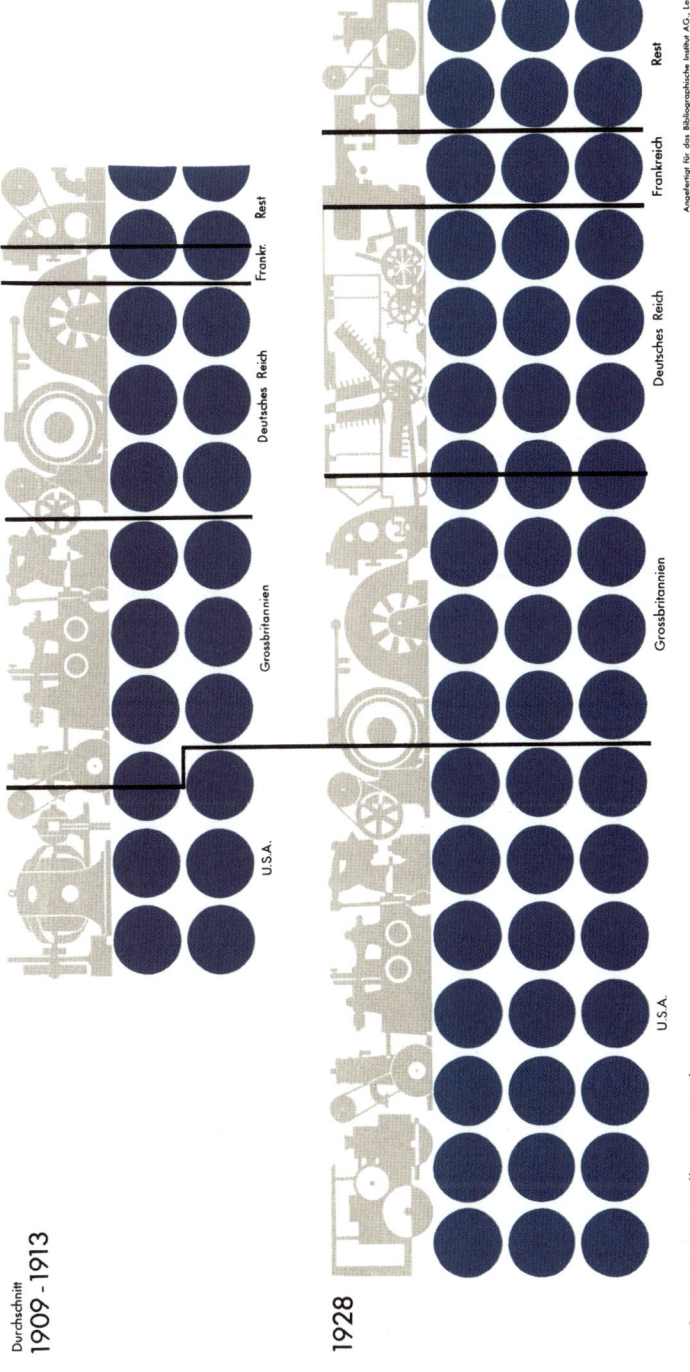

Durchschnitt
1909 - 1913

1928

Jeder Kreis 100 Millionen Mark

249. **Homo technicus**

105 Fritz Kahn— A "Creative Director" of Artistic-scientific Illustration

Helena Doudova in conversation with Uta von Debschitz

Fritz Kahn is known all over the world for his unique visualizations. Where did he derive his concept of popular scientific illustration and how would you characterize his approach?

During the nineteenth and early twentieth centuries, popular science was mainly thought of as a simplified presentation of scientific content. For this reason, the illustrations in non-fiction books resembled those found in academic publications and textbooks. In the foreword to his book series *Das Leben des Menschen* [The Life of Man] Kahn referenced the recent reprint of an encyclopedia of human biology which was produced to high standards but very conventional in its illustrations. He consciously set himself apart from it by formulating the goal that his readers should be presented with an up-to-date "total painting" with the title "Man in the Light of Modern Science". In the foreword to the second edition, he added: "Every age will paint this picture slightly differently."

The term "painting" in itself emphasizes the fact that Kahn wanted to depict human biology faithfully, but not strictly factually. Elsewhere he called this kind of portrayal "artistic-scientific graphics". For him, science, art, and popular culture were complementary rather than contradictory perspectives, and this also explains his interdisciplinary approach and the stylistic range of his illustrations. In some, we find visualization strategies from specialist medical literature. Others are obviously inspired by the culture pages of illustrated newspapers, works of the classical modernism or the advertising aesthetic of the day.

Kahn's joyful affirmation of the subjective, the interdisciplinary and the artistic must have felt like an intellectual breath of fresh air compared to the popular science illustrations of the turn of the century. Many of his more academic illustrations are very painterly and downright experimental for popular scientific representations, and different artistic styles are seamlessly integrated. We can see here a conception of modernity that is completely different from that of Neurath, who saw art as a distraction and aimed for the greatest possible abstraction and standardization in his images.

Kahn was to take up the concept of the painting again on a later occasion. In an unpublished foreword for the book *Design of the Universe* he wrote at the beginning of the 1950s: "Just as the artist paints with the brush a picture of a landscape (…), the scientist paints a design of the universe." But the paintings of science would be "less final" than works of pure fiction. His further remarks make it clear that Kahn understood the theories of science as historically conditioned artefacts, just like the texts and images he himself created in his attempt to convey the scientific "total painting". In the said foreword he compares himself to a reporter who visits a "fashion show" and then tries to give an eyewitness account that is as precise and vivid as possible. He is not interested in objectivity in an absolute sense but rather in a snapshot of human life. This calls to mind the subtitle of the cultural magazine *Der Querschnitt* [Cross Section] from the 1920s: "Magazin für aktuelle Ewigkeitswerte" [Journal of Current Eternal Values].

In Kahn's work, it is above all the visual man-machine analogies that are the most striking. How did this come about?

The original inspiration probably came from the 1921 popular science compendium *Wunder in uns* [Wonders Inside Us], to which Fritz Kahn had contributed three texts. The editor was Walter DeHaas (pen name Hanns Günther), a highly creative editor and publisher who paid close attention to the American book market. It was there that he seems to have discovered the family encyclopedia *Pictured Knowledge*, which contained some illustrations showing the human body and individual organs as workplaces. DeHaas reprinted some of these images in *Wunder in uns*, and for the second edition he even had them redrawn in colour. The fact that he justified these deliberately "unscientific" images in a detailed footnote shows how unfamiliar such illustrations must have been in the prevailing local conditions.

In the early 1920s, Fritz Kahn's publisher Walther Keller founded the publishing house Montana Verlag in Switzerland and put DeHaas in charge. At the end of the period of high inflation, he wanted to position himself in the book market with new, modern themes. In the medically-oriented Montana Verlag, this included sexual education, although this soon drew suspicions of pornography. It is likely that DeHaas, Keller, and Kahn—who had already developed the innovative illustration concept of "vivid representation"— collectively conceived the idea of abstracting the body and its functions to such a degree that they would no longer be perceived as indecent. What was really new, therefore, was this strategy of artistic alienation; the technology depicted in the images was no more than a means to an end. Kahn could get really excited about modern technology, but his concern was neither a glorification of industrial modernity nor the propagation of a mechanistic worldview—and in *Das Leben des Menschen* there are in fact a large number of non-technical illustrations as well as the technical ones. His primary intention was to arouse interest for the wonders of nature, which in his opinion eclipsed the wonders of technology. He pursued this goal by almost any means available.

> *Is there a precedent for the work "Man as Industrial Palace"?*

The underlying motif—the torso with the head in profile view— can already be found in *Pictured Knowledge*. But these older house–body analogies only show scenes from traditional crafts and agriculture; the location of the human body in modern industrial society is Kahn's own enhancement of the motif—the corn mill becomes a factory, the kitchen a laboratory and so on. A direct precursor from Kahn's own production could be "Die Atmung" [The respiratory system] which he developed with his illustrator Georg Helbig.

> *In your illustrated book* Fritz Kahn *you mention Kahn's work as a physician, but you see his professional focus more in the production of popular science texts and illustrations. How did this switch come about?*

Kahn saw himself as a passionate scientist, but dealing with patients probably wasn't his thing. At the age of 23, he was given the assignment for *Leben des Menschen* and tried to develop an innovative concept of visualization together with his illustrators. After the First World War Fritz Kahn initially worked as an obstetrician and surgeon at a large hospital in Berlin-Lankwitz. But in a later autobiographical statement, he hinted at the generous support his employer gave to his book projects, so it seems that Kahn could be released from work when necessary. From the mid-1920s at the latest, when he was producing illustrated newspaper articles and advertising material, Kahn set up a studio in his flat. The file of his restitution claim after the Second World War contains an inventory of the items he had to leave behind when he emigrated in 1933, including the furniture of a design studio with five workstations —for Kahn himself, his secretary, and three illustrators.

After his relocation to Palestine Kahn's work as a physician came to an end. In Jerusalem, he opened a studio called "Hayad" [The Hand], together with a fellow native German, Eliyahu Korngold. In an introductory letter to potential new customers, the two-man company presented itself as one of the most famous studios for artistic-scientific graphics, which had already been active in Germany for twenty years and whose work was regarded as groundbreaking. This statement clearly referred to Fritz Kahn, yet the studio was not named after him, but presented itself as an anonymous service provider—between the head and hand, the hand is after all the executive organ. Hayad's range of services included producing all kinds of graphics, but Kahn also designed an exhibition on school hygiene, advertising material for the Jaray streamliner, a detailed prospectus for the Hebrew University, and his internationally most successful work, *Our Sex Life*.

From today's point of view, I would say that in his collaboration with his illustrators Fritz Kahn developed into a competent creative director because ultimately he was responsible for both the aesthetic concept and the implementation of all his projects. He wrote the texts himself, but he hired professional designers to produce the images. Like an auteur filmmaker or an architect, a creative director does not have to master all the professions under his responsibility, but in pursuit of the concept he must be able to coordinate, lead, and deliver a coherent product. The challenges involved would certainly have suited Kahn's personality better than a hospital day.

> Who was involved in the production of art for *Das Leben des Menschen*? How did Kahn choose his collaborators?

What is most striking in the image production is the sophisticated division of labor. First you have to differentiate between staff and freelance illustrators.

The graphics department at Franckh/Kosmos had a staff of about four who had in all likelihood attended a school for arts and crafts, were chosen by the publisher and created a large number of the text illustrations for *Das Leben des Menschen*, following Kahn's written instructions. As these images were in-house products, the designers remained anonymous. Stylistically, the illustrations were rather conventional, and they can be neglected in any aesthetic appraisal of Kahn's work.

For the more demanding drawings such as wall charts, colored images or cover art, the publisher would employ freelance illustrators who generally had academic training or specialist expertise, e.g. as fine artists or scientific painters. These illustrators worked only occasionally or part-time, they used their own workspace or studio and retained authorship of their work by signing it. From the number of images that can be attributed to individual illustrators, we can infer that Kahn worked closely with some of them over many years. In the selection process residence in Berlin was a decisive factor since it was only immediate personal exchange—ideally at Kahn's own studio—that enabled both sides to learn from one another and to collectively develop up-to-date popular science visualizations.

His publisher gave Kahn free reign in defining his management role, but he would insist on this freedom anyway and, for example, reserve the right to personally select his co-workers. On one occasion, he rejected a designer repeatedly put forward by the publisher, claiming that he "is no more than mediocre". This hints at a significant difference in dealing with illustrators. For the publisher Franckh'sche Verlagshandlung, they were above all to add value to the actual product and cost as little as possible. Thus a memo to Kahn read: "Schmitson wants money again. We sent him a penny." By contrast, Kahn saw his co-workers as highly qualified partners, who were to be adequately remunerated for their demanding activities. Wherever he could, he was happy to pay them above the usual wages.

What skill sets did Kahn expect from his illustrators? How did he work with them?

Previous knowledge of medicine and scientific illustration was desirable, but not essential. Apart from Arthur Schmitson, a renowned scientific illustrator in his own right, none of his co-workers had any significant experience in the field of human biology.

The working process during the production of images for *Das Leben des Menschen* can be reconstructed from the statements of co-workers in different creative periods, which are all largely in agreement.

First Kahn would introduce the topic in question, usually in combination with a central design idea, for which he presented existing images or his own sketches as needed. He provided the designers with the necessary background knowledge by way of specialist literature. They would study this independently, thus specializing in particular fields. Not only were they expected to familiarize themselves with the scientific material, they also had to learn about the specific conventions of visual representation in natural science, art, and popular design in order to be able to combine them in a new way when required.

Depending on the complexity of the visualization, the designer would create several designs in close coordination with Kahn, which often led to new ideas for images. Several motifs exist in different versions, showing that they have been revised or modified several times. Sometimes this could even get too much for the illustrators; Roman Rechn, for example, later complained that Kahn had made him produce new ideas for a single problem for weeks on end.

During this phase of the work, the designers could also contribute their own ideas, expertise, and artistic signature. Helga Malling Van Roey, who had worked as a senior graphic designer on Kahn's last book

The Human Body, described Kahn to me as dealing with his co-workers in a very relaxed way, although he could also "make a fuss" and not all his instructions were executed without resistance. If he asked for things that were "too wild," she would reply: "We can't do it like that—*you're* the scientist, but *I'm* the designer!"

Through this constant high-level interaction, both sides broadened their professional horizons—the illustrators acquired a comprehensive knowledge of human biology and Kahn increasingly acquired his own design skills.

In view of the "incessant intellectual activity" that Kahn obviously expected and his demand to always be state-of-the-art in terms of content and design, it is not surprising that many of his employees had an academic background. Above-average creativity was also important because the illustrators had to deal with entirely new areas of research, especially in the field of physiology. In extreme cases, the content concerned subjects which had not yet been scientifically depicted, and for which they might even have to develop original conceptual imagery since they led into areas beyond the representable. This intellectual flexibility was the actual core competency of the artistic and scientific illustrators.

> *Kahn worked with many different illustrators. Who were his most important collaborators and what is their most distinctive work?*

In Kahn's productive Berlin years, from 1913 to 1932, the closest circle consisted of six people, all of whom had an academic or equivalent education and were extremely versatile in terms of style. Within this narrow circle, two "generations" can be distinguished, each spanning about ten years. The first decade, half of which Kahn spent abroad during his military service, was characterized by the strategy of "vivid representation." It was marked by exceptionally dynamic illustrations, which were intended, in particular, to create visualizations of physiological processes inside the human body.

Arthur Schmitson, who had illustrated numerous medical atlases on a wide variety of subjects, is considered the most important figure of "vivid representation." Outstanding examples of his work include his image sequences "Märchenreise auf dem Blutstrom" [Fabulous adventures on the bloodstream] and "Reiseerlebnisse einer Wanderzelle" [Traveler's tales of a migratory cell].

Georg Helbig, an artist and miniature painter with a keen interest in natural science, initially produced rather conventional illustrations for Kahn's debut works *The Milky Way* and *The Cell*. *The Life of Man*, however, also contains some pioneering works such as "The Respiratory System."

The painter, art teacher, and graphic designer Toni N. Haken was the only woman among Kahn's illustrators. She developed numerous highly complex illustrations of the digestive and nervous system for him, but also illustrations in the style of contemporary advertising posters.

I am mainly interested in the second generation, which was responsible for the image of the human being as a machine. What did each of them contribute to this pictorial language?

The second generation of illustrators, which shaped Kahn's visual output from 1924 to 1933, was very open-minded toward classical modernism and the flourishing popular culture. In addition to their industrial associations, the human-machine analogies also contain numerous references to urban life in general and the Berlin of the late 1920s in particular.

Fritz Schüler was a full-time architect who specialized in exhibitions for leading electrical companies from the 1920s onwards. At the 1929 Barcelona International Exposition, he worked together with Ludwig Mies van der Rohe on the pavilion of the German electricity industry. The building was designed by Mies van der Rohe, the exhibition architecture by Schüler. Among his work for Fritz Kahn, Schüler drew numerous industrial and metropolitan scenes and the wall chart "Man as an Industrial Palace."

Ottomar Trester, a painter and art teacher, worked as a graphic artist at the publishing house Scherl Verlag. It seems that he was Kahn's specialist for diagrams and the use of writing within the image. Among his characteristic works are his statistics on the consumption of luxury foods, an image sequence on digestion and the new edition of the "Industriepalast" in 1931. Trester and Schüler also worked with Kahn to produce illustrations for pharmaceutical companies and newspaper publishers.

Like Fritz Schüler, Roman Rechn had originally studied architecture, and both had a highly developed sense of spatial imagination. Although Rechn initially worked in technical planning departments, he had more affinity with arts and crafts and after an unsuccessful application to the Bauhaus he worked as a commercial artist. For *Das Leben des Menschen*, Rechn created many complex images, including the collages on the dust covers of volumes I–IV.

Fritz Kahn was expelled from Germany in 1933. How were his works dealt with during the Nazi era?

Kahn's case is a really good example of the existential challenges facing persecuted writers at the time, but also of the way political pressure could affect publishing practice.

Like many other dissident intellectuals, Kahn was stripped of German citizenship under a pretext. They lost not only their homeland and their livelihood, but also all legal protection—they were to all intents and purposes put beyond the law.

In the summer of 1936, the Nazis intensified political persecution, especially of the Jews, and in this context the remaining stocks of *Das Leben des Menschen* were impounded by the police. According to the publisher's figures a total of 131,000 books had been printed by then—a considerable quantity for an encyclopedia. Nearly 14,000 copies were confiscated and destroyed, and the work later appeared on the "List of harmful and undesirable literature."

As already mentioned, Fritz Kahn and Walther Keller continued to work on joint projects even after 1933, via the Swiss publishing house Montana Verlag. When *Das Leben des Menschen* could no longer be sold in Germany, they decided together with Montana's senior manager Walter DeHaas to produce a new edition of this work for the international market. Shortly afterwards, Keller had to sell Montana, presumably due to political pressure. The enforced political synchronization of the German publishing industry meant that he and many other publishers of persecuted writers were trapped in a conflict of interest: on the one hand, they felt committed to their authors, perhaps even personally connected with them; on the other hand, they had to make a profit with their products and in many instances saw themselves forced to cooperate with the Nazi regime.

The commercial success of *Das Leben des Menschen* was largely due to the illustrations developed by Kahn. For this reason, Keller arranged with the Reichsschrifttumskammer (National Chamber of Literature) that he could continue to use the images, which were ostensibly banned, if he attributed them to "Bildarchiv Franckh" (Image archive Franckh). Denying Jewish creative artists like Kahn the authorship of their works was one of the Nazi regime's common persecution strategies, aimed at the economic exploitation and ultimately the elimination of the person concerned. In order to legitimize the obvious copyright infringement, Keller had Roman Rechn confirm in writing that the ideas for the pictures were not originally Kahn's, but those of his illustrators.

Keller had originally agreed with Kahn that the existing illustrations could be used for new foreign editions of *Das Leben des Menschen*. After the arrangement with the Reichsschrifttumskammer, however, he only returned to Kahn the text rights of *Das Leben des Menschen*, which by then had become virtually worthless. Thus Kahn was deprived of any legal access to the pictures he had developed and was forced to have new ones made at his own expense.

In 1938, Franckh'sche Verlagshandlung published two books with illustrations by Kahn: an abridged version of *Das Leben des Menschen* entitled *Der Mensch und sein Leben* [Man and his Life], which contained an explicitly antisemitic chapter on the study of race, as well as a *Hand- und Lehrbuch der Krankenpflege* [Nursing Manual and Textbook], which was equally influenced by National Socialism. The author was Gerhard

Venzmer, a practicing doctor who was also editor-in-chief of *Kosmos* magazine and who, after Kahn's emigration, became the leading author of popular medical topics at Franckh'sche Verlagshandlung.

Kahn immediately complained about Venzmer's cynical plagiarism, but Keller would only offer him royalties for the use of his pictures. Since Kahn was not able to defend himself legally at that time and his economic circumstances were precarious, he accepted the offer. In 1939/40 he himself published a new edition of *Das Leben des Menschen* under the title *Der Mensch, gesund und krank* [The human being in health and sickness]. Besides new illustrations, it also contained some from *The Life of Man*, albeit with slight changes and variations. To protect himself against future copyright infringements, Kahn retained the rights to this work and labeled every illustration with an "fk©" sticker.

It was not until 1949, when the German Restitution Law regulating the restitution of lost property and the payment of damages to victims of Nazi persecution came into force, that Kahn had the opportunity to file a lawsuit against Franckh'sche Verlagshandlung as well as Venzmer.

What was the result of this court case?

It was settled out of court in 1951, i.e. without any recriminations or reparations; Kahn's authorship was never in any doubt. Since Franckh'sche Verlagshandlung could not provide proof that it had actually transferred any royalties to Kahn during the Nazi era, it had to pay him DM 12,000 in "outstanding author's remuneration." Venzmer was no longer permitted the use of the pictures, but just three months after the judgment he published the fourth edition of *Der Mensch und sein Leben* with a sanitized chapter on race, and new, rather mediocre illustrations.

The moral question, i.e. to what extent Keller's, Rechn's and Venzmer's collusion in Kahn's political persecution was voluntary or under duress, was probably as difficult to answer then as it is today. Keller felt a commitment to Kahn, and on completion of *Das Leben des Menschen* he even spoke of the relationship between publisher and author as being like a marriage. After the restitution procedures, he seemed eager to seek personal reconciliation too; at least he offered Kahn a resumption of their cooperation and an updated edition of his book. This never materialized since Kahn had to return to the United States for brain surgery and Keller passed away, but the invitation to publish in Germany once again was a gesture that meant a lot to Kahn as a writer in exile.

[*The conversation with Uta von Debschitz, co-curator of the exhibition "Fritz Kahn—Man Machine" (2010) was conducted on May 15, 2017 in Berlin.*]

115 The Isotype Work
Otto Neurath, 1943

Editor's note by Christopher Burke:
This text is taken from a typescript dated 23 May 1943, which is held in the Otto and Marie Neurath Isotype Collection at the University of Reading (UK). It was written (in English) around the same time that Otto Neurath was outlining grand plans for a "visual thesaurus" to be made with Isotype—a kind of graphic encyclopedia. The text below was probably intended to give the background of Isotype to those whom Neurath sought to interest in backing the project. Also around this time, Neurath was seeking support for establishing an Institute for Visual Education, which he mentions briefly in the text below.
So this text was intended for private circulation and not for publication. Consequently, Neurath's English was unrefined. In the version given here I have tried to correct ungrammatical passages and to clarify some points, without changing the essence of his meaning. Neurath stated that this was what he wanted an English editor to do for his writing (see the preface to his visual autobiography, From Hieroglyphics to Isotype *[London, 2010, p. xxi]).*
For example, Neurath's Germanic use of verb tenses and commas has been corrected. He also used the original German term for the transformer—Transformator—and so the English term has been used instead. His frequent, informal use of 'etc.' has been retained. Emphasis made using capitalization in the typescript has been replaced by italic.
Neurath's mention of the "oceanic feeling" signals an awareness of the writings of his Viennese contemporary, Sigmund Freud. The first paragraph of Neurath's 'introductory remarks' (omitted here) is quite unclear and rather superfluous: he seems to be saying that it was his duty as director of the Isotype Institute to protect its interests against competing activities, in which he may also have been involved; in other words, to keep the Institute's interests separate from his own, to some extent. He then continues as follows ...

Introductory remarks

I, personally, have been occupied for many decades as a Social Scientist, mainly interested in planning on the one hand, and in theoretical analysis on the other; then as a member of what is usually called the Vienna Circle, I have been concerned with Logical Empiricism—that is, with the analysis of scientific language and language in general as a means of communication. Both activities have sometimes been connected with Isotype work. A selection from my writings may illustrate that.
> *[Here Neurath included a lengthy bibliography of his writings, which can now be found in published sources on, for example, Empiricism and sociology.]*

My activities as writer and research worker led me time and again to do some editorial work and to become managing director or secretary of various institutes and museums. (Besides functions in administration I have been Privatdocent [sic; lecturer] of the University of Heidelberg, and I taught economics and sometimes history at the Commercial Academy, Vienna [Neue Wiener Handelsakademie].)

I became editor-in-chief of the *International Encyclopedia of Unified Science*, managing editor of the *Journal of Unified Science*, and editor-in-chief of the *Library of Unified Science* (Journal, 8 volumes; Library, 9 volumes published).

Organizing Isotype work

As Secretary General of the Austrian Housing and Garden Plot Association [Österreichische Verband für Siedlungs- und Kleingartenwesen] (about 20,000 members, mostly in co-operative housing societies) I proposed the creation of a Museum for Housing and City Planning [Museum für Siedlung und Städtebau] in Vienna (1923), after a very successful exhibition in the centre of the city. We knew from experience that hundreds of thousands of people are prepared to look at charts, models, and photos etc., who would not be prepared to read even the simplest booklet or to look at a picture book. Exhibitions have a particular charm and attractiveness.

I suggested making this a model museum. A world-famous architect [Josef Frank] co-operated with us, we arranged attractive photos and models, we put real walls and real furniture before the visitor. But all these coarse details were completed by our charts, which, in a symbolic way, told the story of housing, and of the social background. Usually housing exhibitions deal mainly with the "surface" and not with the basic social facts.

There was a section about health, and another about social history and the social sciences in general.

To create enthusiasm we have to do something for the "oceanic feeling," for humanizing knowledge, connecting the visitor with mankind, with past and present, with present and future. The individual has to find himself in the exhibition, but also his dreams and hopes, his fears and dangers.

The exhibition was completely successful and the town councillors, interested in our housing organization, treated this kind of enlightenment seriously. I explained to them that in a democracy we can only expect help from citizens who understand a problem and are able to argue pro and con. Newspapers reach only their subscribers, the opposition does not read what "the others" have to say. The readership of books is small—the plain man in the street does not even buy books—but everybody enters exhibitions, without any distinction of party etc. It is a remarkable fact that exhibitions are regarded as "neutral." They reach the broadest masses.

Therefore I suggested I should be given an opportunity to create a museum of international standard, with all departments necessary for progressing at full speed. In 1924 the Gesellschafts- und Wirtschaftsmuseum [Social and Economic Museum] was founded. I became the director and had every opportunity to select my collaborators and to go on without limitations of any kind. After some deliberation, we decided to make the Museum an independent institute attached to the municipality (which nominated the accountant). Ample funds were granted; and after a short time schools and governments from abroad asked for consultation and materials. For this purpose we founded another body, of which I became managing director, too: the Mundaneum Institute Vienna (later on Mundaneum Institute The Hague), and when we thought about the transfer of our international work we founded together with Dutch friends the International Foundation for Visual Education (1933) according to Dutch law, with a permanent acting secretary in Amsterdam, where we got an opportunity to display material in a kind of technical museum and in a university institute, where we got a working room, too.

The "volume" of our Vienna activity may be pictured by saying that we got about 200,000 Austrian shillings from various sources, besides "free" exhibition rooms, and much other help: wardens paid by the municipality etc. 200,000 Austrian shillings are equal in purchasing powers perhaps to 15,000 pounds a year [in 1943].

We had at our disposal: a central museum in the city hall [Neues Rathaus], with our symbolic charts, iron charts with (changeable) magnets, models, documentary photos etc.; branch exhibits in a suburb of Vienna and in the centre of the city, besides exhibits in various places, schools etc., travelling exhibitions throughout Europe, Czechoslovakia, Norway, Germany, England, etc. In one suburb of Vienna the production of charts and the research apparatus were concentrated. A staff of two dozen and sometimes more collaborators worked together with the Museum for many years.

A few words about the sections of this particular part of our Museum: we had about a dozen big rooms at our disposal. The Museum was in permanent contact with scientific experts, cartographers, ethnologists, historians of art and technology, astronomers, physicians, etc., etc. In the meetings, we discussed possible educational material that the Museum wanted to prepare for:

1). Permanent exhibitions, travelling exhibitions etc. In this way, you reach the maximum number of people within a relatively short time. In our well organized "Zeitschau" (March of Time) we received 2,000 persons every day, 60,000 per month. We do not know of any way to reach the masses if they are indifferent: the visitors could take away charts printed on loose sheets, and children often asked for heaps of such material for the classroom. Our exhibition "Rondom Rembrandt" at The Hague, Amsterdam, and Rotterdam (photos, Isotypes, apparatuses—very important, because this would attract the child in any person) received 10,000 visitors who would not read even the simplest booklet on Rembrandt and his time, nor look at a picture book.
2). Leaflets for distribution to school children, adults in adult-education classes, in exhibitions etc.
3). Booklets and books, collections of charts with tables and short notes, no text.
4). Periodicals of the same type.
5). Charts prepared for other people's books, for official reports etc., for periodicals and newspapers.

One of our first principles was to make even the smallest chart as good, as original, and as charming as possible.

After the collection of the scientific material, including documentary photos, prints, etc., the whole matter was shifted to what we called the "transformation" department. A representative of this department was in permanent contact with the scientific experts. The transformation department is, so to speak, the trustee of the visitors and readers, people usually forgotten in our museums, which present what they have and not what the public wants to see.

The transformation department analysed the educational possibilities and therefore required experimental studies. The Vienna municipality provided a school in which we could test our material. Our material was applied in all branches of the curriculum. In history, for example, the teacher got an iron blackboard, on which he fixed (by means of magnets) maps on thin paper, and on this surface the teacher or the pupil could distribute symbols of, say, population mounted on magnets. Charts on the walls, and sheets in the hands of the pupils, who applied the method to the daily routine of the school. Kindergartens not only in Vienna but also in other cities used our symbols in a specific way.

Then teachers came to us and we discussed with them how to test pupils in all schools of Vienna, depending to what extent the teachers were interested in the new method.

School classes visited the Museum and exhibitions. Scientists tested our charts in laboratories and studied the memorizable qualities of Isotype, for example. The transformation department used all this experience and the contact with teachers, scientists, and children. The Museum was mainly open in the evening but not only for adults, also for children of any age. We found out that even small children of 5 years of age liked to look at our material and to grasp as much as possible of the contents.

The transformation department produced models, too, and selected documentary material or arranged for it be produced by specialists.

A well-stocked library enabled not only our staff to find scientific data, but also readers from the outside who had some connection to our institute, mainly teachers but also private persons who wanted to consolidate the knowledge they had acquired at our exhibitions.

Connected with the library was a big collection of Isotype lantern slides together with documentary lantern slides.

Our photographic department made photos and collected those we selected from other sources. For example, we prepared for the municipality and other bodies a series of documentary photos on various occupations, because children and parents want to know what it means to become a plumber, a tailor, a joiner, etc. Together with statistical charts such series are very educational and helpful. The photographic department co-operated with specialists in this field and tried to evolve particular methods of presentation, too. We sometimes combined photographs with statistical charts. These and similar activities can be executed only if all the crafts are under one roof, as it were.

Of course, we had machinery for copying prints, maps, etc., as well as presses for printing symbols and wording [for making exhibition charts], and for printing large numbers of small-scale leaflets reproducing our charts.

A big department was the graphic department, composed of specialists in design, linoleum-cutting, wood-cutting, and other crafts. The chief of the department [Gerd Arntz] was a man of extraordinary abilities, who worked with us for more than a decade. He, unfortunately, remained in Holland, and therefore we had to teach the skills to new collaborators here. It requires years before collaborators may act without permanent consultation, but even then only an institute, not single individuals, is able to perform the task; one could compare Isotype-making with map-making.

The transformation department discusses with the graphic department the execution of the "transformation" design. The Transformer forms the bridge between the scientists and the designer, who in our Museum did not work together. The Transformer has to fill the gap which usually appears between scientist and designer, neither of whom are educationalists, and who do not know each other's business, whereas the Transformer has to be scientifically trained and sufficiently trained in the details of designing for anticipating the educational effect in an exhibition or in a book.

The Museum organized the distribution of graphic material partly by its own staff and partly through the usual channels, such as publishers. In no case did it allow any interference from that side. Our institutes through all these years co-operated in various ways with scientists, writers, governments, publishers, institutes etc. all over the world. We have been consultants about and makers of visual aids for Mexico and Norway, Sweden and the USA, the USSR and Czechoslovakia, Yugoslavia and France, the Netherlands and Great Britain, Poland and Belgium, etc., etc.

The following types of co-operation appeared to be fruitful and without friction:

1). The Isotype Institute prepares a complete exhibition, a complete book—the whole material: charts, photos, tables, explanations. In this way we published *Die bunte Welt*, a book for children, *Gesellschaft und Wirtschaft*, a big atlas composed of 100 charts, tables and explanations, etc. In these cases, the publisher accepts the master as it is; he does not suggest anything.

2). The Isotype Institute collaborates with authors, governments etc. in providing charts, which may be combined with text and other material provided by other people. In this way we prepared charts for a Dutch government booklet on public health, and, together with the National Tuberculosis Association, New York, we prepared two exhibitions and booklets. In this way also we co-operated with P. Sargant Florence & Lella Secor Florence [on the Adprint series, America and Britain, 1943–44]. The co-operation with the National Tuberculosis Association required 6 months of discussions of all the details, careful analysis of the "field" and adaptation to the American standard. Here we had experience of how to reach the masses who hardly read anything about tuberculosis. Our American Vice President [Mary van Kleeck] told us how much the people in Alaska, in Texas and the South liked our charts.

3). The Isotype Institute provides single charts for certain purposes from its collections, without particular collaboration: e.g. illustrations for a translation of a book by [H.G.] Wells.

The co-operative attitude has been the basis of our organizations; on the other hand we never made adaptations to the wishes of single publishers etc. We regard commercial organizations as very important and would like to find a publisher, or better a group of publishers, who would be prepared to publish all our stuff, because then the various items could better support one another. Up to now we have not found such an opportunity for spreading the humanization of knowledge and judgement.

Isotype plans

General remarks:
We think that the Isotype technique can do a lot for the humanization and democratization of knowledge. Therefore we should prefer to publish charts plus photos with explanations and tables, but without any text. The selection of charts and photos has to be made exclusively by the Institute, the experts of the Institute and the committees of the Institute. Only educational principles can be regarded as essential in preparing such a thesaurus. The collection *Gesellschaft und Wirtschaft* is an example of how to make such a thing.

Therefore, we shall always try to remain an independent, non-commercial body, prepared to make agreements with other organizations and to discuss publication possibilities with them—i.e. with publishers, and representatives of the various channels of propaganda and education. But the Institute's own body should remain free of all these influences. That is no obstruction to any kind of co-operation, only the clear definition of a line, which has proved useful in two decades.

We make not the slightest objection to the use of this material—charts, maps and photos, technical designs etc.—for any kind of publishing. If the thesaurus has been published, writers may add textbooks or articles, they may write explanatory texts etc., but the primary body of the Isotype thesaurus has to remain free of any kind of additional statements—even of my own. The people interested in the thesaurus material may use it in different combinations. That is a question of organizing the copyright etc.—a matter for the publisher, not for the Isotype Institute. Both are separated carefully. That is our unchanged policy through two decades. This policy enabled us to co-operate with many different types of institutes, governments, writers, and publishers.

We are as "liberal" as possible in co-operating with other people and institutions, otherwise we cannot continue our world-wide contacts, but we cannot be liberal within our institute's activities: there we have to take care of our purely educational and scientific attitude in the most rigid way. It is only a question of practice and skill, how to remain undisturbed within one's own field and on the other hand to have contacts with almost everybody.

Special proposals:
I think that my wife and I, as Secretaries and Directors of Studies of the Isotype Institute, should apply our experiences to the new situation, as we did very often in the past. We found out that a multiplicity of institutes has many advantages. For example, in 1934 there existed three independent institutes, each of them with particular purposes and particular contacts. The Gesellschafts- und Wirtschaftsmuseum, supported by the municipality, could not remain untouched by political changes in Austria. It was a Viennese and Austrian institute. The Mundaneum Institute, which made the international contacts for the Gesellschafts- und Wirtschaftsmuseum, could not survive much longer than the Museum. But the International Foundation for Visual Education could remain wholly untouched. We had an office in Vienna for months after the end of the Museum and the Mundaneum, with the Dutch flag on our doorstep. The International Foundation was the legal successor of the Mundaneum Vienna, which was an Austrian institute, but the authorities accepted, as we suggested, that the International Foundation would automatically become the legal heir of the Mundaneum Vienna. In this way we got the international material out of Austria and some of our collaborators came with us.

We think that also in the future, whatever may happen, it would be a good thing to have a scientific and educational "Institute for Visual Education"—e.g. attached to a university—and an Isotype Institute which may have contacts that do not fit into the pattern of a more official institute. Besides that, the production of visual aids should be necessarily connected with research work in visual education, in organizing it on a world-wide basis. Just such reasons led us to the creation of more than one institute in Vienna. There are many contacts which are serious and honourable, but just not the kind of contacts a municipality wants to support, as such.

Furthermore, the plan of the Isotype thesaurus has been the plan of our Institute for decades. It evolved from a pre-Isotype plan for making a kind of general knowledge collection for the man in the street, a project kindly supported by Einstein long ago. Then we changed this into the thesaurus plan.

When I became editor-in-chief of the *International Encyclopedia of Unified Science* (University of Chicago Press), I wanted to build up this encyclopedia as a kind of logical counterpart to our thesaurus, which is destined for the man in the street, whereas the encyclopedia is destined for students and research workers who want to know more about scientific language and other scientific tools. (9 out of 11 monographs have already been published within the first series "Foundations of the unity of science"; the agreement with the press provides for 60 more monographs of the second series.) On page 25 in the first monograph I mention our thesaurus plan.

I think a co-operation of our Unity of Science congresses (of which I am permanent secretary) with the Isotype Institute would be fruitful, because there are remarkable links between the unification of scientific language in an empiricist way and the unification of our visual language in an empiricist way by Isotype. (The Unity of Science Institute worked as part of the Mundaneum The Hague.) Whereas in the first case we have to compete with other aids, the Isotypes are without competition.
Up to now the following international congresses of our Unity of Science movement have taken place: 1934 Prague, 1935 Paris, 1936 Copenhagen, 1937 Paris (Encyclopedia Conference), 1938 Cambridge (England), 1939 Cambridge (USA), 1941 Chicago.

[This text was accompanied by some examples of Isotype work when sent out, and a final note requested that it be returned by registered post.]

125 Isotype after 1945

Helena Doudova in conversation with Eric Kindel

Is Isotype a universal language? Marie Neurath and the Isotype Institute did work in West Africa, including in the Western Region of Nigeria, Gold Coast, and Sierra Leone. How did Isotype function in these different countries and cultures?

Isotype may be more accurately described as "international", the first word encoded in the ISOTYPE acronym. To describe Isotype as international is to affirm its place in the world, a system that could be applied across national, cultural, and linguistic boundaries. By contrast, "universal", a term rarely used by those involved with Isotype, suggests an abstract, singular, and idealized concept—one size fits all (and everything) regardless of mitigating circumstances. The term lacks sufficient reference to people; it is located instead in a philosophical realm, or perhaps a mathematical or technological one. Similarly, Isotype has some language-like features, but it is not a language.[1]

Isotype was a flexible and open-ended system: it could be adjusted and varied according to particular contexts and tasks. Nevertheless, the work done by Marie Neurath and the Isotype Institute in West Africa in the 1950s presented a considerable challenge to the international claims made for Isotype. The social, cultural, technological, and linguistic circumstances in those territories required adjustments to the Isotype approach and its iconography so that it could be understood by the people who lived there. Marie Neurath wrote about the work in West Africa; she concluded that in "[b]ecoming citizens of the world we gradually recognised that our symbolism was often international for western man only. More than before I recognised this when I had to work out ways of informing the Nigerian people about health, education, agriculture, voting etc., in visual terms. Man, woman, house, plants, markets, trees all had to be drawn in a different way to be understandable in that country. Also the approach, the speed of information, the colour scheme, the ways to catch the attention—all had to be different."[2]

---

[1] Christopher Burke has addressed this topic in his essay "The linguistic status of Isotype", in Heinrich, Nemeth, Pichler, and Wagner (eds), *Image and Imaging in Philosophy, Science and the Arts*, Publications of the Austrian Ludwig Wittgenstein Society, new series, vol. XVII (vol. II) (Frankfurt/Paris/Lancaster/New Brunswick: Ontos Verlag, 2011), pp. 31–58.

[2] Cited in Eric Kindel, "Isotype in Africa: Gold Coast, Sierra Leone, and the Western Region of Nigeria, 1952–1958," in Burke/Kindel/Walker (eds), *Isotype: Design & Contexts, 1925–1971* (London: Hyphen Press, 2013), pp. 495–96.

Does Isotype still have a role today?

The features and iconography of Isotype work are specific to those who produced it, their historical context, and the production techniques they employed. These no longer apply today in the same way and so any attempt to simply recreate Isotype will would be anachronistic; it was of its time. The body of Isotype work, however, in its extent and diversity, does provide guidance for the meaningful and comprehensible visualization of social facts and processes. Its method of "transformation", its principles of graphic representation and configuration, and its intelligent technical formation all retain their instructive value and this can benefit many areas of graphic communication today. So the "lessons" of Isotype are best discovered not in revival but in new and principled applications of its underlying approach.[3]

> *Do you think Isotype pictograms work well on their own in contemporary media and modes of reproduction? Or is Isotype more than its ubiquitous pictograms because it shows complex social data and contexts?*

Reducing things to a simple visual form without introducing ambiguity, trying to reach an essential representation—this is useful work in graphic communication that has many applications across print and digital media. But pictograms often fit into larger systems of meaning, and so while individually their design may be intelligent and attractive, they may at the same time lack a greater purposefulness. This applies equally to Isotype pictograms and other instances of simplified graphic depiction found in Isotype work. While their independent design is of interest and value, to see them only on their own is to overlook their place in a larger process of meaning production.

> *What was the history of Isotype after the death of Otto Neurath? Did Marie Neurath continue to collaborate with Gerd Arntz and the original core team?*

When the Neuraths left the Netherlands in 1940, Gerd Arntz remained behind and after a period working for the Nederlandse Stichting voor Statistiek (NSS) he was conscripted into the German army. In Britain, Otto and Marie Neurath established the Isotype Institute in 1942 and began assembling a new team to support Isotype work. After the war, Arntz returned to the NSS, producing pictorial statistics using Isotype pictograms he had previously designed. In 1947, the Isotype Institute came to an agreement with the NSS that the Dutch organization could continue

[3] Robin Kinross has written on this topic in his chapter "Lessons of Isotype", in Marie Neurath/Robin Kinross, *The Transformer: Principles of Making Isotype Charts* (London: Hyphen Press, 2009), pp. 96–116.

using Isotype pictograms and making pictorial statistics with them. After the death of Otto Neurath in 1945, Marie Neurath became sole director of the Isotype Insitute and remained highly productive, working with a team of collaborators on several series of children's books and on other projects, including those in West Africa. These show how Marie Neurath developed Isotype independently, following its basic approach but also refining and evolving its techniques of graphic presentation. In 1971 she retired and gave the accumulated material of the Isotype Institute to the University of Reading. The Isotype Institute continued until 1981 when it was dissolved.

[The conversation with Eric Kindel, curator of the Otto and Marie Neurath Isotype Collection, University of Reading, took place on August 2, 2016.]

.

129 Gender Relations

Visual essay: Patrick Rössler

Immer dasselbe, immer dasselbe.

Gnädige Frau, Sie und wir stehen auf einem Platz, von dem drei Wege in die Welt laufen:

Auf dem einen marschieren Männer und Frauen mit Zopf und Perücke und stimmen den Refrain an von der „guten alten Zeit".

1

Auf dem andern wandern die Snobs und verkünden mit herabgezogenen Mundwinkeln, daß man in Paris sich neuerdings die Augenwimpern mit Fliegenbeinen verlängert, und daß Gloria Swanson das Vorbild für jede Lady sein müsse.

2

Gnädige Frau, Sie fühlen es genau so gut, daß „die gute alte Zeit" unwiederbringlich vorüber ist, daß eine Dame ihr Vorbild nicht aus Hollywood bezieht. Sie wissen, daß es einen dritten Weg gibt, **den Weg der wirklichen Dame.**

3

above: Irmgard Keun: *Das kunstseidene Mädchen* (Berlin, 1932)
below: Advertisment for the magazine *die neue linie* (September 1930)

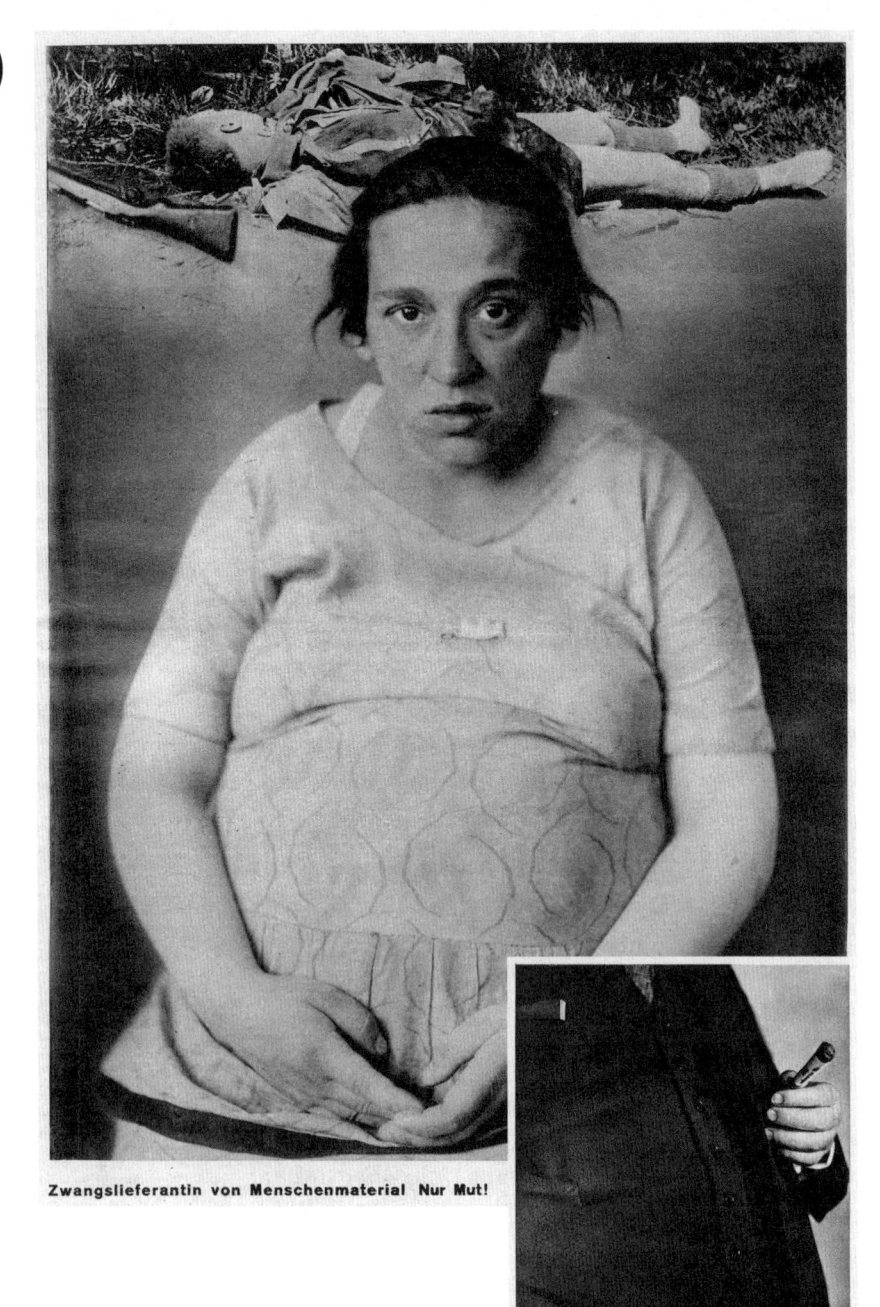

Zwangslieferantin von Menschenmaterial Nur Mut!

above: John Heartfield: Forced supplier of human material;
montage in *Arbeiter-Illustrierten Zeitung* (no. 10, March 1930)
below: Aenne Biermann, The Boss; photo in *Revue des Monats* (no. 7, May 1931)

above: Hans Söhnker as photo reporter in *Auf Wiedersehen, Franziska* (photo: Terra, 1941)
below: Brigitte Helm, Ufa press photo (around 1932)

132

Enjoyment of life alone…, cover image of the catalog of Reichsverband für Freikörperkultur [Reich Association for Naturism] (1932)

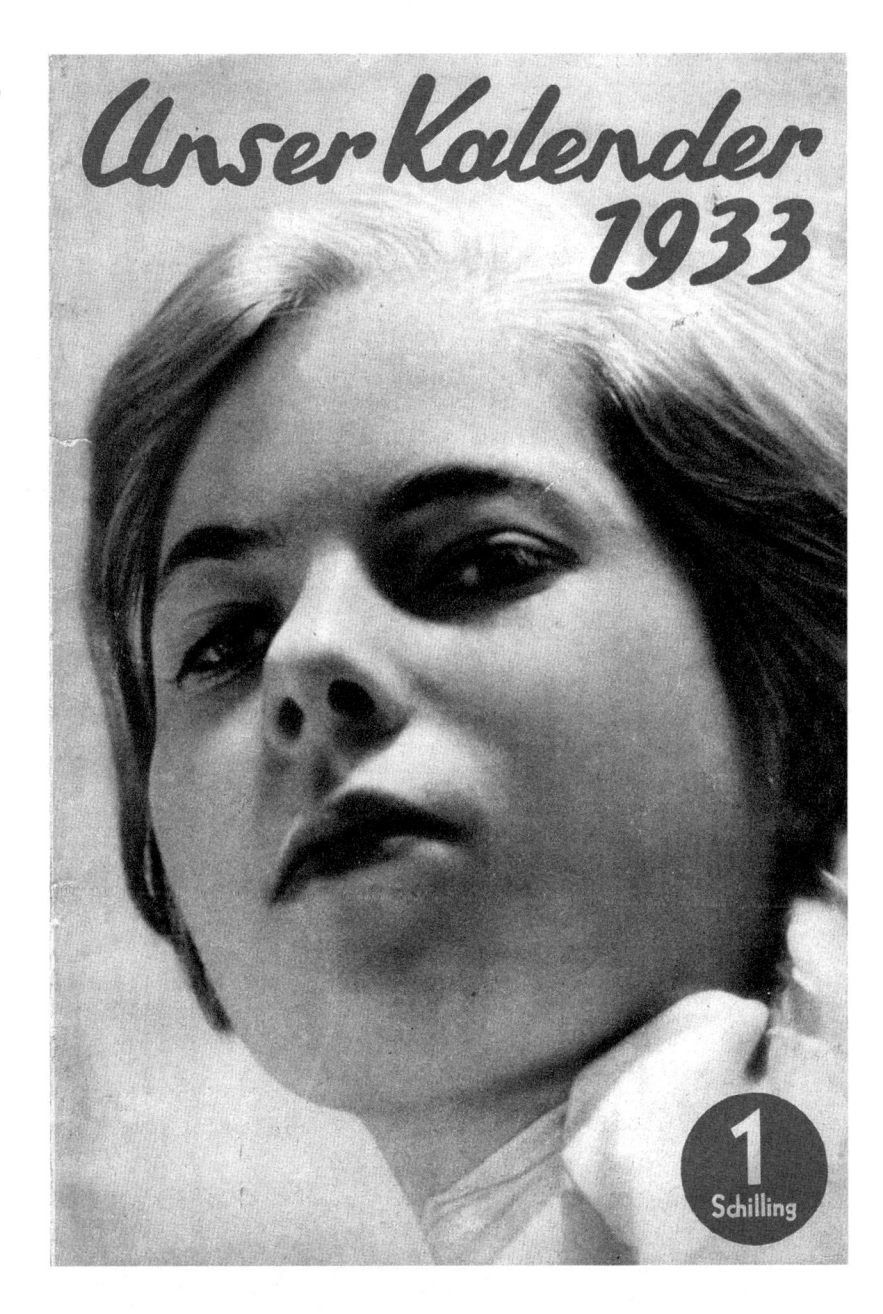

Cover image of *Unser Kalender 1933*, publishing house Vorwärts
(Vienna 1932), photographer unknown

134

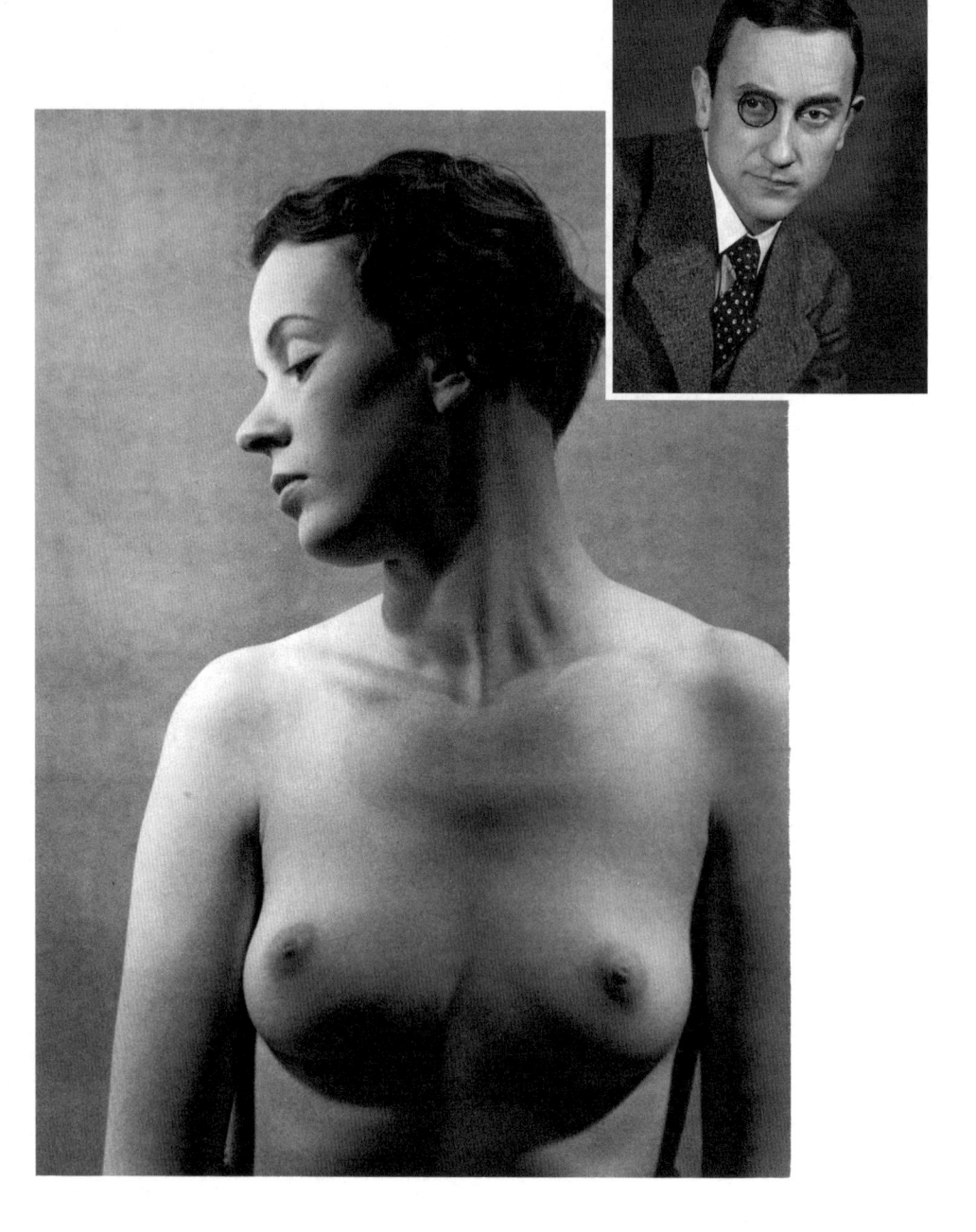

above: Eberhard Posner, self portrait (around 1934)
below: Eberhard Posner, nude portrait of his wife (around 1935)

135

above: Paul W. John: At the beach Wannsee (around 1933)
below: Farm girl on a course of the Reichsnährstand, [Reich Alimentation Estate]
Cover image of the magazine *Koralle* (no. 40, October 1940)

136

above: You or I! (combat aviator); cover image of *Die Woche* (no. 42, October 1938)
below: German Girls 1940; cover image of *Erika* (no. 35, August 1940)

137 Biographies

138 Fritz Kahn

Doctor, author of popular nonfiction books, creative director
(b. 1888 in Halle, d. 1968 in Locarno)

1907–12	Medical studies in Berlin, observer on various science and humanities courses
1910	Writer of popular science articles for feature pages of national press
1913	Hospital doctor in Berlin-Lankwitz, specializing in gynaecology, start of sideline as nonfiction author
1914–18	Participation in World War I as a doctor in the medical service, followed by period in sanatorium in Algeria, return to position as obstetrician and surgeon
1924	Greater social and political involvement: founding of a Jewish humanist lodge, presidency of Jewish Elderly Care
1925	Publisher of the political information pamphlet "Sammelblätter jüdischen Wissens" and editor of the *Encyclopaedia Judaica*
1926	Scientific adviser for the exhibitions "GeSoLei" in Düsseldorf und "Die Ernährung" in Berlin
1933	Expulsion by the National Socialist regime und emigration to Palestine; in the following years official confiscation and ban of his works
1934	Establishment of the design studio Hayad in Jerusalem, exhibition "Hygiene des Schulkindes"
1936	Move to Neuilly-sur-Seine
1939	Flight to Bordeaux, temporary internment in Libourne, flight to Spain
1940–41	Emigration to the USA with the help of the Emergency Rescue Committee und thanks to recommendation by Albert Einstein
1956	Return to Europe (Switzerland and later Denmark)
1968	Death in a sanatorium after a long illness (January 14)

Selected publications:

Die Milchstraße (Stuttgart, 1914); *Die Zelle* (Stuttgart, 1919; *The Cell*, New York, 1923); *Die Juden als Rasse und Kulturvolk* (Berlin, 1920); *Das Leben des Menschen*, vols I–V (Stuttgart, 1922–31); *Unser Geschlechtsleben* (Zurich, 1937; *Our Sex Life*, New York, 1939); *Der Mensch, gesund und krank*, vols I–II (Zurich, 1939–40; *Man in Structure and Function*, vols I–II, New York, 1943); *Das Atom* (Zurich, 1949); *Das Buch der Natur* (Zurich, 1952); *Design of the Universe* (New York, 1954); *The Human Body* (New York, 1965); *Der menschliche Körper*, Munich / Zurich, 1967)

139 Otto Neurath

Economist, theoretical scientist, workers' educator
(b. 1882 in Vienna, d. 1945 in Oxford)

1901–05	University studies in Vienna and Berlin: mathematics, physics, history, sociology, economics
1907–14	Teacher at the Neue Wiener Handelsakademie (New Vienna College of Commerce)
1911–13	Research trips for the Carnegie Foundation in Eastern Europe and the Balkans
1912	Marriage to Olga Hahn (d. 1931)
1914–18	Military service; doctorate in Heidelberg; appointed director of the German Museum on War Economy in Leipzig
1919	President of the Central Planning Office in Munich under the Bavarian soviet republic; return to Vienna
1919–24	Active participation in the housing movement in Vienna
1924–34	Foundation and direction of the Social and Economic Museum in Vienna
1927	Start of collaboration with Gerd Arntz
1929	Main author of the Vienna Circle manifesto
1931–34	Consultant and instructor at the Russian Institute for Pictorial Representation of Statistics, together with members of his team
1933	Foundation of the International Foundation for Visual Education in The Hague
1934	Emigration to The Hague
1934–40	Work on visual education (Isotype) and in the Unity of Science movement; editor-in-chief of the *International Encyclopedia of Unified Science*
1940	Flight to England, internment
1941	Marriage to Marie Reidemeister
1942	Foundation of the Isotype Institute (Oxford, with Marie Neurath)
1945	Sudden and unexpected death (December 22)

Selected publications:

Antike Wirtschaftsgeschichte (Berlin, 1918); *Wirtschaftsplan und Naturalrechnung* (Berlin, 1925); *Die bunte Welt* (Vienna, 1929); *Gesellschaft und Wirtschaft. Bildstatistisches Elementarwerk. 100 Bildtafeln* (Leipzig, 1931); *Empirische Soziologie* (Vienna, 1931); *Technik und Menschheit* (Vienna/Leipzig, 1932); *Bildstatistik nach Wiener Methode in der Schule* (Vienna/Leipzig, 1933); *Einheitswissenschaft und Psychologie* (Vienna, 1933); *International Picture Language* (London, 1936); *Basic by Isotype* (London, 1937); *Modern Man in the Making* (New York, 1939)

140 Team Kahn

Roman Rechn
Graphic designer (b. 1892 in Werro/Estonia, d. 1945 in Hagenow)

1909–15 Study of architecture at the Technical University in Riga (presumably without completing degree)
1915–19 Building and graphic design work in Russia, including Moscow
1920–23 Graphic designer in Berlin, including at Siemens-Schuckert und Ullstein Verlag
1923 Workshop for craft industry in Hamm, exhibition at the Leipzig Fair
1924 Application to the Bauhaus in Weimar (rejected principally for reasons of age),
1926–30 Collaboration with Fritz Kahn, around 30 illustrations in *Das Leben des Menschen*, vols IV–V; then freelance graphic designer (not a member of the Reich Chamber for Fine Arts)

Fritz Schüler
Architect (b. 1887 in St. Petersburg, d. 1954 in Berlin)

1912 Architecture diploma at the Technical University of Karlsruhe; then building expert in St. Petersburg
1913–15 Independent architect in Riga
1918 Architect in Berlin, working on housing developments and exhibitions
1929 Internal design for the pavilion of Deutsche Elektrizitätswirtschaft (Architect: Ludwig Mies van der Rohe), for the World Exposition in Barcelona
1925–33 As a sideline, collaboration with Fritz Kahn, around 30 illustrations in *Das Leben des Menschen*, vols III–V
1934 Exhibition architect at Reichselektrowerke; member of the NSDAP and the Reich Chamber for Fine Arts

Ottomar Trester
Graphic designer (b. 1888 in Wiesbaden, d. 1958 in Berlin)

Education at the Royal School of Art in Berlin
Graphic designer at Scherl Verlag
1924–32 As a sideline, collaboration with Fritz Kahn; around 90 illustrations in *Das Leben des Menschen*, vols III–V
1933 Freelance science illustrator and graphic designer in advertising, not a member of the Reich Chamber for Fine Arts

141 Team Neurath

Marie Reidemeister (later Neurath)
Mathematician, transformer, director of the Isotype Institute
(b. 1898 in Braunschweig, d. 1986 in London)

1917–24	University studies (mathematics, physics), art school
1925	Joins Otto Neurath to work for the Social and Economic Museum in Vienna
1931–33	Instructor in transformation, Moscow
1934	Emigration to The Hague, work for the International Foundation for Visual Education, The Hague
1940	Flight to England, internment
1941	Marriage to Otto Neurath
1942	Foundation of the Isotype Institute (Oxford, with Otto Neurath)
1948–72	Move to London, collaboration on several publications, films and book series
1953	Production of visual material for civic education (for the Government of Western Region, Nigeria)
1959	Co-editor, volumes of the Vienna Circle Collection

Selected publications:
Visual History of Mankind (Book series, London, 1947–63); *Wonders of the Modern World* (Book series, London, 1948–61); *They Lived Like This* (Book series, London, 1964–71)

Gerd Arntz
Artist, graphic designer (b. 1900 in Remscheid, d. 1988 in The Hague)

1919–20	Studies at art school run by L. von Kunowski in Düsseldorf
1920	First contact with F. W. Seiwert and the Cologne Progressives, first woodcuts
1925	Solo exhibition *Der neue Buchladen*
1926	Participation group exhibitions in Moscow, Cologne, Düsseldorf; first meeting with Otto Neurath
1929	Appointment as chief graphic designer of the Social and Economic Museum; move to Vienna
1931–34	Periodic visits to work at the Isostat Institute in Moscow
1934	Move from Vienna to The Hague
1940	Chief graphic designer at the Netherlands Statistical Foundation
1943	Conscription into the Wehrmacht
1946	Return to the Netherlands Statistical Foundation
1951–62	Work for Unesco in the field of pictorial statistics

Authors

Christopher Burke is Research Fellow at the University of Reading. His principal area of research is German typography of the early twentieth century. He is the co-editor of Isotype: Design and Contexts, 1925–71 (London, 2013).

Uta von Debschitz is a former architect and cultural journalist. Together with her brother Thilo von Debschitz she published the first illustrated monograph on Fritz Kahn (*Fritz Kahn—Man Machine*, Vienna, 2009, new, expanded edition Cologne 2013 and 2017), and curated an exhibition of the same name at the Berlin Museum of Medical History (2010).

Helena Doudova is an art historian and curator. As a Fellow of the International Museum Program she organized the exhibition *Image Factories. Infographics 1920–1945: Fritz Kahn, Otto Neurath et al.*

Vilém Flusser was a philosopher and expert on media theory (d. 1991). He has taught at universities in Brazil, France and Germany. His most important works include *Ins Universum der technischen Bilder* (Göttingen, 1985) and Kommunikologie (Mannheim, 1996).

Stephanie Jacobs is the Director of the German Museum of Books and Writing of the German National Library. She is the author of numerous texts and exhibitions, including *Zeichen—Bücher—Netze. Von der Keilschrift zum Binärcode* (Göttingen, 2016).

Eric Kindel is head of the Department of Typography & Graphic Communication at the University of Reading (UK). He is curator of the Otto and Marie Neurath Isotype Collection and co-editor of *Isotype: Design and Contexts, 1925–71* (London, 2013).

Patrick Rössler is professor of Media and Communication Studies at the University of Erfurt. His focus and publications deal with media history, modern typography and the Bauhaus including *Herbert Bayer: Die Berliner Jahre—Werbegrafik 1928–38* (Berlin, 2013).

Bernd Stiegler is Professor of Modern German Literature at the University of Konstanz, with a focus on the twentieth century in the media context. From 1999 to 2007 he was head of the science publishing program at Suhrkamp Verlag. Numerous publications, including *Der montierte Mensch. Eine Figur der Moderne* (Paderborn, 2016).

Colophon

Image Factories. Infographics 1920–1945
Fritz Kahn, Otto Neurath et al.

Editors: Helena Doudova, Stephanie Jacobs, Patrick Rössler

Texts: Christopher Burke, Uta von Debschitz, Helena Doudova, Vliém Flusser, Stephanie Jacobs, Eric Kindel, Otto Neurath, Patrick Rössler

Graphic design: Kay Bachmann

Lithography: Carsten Humme

Translations: Jan Caspers (Patrick Rössler / Stephanie Jacobs, Uta von Debschitz, Bernd Stiegler), Paul Feigelfeld (Vilém Flusser)

Copyediting and proofreading: Margaret May

Printing and binding: Pöge Druck, Leipzig

Published by:
Spector Books
Harkortstraße 10
04107 Leipzig
www.spectorbooks.com

Distribution:
Germany, Austria: GVA, Gemeinsame Verlagsauslieferung Göttingen GmbH & Co. KG, www.gva-verlage.de
Switzerland: AVA Verlagsauslieferung AG, www.ava.ch
France, Belgium: Interart Paris, www.interart.fr
UK: Central Books Ltd, www.centralbooks.com
USA, Canada, Central and South America, Africa, Asia: ARTBOOK / D.A.P. www.artbook.com
South Korea: The Book Society, www.thebooksociety.org
Australia, New Zealand: Perimeter Distribution, www.perimeterdistribution.com

Biographies of Fritz Kahn, Roman Rechn, Fritz Schüler and Ottomar Trester compiled by Uta von Debschitz.

© 2017 the editors and the authors; Spector Books, Leipzig
© Kosmos; www.fritz-kahn.com (cover: "Man as Industrial Palace", pp. 1–5, 9–14, 23, 25, 27–28, 74–75, 78–79, 86–87, 89, 100)
© VG Bild-Kunst, Bonn 2017; Gerd Arntz (pp. 73, 76–77, 80–81, 84–85, 88, 90–91, 94–95, 98–99, 102–103, 147–158, 167–176)
© Otto and Marie Neurath Isotype Collection, University of Reading (pp. 73, 80, 84–85, 88, 90–91, 94–95, 98, 102–103, 145–158, 163, 168–176) and the edited version of the text by Otto Neurath "The Isotype work"
© Miguel Flusser; Vilém Flusser, "Imagination and (the) Imaginary," 1977, Vilém Flusser Archiv, Berlin (Reference number: (SEM REFERENCIA)_2446), original language: German
© Uta and Thilo von Debschitz, Berlin/Wiesbaden 2017 (pp. 17–22)
© Fritz Kahn—Kahn Family, 2017 (pp. 4 b., 6–8, 24, 26, 29–32, 78, 82–83, 92–93, 96–97, 101, 104)
© VG Bild-Kunst, Bonn 2017; cover Gerd Arntz (pp. 73, 76–77, 80–81, 84–85, 88, 90–91, 94–95, 98–99, 102–103, 147–158, 167–176)
© Österreichisches Gesellschafts- und Wirtschaftsmuseum in Wien (pp. 73, 76–77, 80–81, 84–85, 88, 90–91, 94–95, 98–99, 102–103)
© Zentralbibiothek Zurich (pp. 15–16)
© Landesarchiv Berlin (p. 140)
© Family Trester (p. 140)
© Vienna Circle Foundation (p. 139)

First edition
Printed in Germany
ISBN 978-3-95905-179-8

With financial support: GESELLSCHAFT FÜR DAS BUCH e.V. DEUTSCHE NATIONALBIBLIOTHEK

DEUTSCHES BUCH- UND SCHRIFTMUSEUM DEUTSCHE NATIONALBIBLIOTHEK KULTURSTIFTUNG DES BUNDES UNIVERSITÄT ERFURT

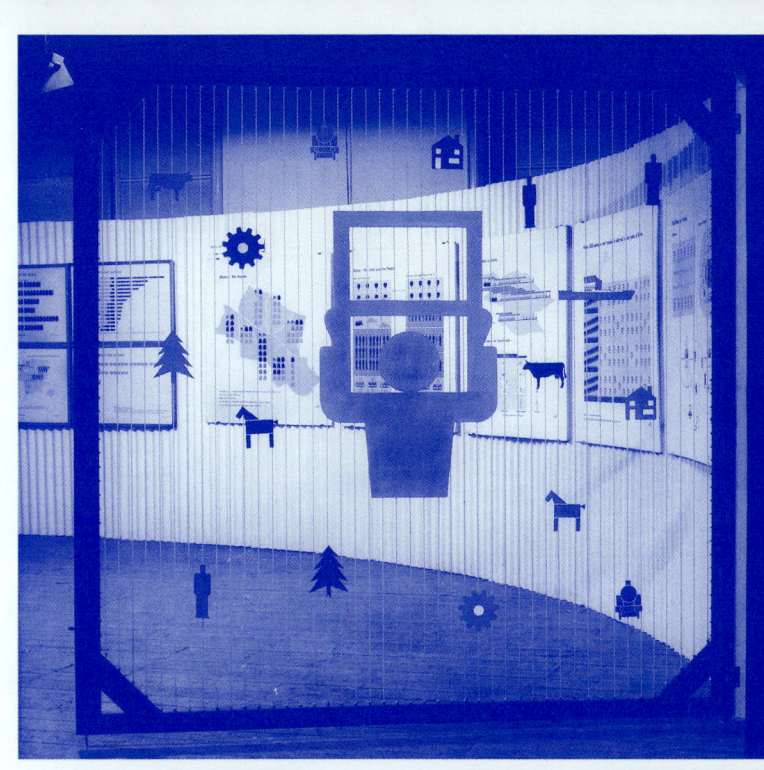

ISOTYPE EXHIBITION

Showing its uses in:-
INDUSTRY · COMMERCE
PUBLIC INFORMATION
EDUCATION

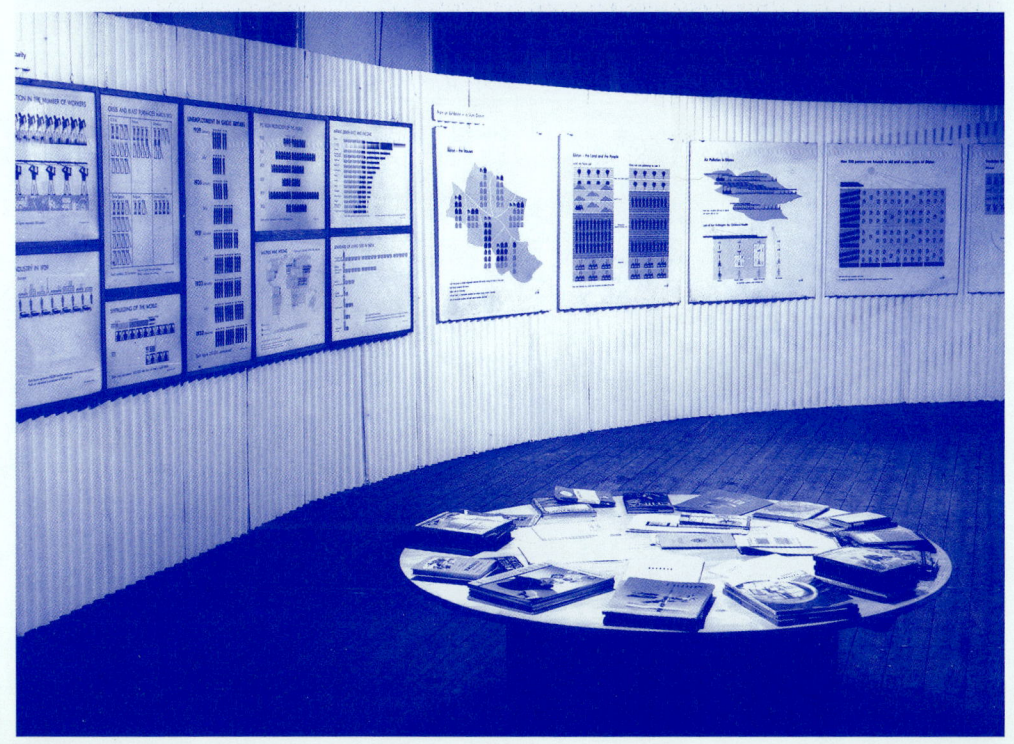

MENSCHHEIT
ERD UND GESELLSCHAFTSENTWICKLUNG

WOHNDICHTE UND
TUBERKULOSEKRANKE IN WIEN
ZEITZONENPLAN DER WIENER STRASSENBAHN
ERWERBSTÄTIGE BEVÖLKERUNG ÖSTERREICHS
OHNE BURGENLAND 1923

147

Soziale Gliederung der Berliner Bevölkerung

Arbeiter und Hausgehilfen Angestellte Selbständige und Berufslose

Jede Figur 100000 Menschen
Jede Reihe 1000000 Menschen

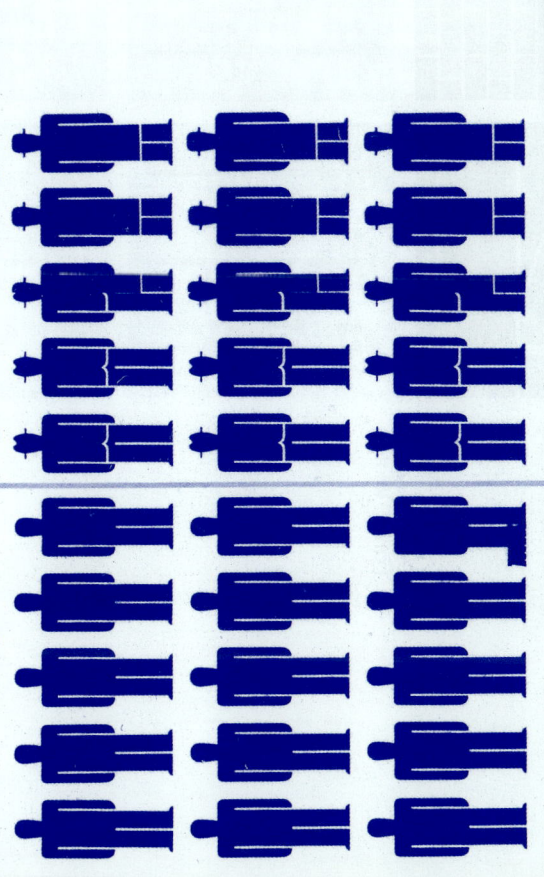

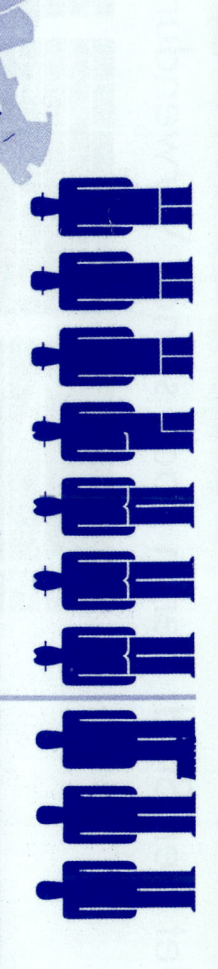

148

Gebiet der Stadt Berlin nach seiner Verwendung 1930

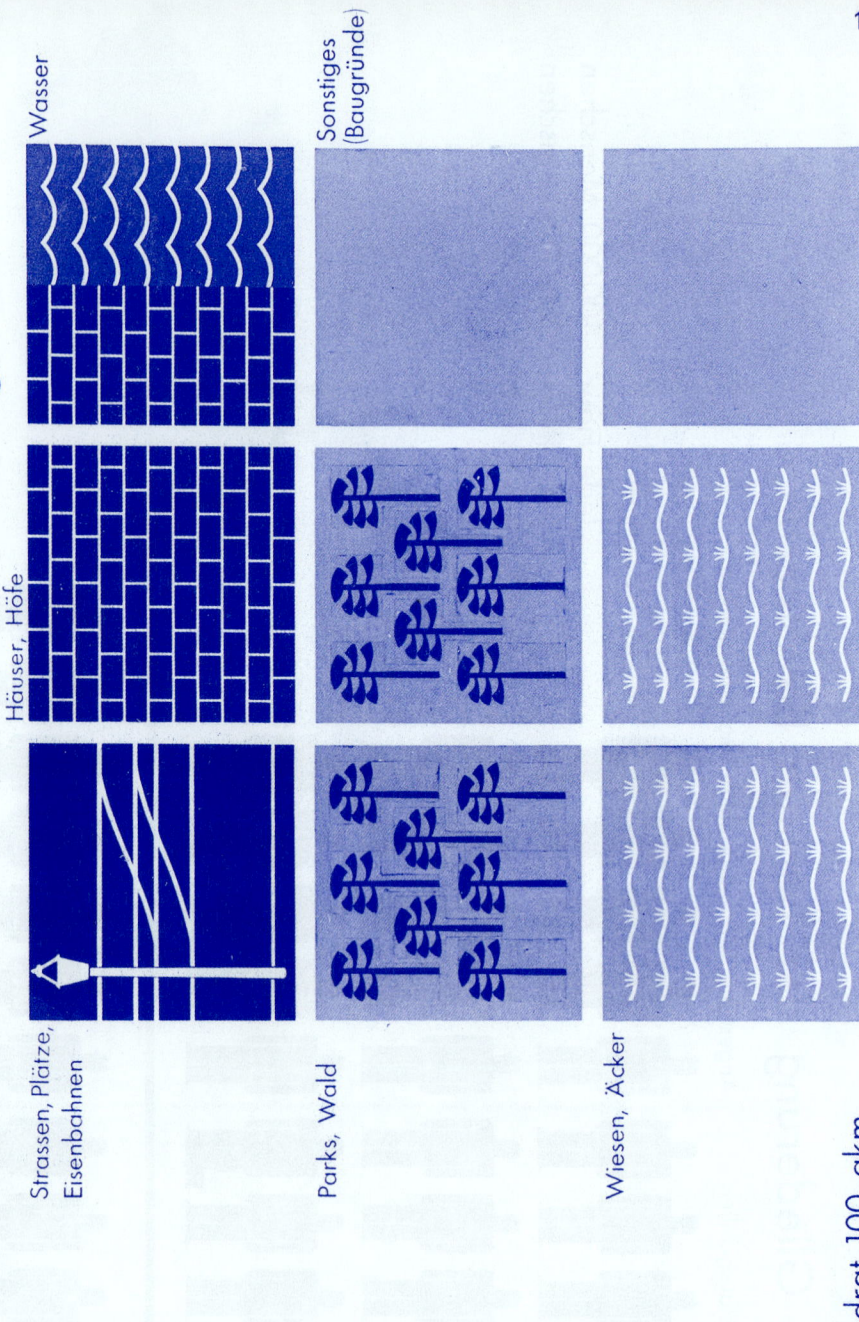

Wasser

Häuser, Höfe

Strassen, Plätze, Eisenbahnen

Sonstiges (Baugründe)

Parks, Wald

Wiesen, Äcker

Jedes Quadrat 100 qkm

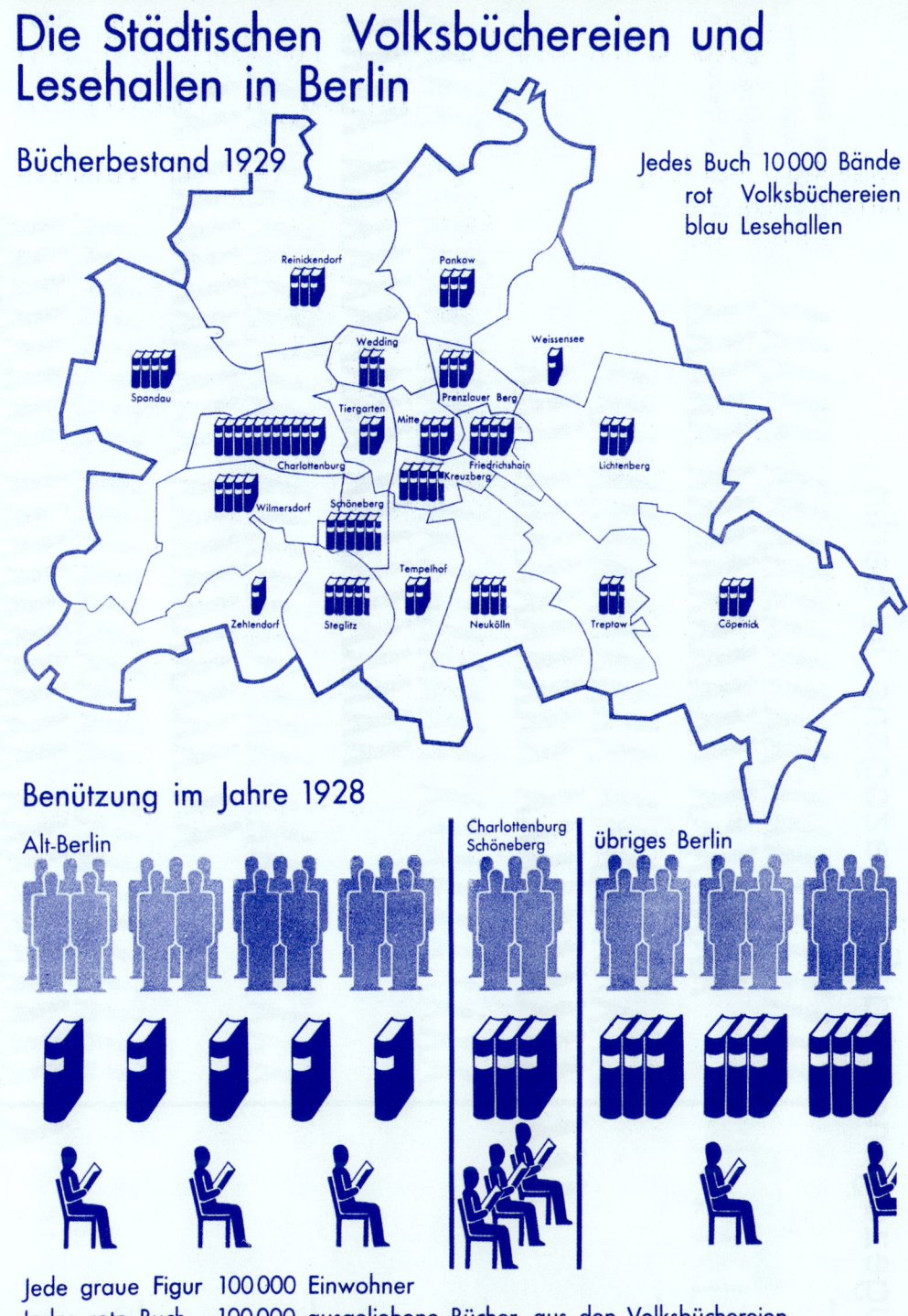

Die Städtischen Volksbüchereien und Lesehallen in Berlin

Bücherbestand 1929

Jedes Buch 10000 Bände
rot Volksbüchereien
blau Lesehallen

Benützung im Jahre 1928

Alt-Berlin | Charlottenburg Schöneberg | übriges Berlin

Jede graue Figur 100 000 Einwohner
Jedes rote Buch 100 000 ausgeliehene Bücher aus den Volksbüchereien
Jeder Leser 100 000 Besucher der Lesehallen

Zugezogene und Fortgezogene in Berlin

Jede rote Figur 10000 Zugezogene
Jede schwarze Figur 10000 Fortgezogene

1921
1923
1925
1927
1930

151

Geburt und Tod in Berlin

1921
1923
1925
1927
1930

Jedes Kind 10000 Lebendgeburten
Jeder Grabstein 10000 Sterbefälle

Eheschliessungen

1920
1922
1924
1926
1929

Jedes Brautpaar 10000 Eheschliessungen

Arbeitslose in Berlin

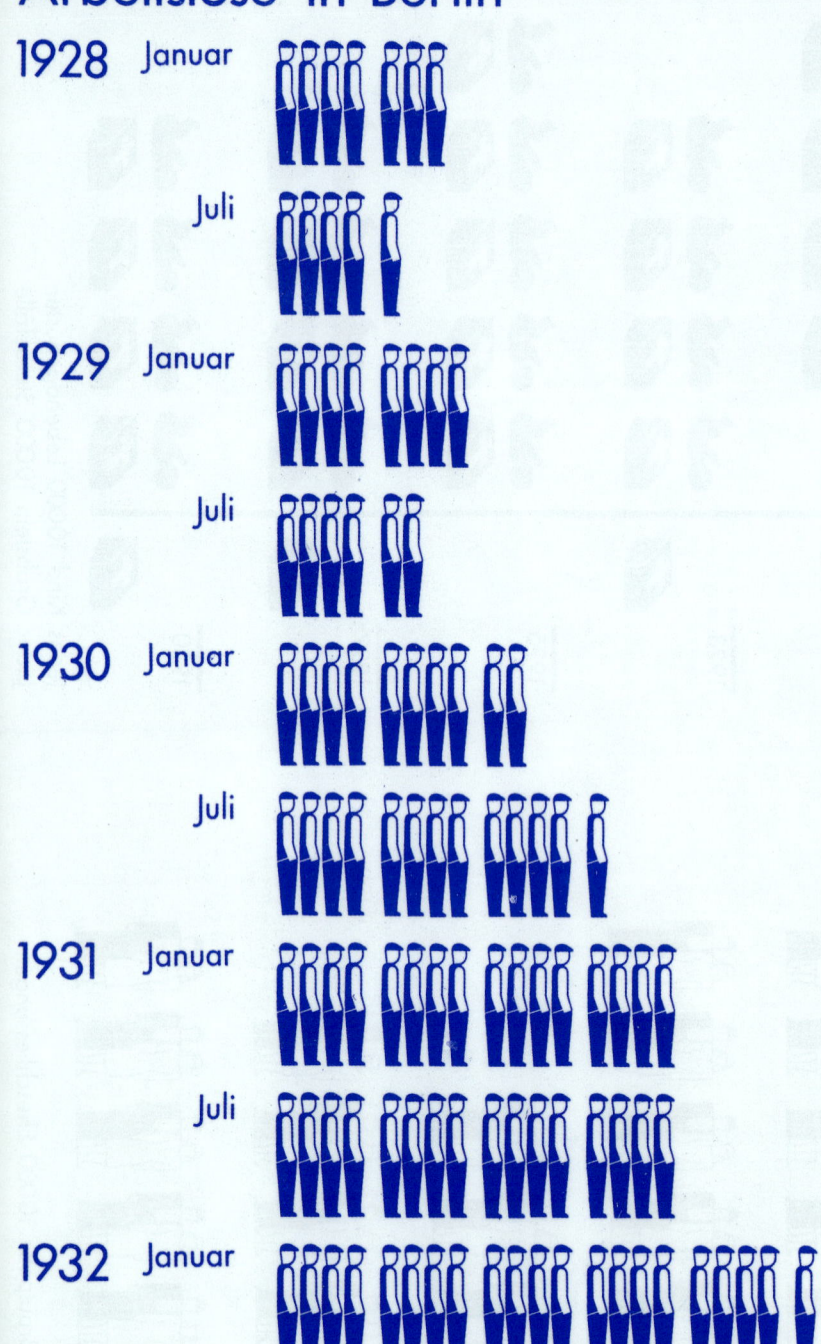

1928 Januar

Juli

1929 Januar

Juli

1930 Januar

Juli

1931 Januar

Juli

1932 Januar

Jede Signatur 25 000 Arbeitslose

153

Die städtischen Warmbadeanstalten im heutigen Berlin

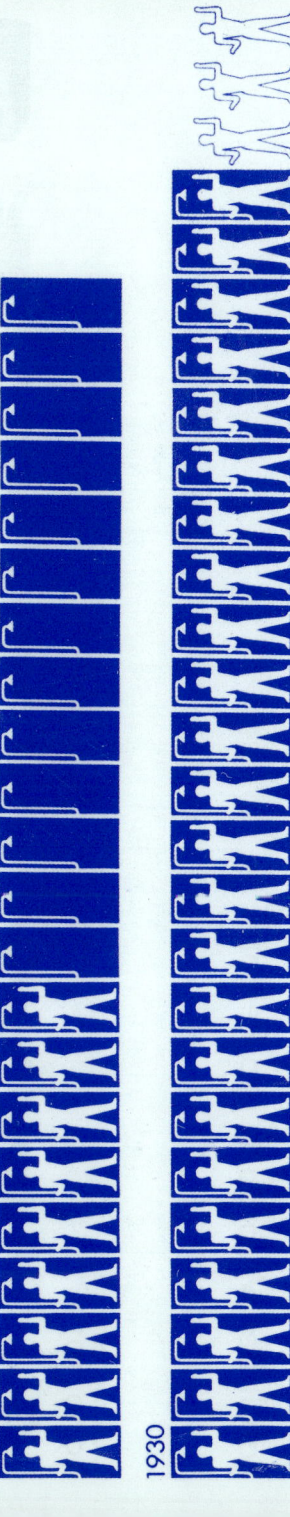

1895

1905

1915

1923

1930

Jede Brause ein städtisches Warmbad   Jede Figur 250000 Besucher

Fleischverbrauch in Berlin vor und nach dem Kriege
Jährlicher Verbrauch pro Person

Durchschnitt
1909-1912

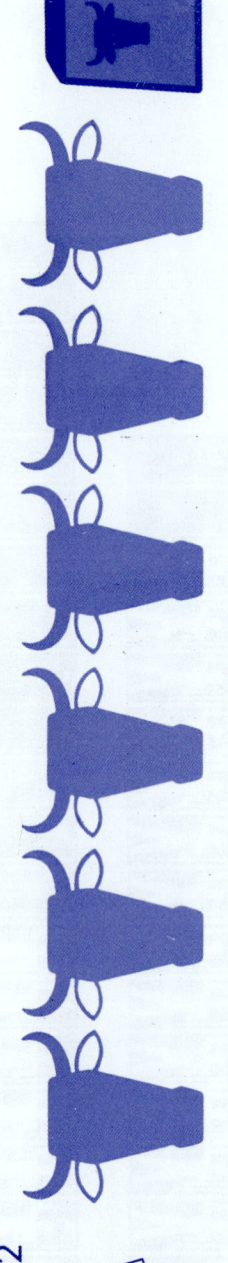

Durchschnitt
1926-1929

Frischfleisch

Gefrierfleisch und Fleischwaren

Jede Signatur 10 kg Fleisch

Konsum-Genossenschaft
Berlin und Umgegend e. G. m. b. H.

1899/1900 Gründung

1909/10

Jede Scheibe 10 Millionen RM Umsatz
Jede Kasse 50 Abgabestellen
Jede Frau 25000 Mitglieder

blau Lebensmittel
rot Fleisch
grau Manufakturwaren etc.

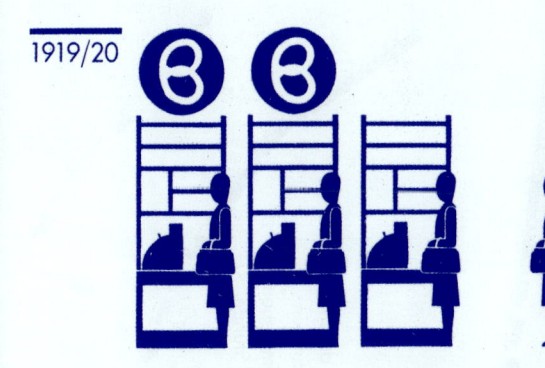

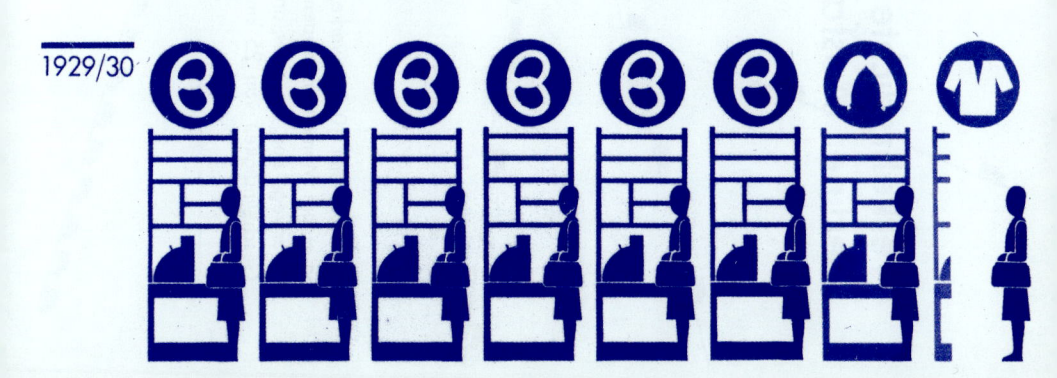

1919/20

1929/30

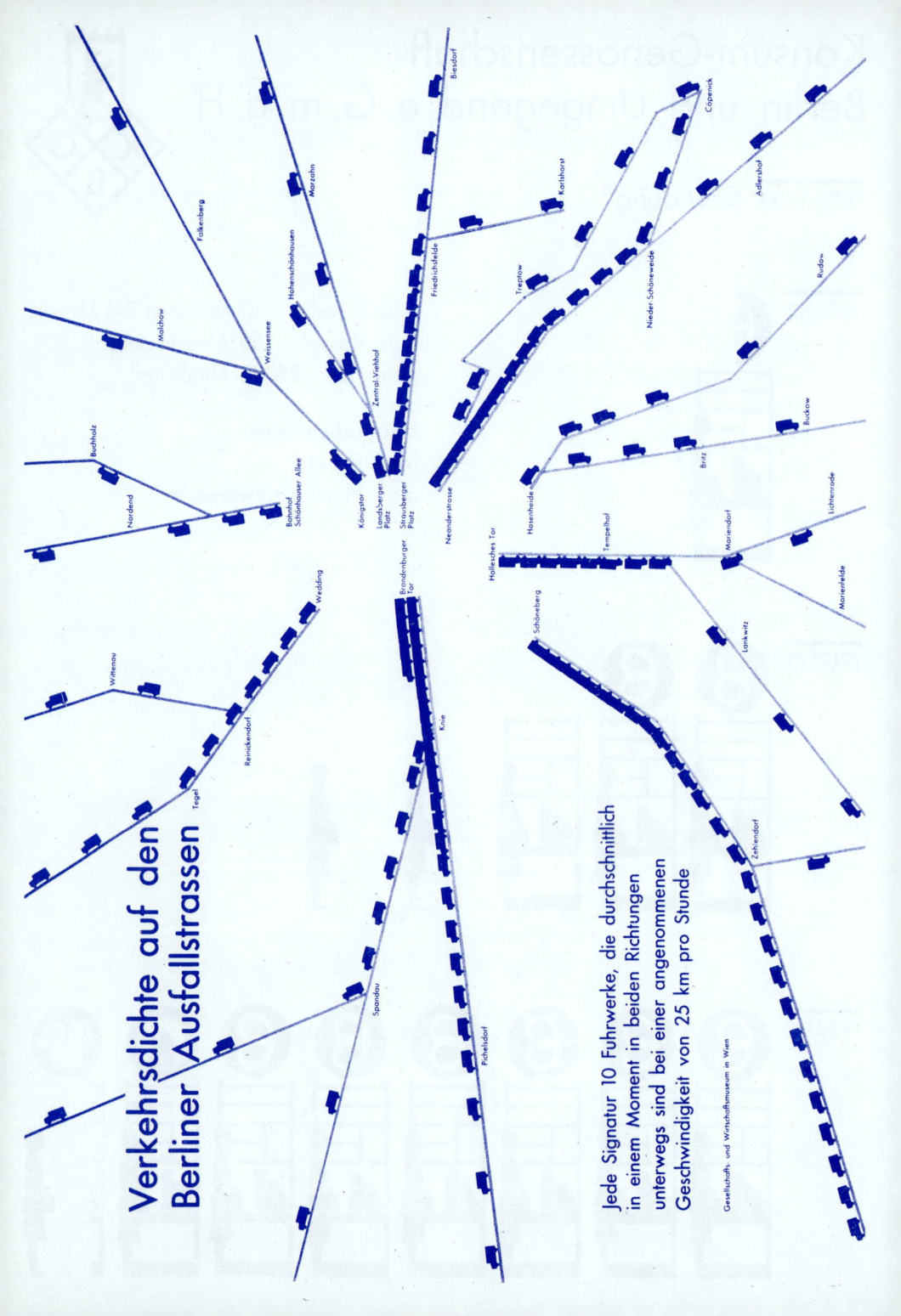

Verkehrsdichte auf den Berliner Ausfallstrassen

Jede Signatur 10 Fuhrwerke, die durchschnittlich in einem Moment in beiden Richtungen unterwegs sind bei einer angenommenen Geschwindigkeit von 25 km pro Stunde

Gesellschafts- und Wirtschaftsmuseum in Wien

Krafträder und Automobile in Berlin

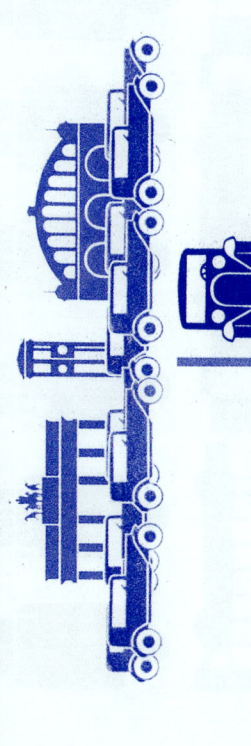

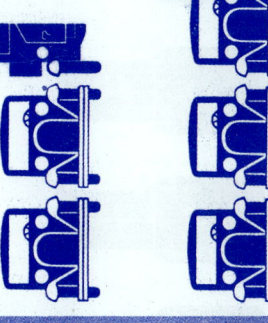

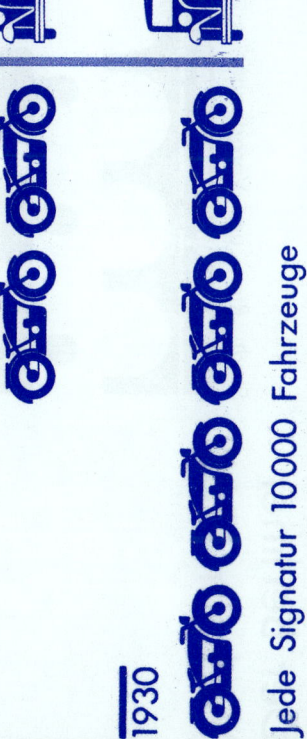

1921

1924

1927

1930

Jede Signatur 10000 Fahrzeuge

Der Berliner Verkehr 1930

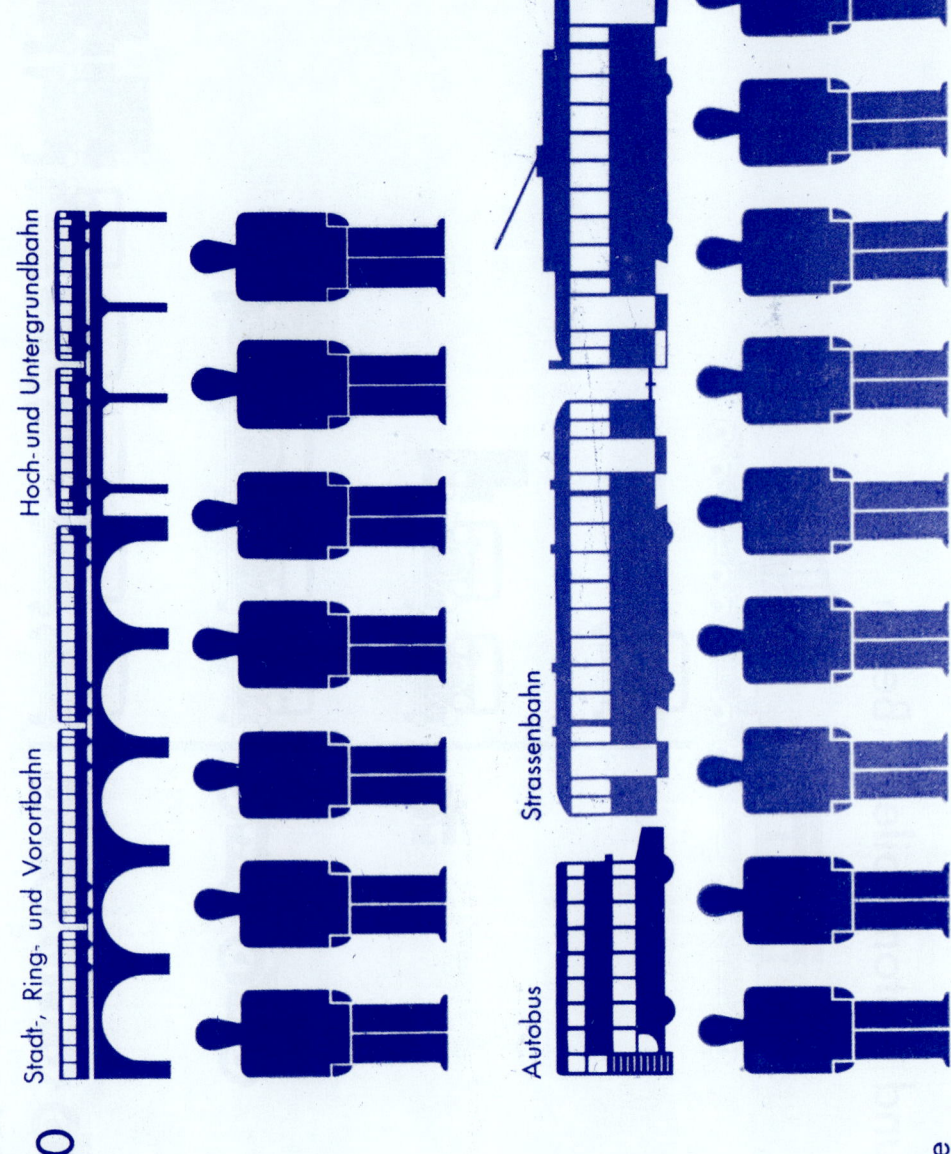

Stadt-, Ring- und Vorortbahn

Hoch- und Untergrundbahn

Strassenbahn

Autobus

Jede Figur 100000 Fahrgäste

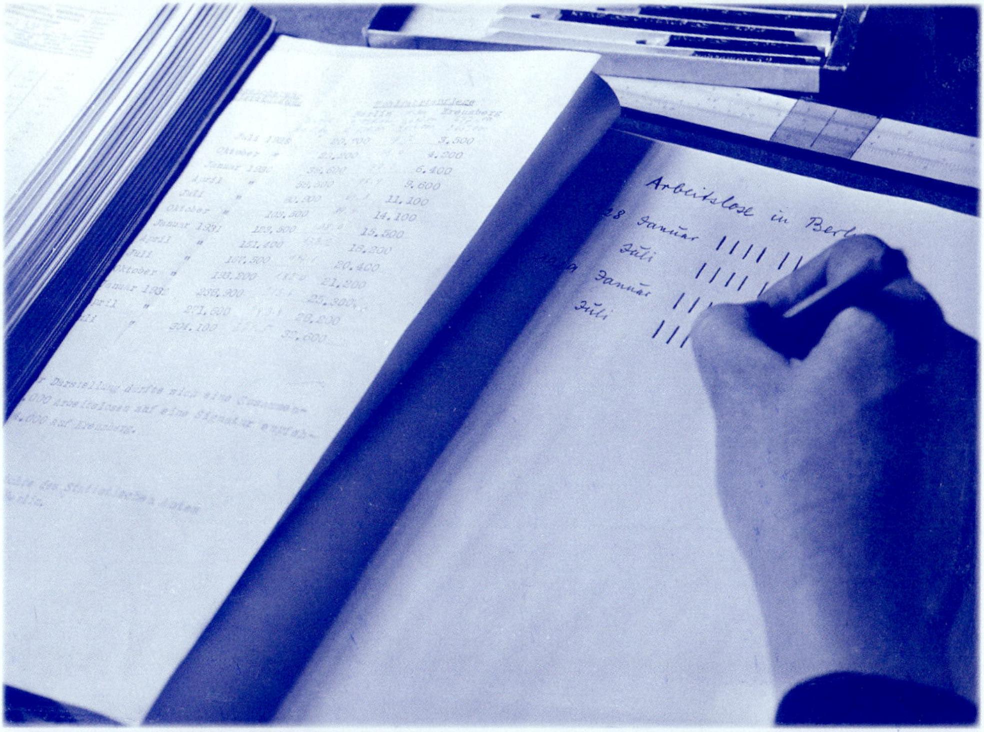
Arbeitslose in Berl
28 Januar
Juli
Januar
Juli

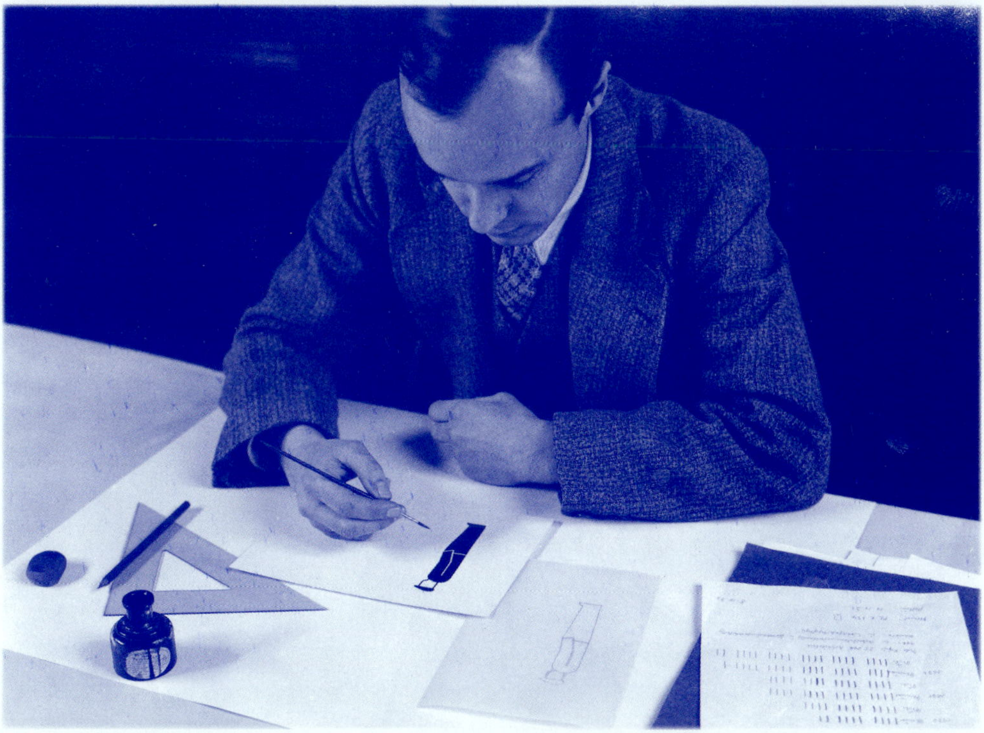

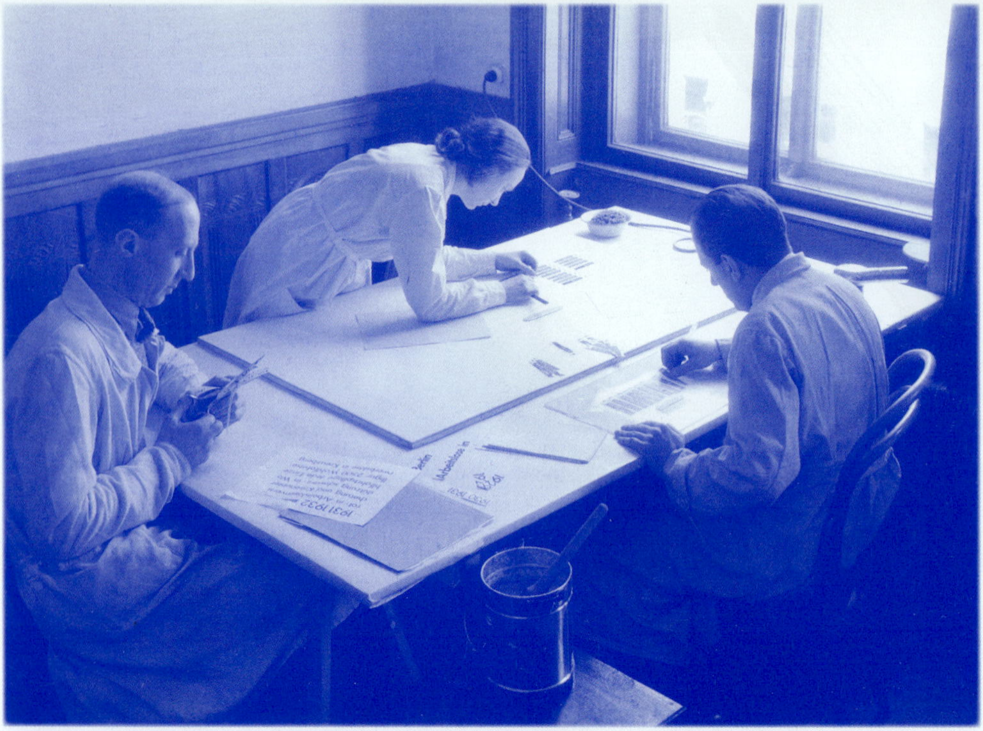

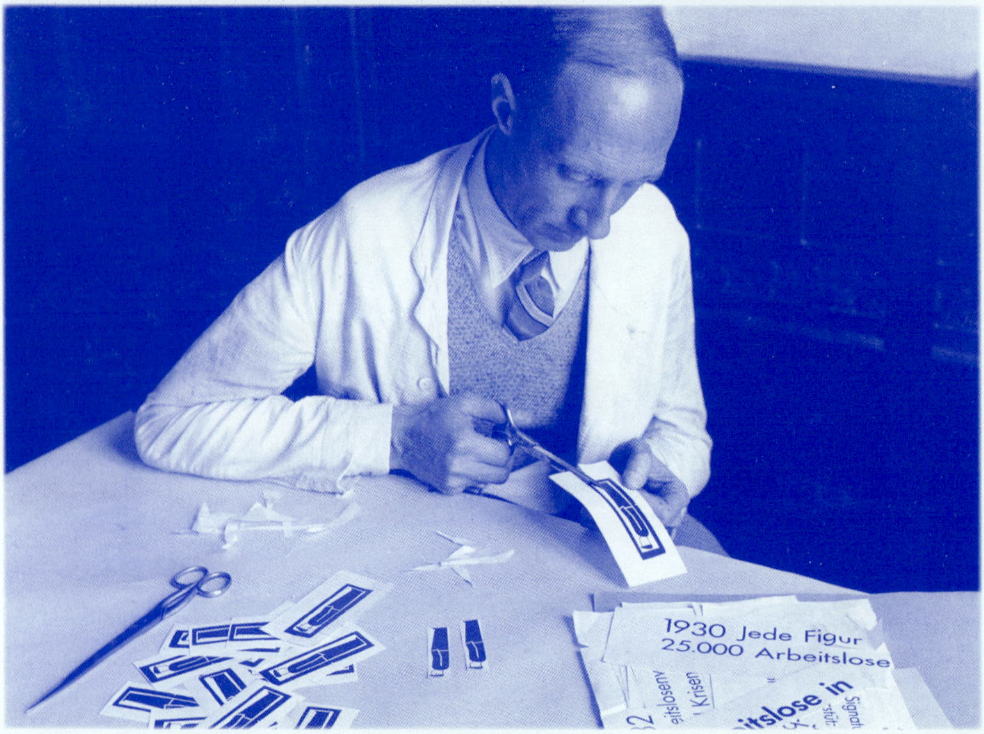
1930 Jede Figur
25.000 Arbeitslose
Krisen

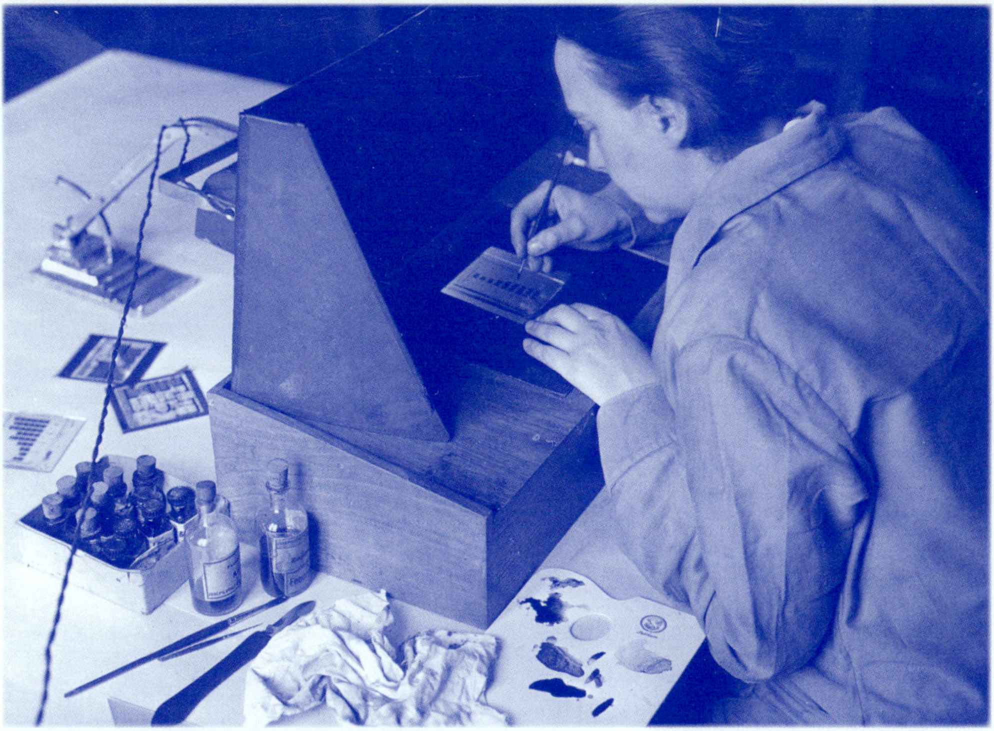

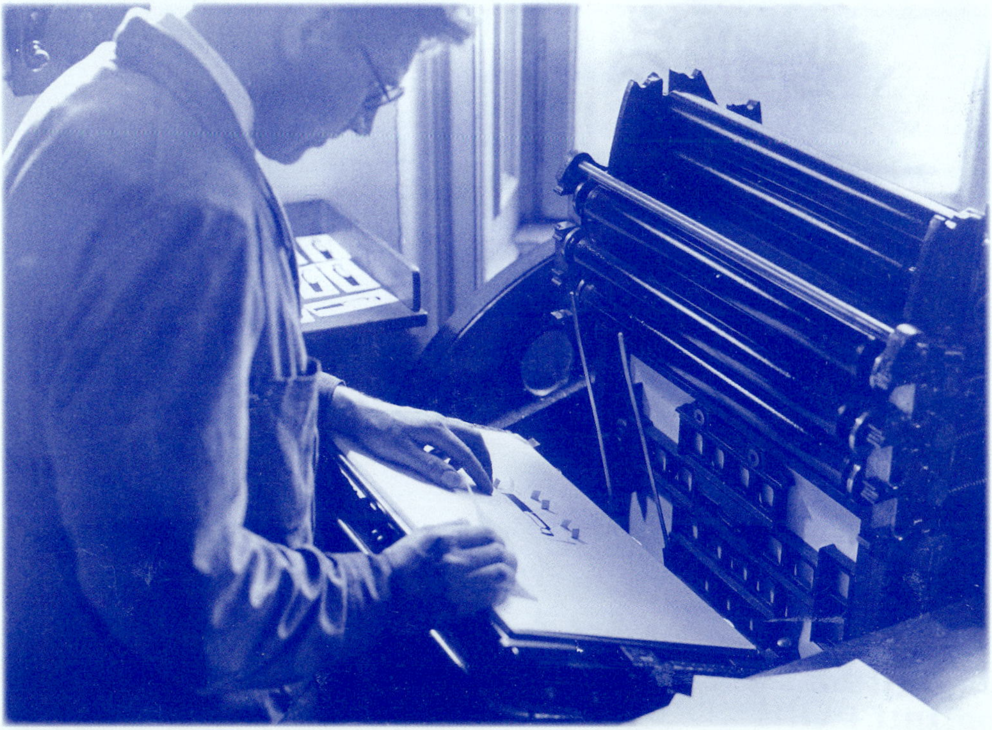

Graphic communication

Income Groups, Great Britain
New Generation
United States
Deaths from Tuberculosis
Imports
Rickets
THESE
OF PL

A Few Ounces ~~YOU FILL THE GAP COMPLETELY.~~ A Day

1. ~~This is the~~ A ship ~~- which brings a load.~~

    ~~The~~ A torpedo blow - which sinks the ship.

    ~~This is~~ A crate - ~~brought in the ship.~~ part of the load

    A ~~salvage~~ sack - one hundredweight.

    Two thousand sacks - make a hundred tons.

    Forty-five times ~~this - is~~ hundred tons make one shipload.

    a family perhaps your own.
    ~~In it has not least - there are yourselves.~~

    Sailing from America - ~~the~~ ships start over fleets
    guarded by ~~American~~ the ~~and British destroyers and planes.~~
    Warships on either side
    ~~Destroyers on either side~~ - escort the convoy.

    Planes overhead - keep watch on the sea.

    Danger
    Here in mid Atlantic - ~~a U-boat~~ is lurking.

    Crash of torpedo - and a ship is sunk.

    Lives are lost - and so are the shiploads

    loads which are wanted - in factories at home.

    Crash goes ~~another.~~ Another ship is sinking.

    Crash goes a third! A third ship is sunk.

    ~~Convoy nearing Britain - the escort is not needed now.~~

    Soon all the shiploads will be safe in port.

    Here is a lighthouse - ~~at last a~~ landfall. a for

    Some ships are lost - but the convoy is ~~here.~~ fine

2. On the shore

    factories are waiting,

    ~~whistles are ~~~~~~,~~

    they waiting for the crates,

    ~~screaming at the ships.~~

164

WORLD of PLENTY

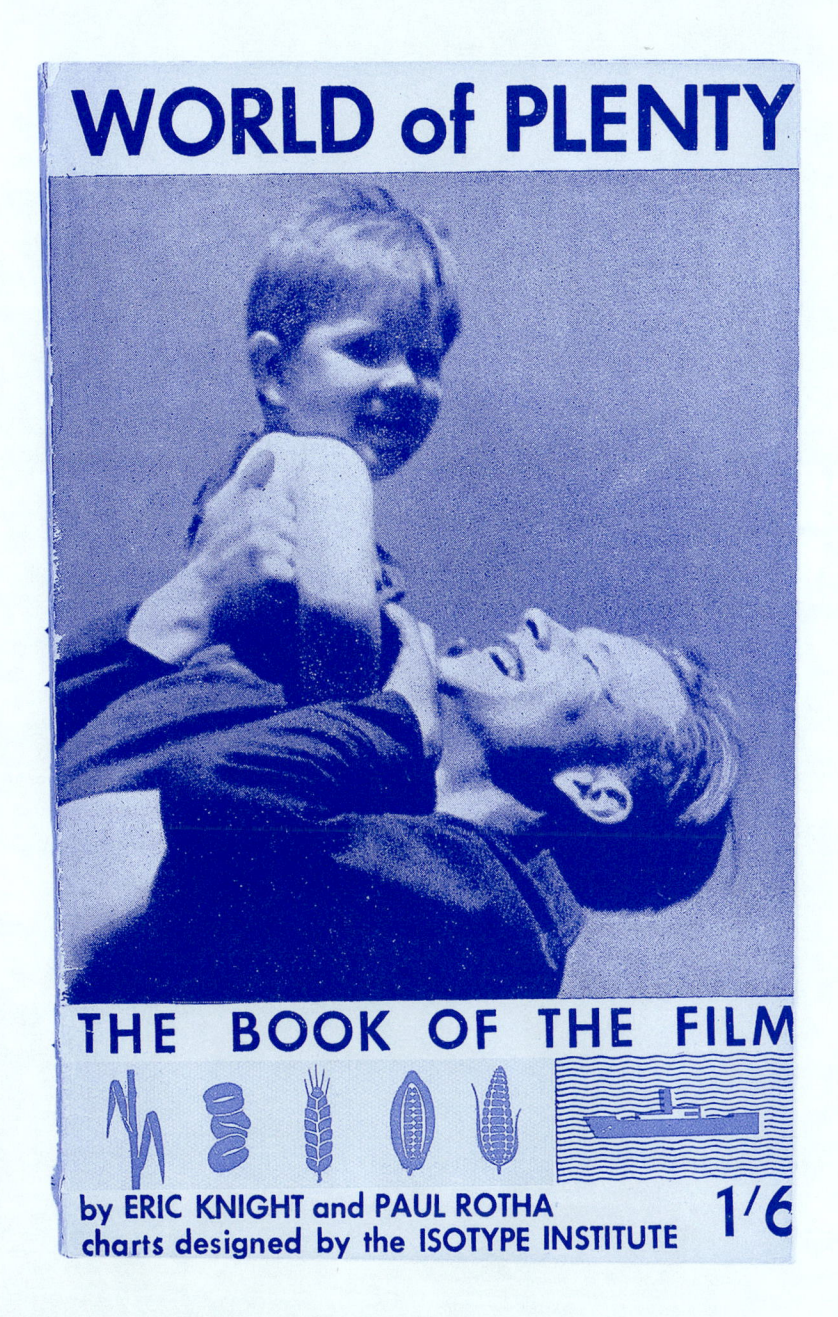

THE BOOK OF THE FILM

by ERIC KNIGHT and PAUL ROTHA
charts designed by the ISOTYPE INSTITUTE

1/6

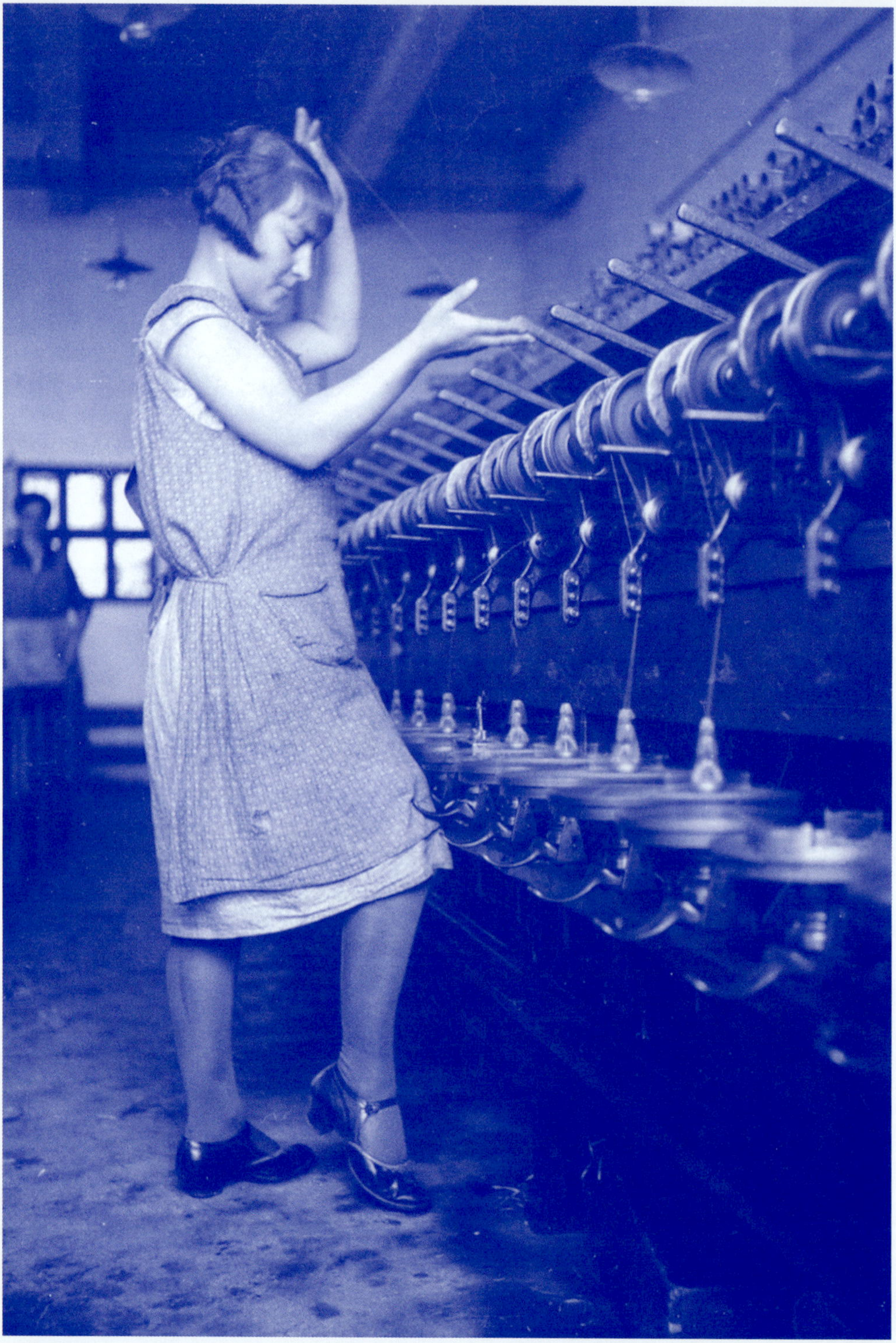

Schützet eure Haare vor der Spindel

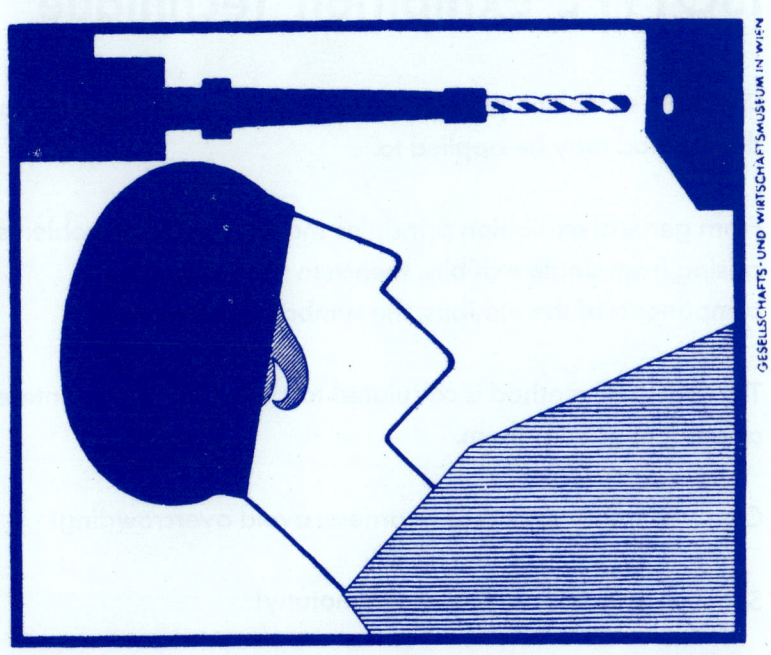

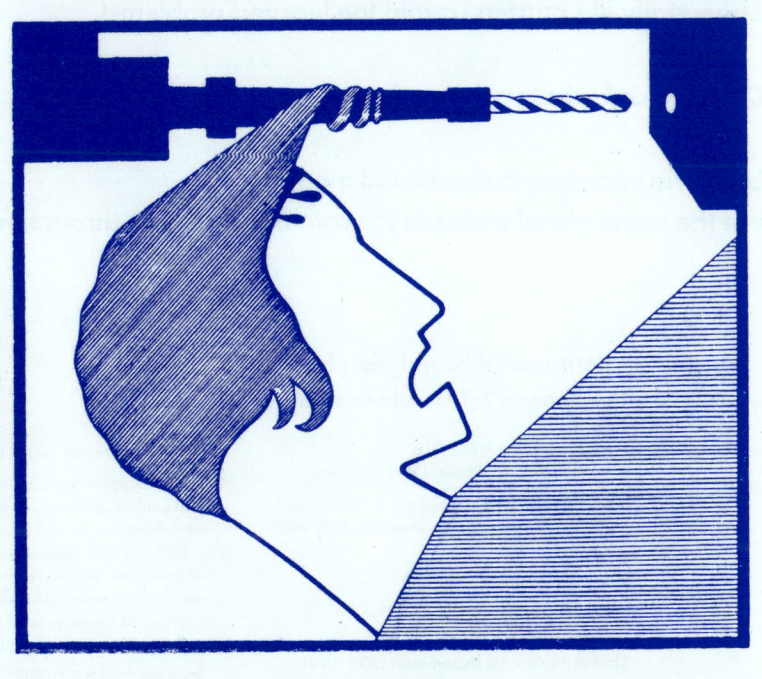

ISOTYPE Exhibition Technique

ISOTYPE exhibition principles are the same whatever purpose the method may be applied to.

From general exhibition principles the way leads to problems arising from single exhibits, thence to the functional components of the exhibits, the symbols in particular.

The ISOTYPE method is calculated to look after visitors' interests and not to govern them.

Combine multiplicity and clearness; avoid overcrowding!

Satisfy many interests; avoid monotony!

Stress daily life matters; avoid too learned problems!

Do not word what you can visualize!

Unify visualization in charts and models,
use the same visual dictionary, grammar and style throughout!

International Foundation for Visual Education
Headquarters: 267 Obrechtstraat, The Hague, Holland

ISOTYPE

President: MARY L. FLEDDÉRUS
Director, International Industrial Relations Institute

Vice-President for U.S.A.: Dr. H. E. KLEINSCHMIDT
Director of Personnel Training, Department of Health,
City of New York

Director: Dr. OTTO NEURATH

General Secretary: MARIE REIDEMEISTER
Chief of the Transformation Department

Chief of the Graphic Department: GERD ARNTZ

Consulting Architect: Dr. JOSEF FRANK

Advisory Committee for the United States:

Mrs. ANN REED BRENNER, Secretary, Survey Association, Inc.
JOHN M. GLENN, Secretary to the Board of Trustees, Russell Sage Foundation
Mrs. HENRY ITTLESON, President, The Vocational Adjustment Bureau for Girls
Dr. A. JOHNSON, Director, The New School for Social Research
WALDEMAR KAEMPFFERT, Science Editor, The New York Times
MARY VAN KLEECK, Director of Industrial Studies, Russell Sage Foundation
K. LONBERG-HOLM, Architect and Research Counsellor

Secretary: HELEN B. RUSSELL
Room 705, 130 East 22nd Street, New York, N. Y.

Vivid Combination: Museum and Zoo

Whale and Whaling

Permanent Exhibition

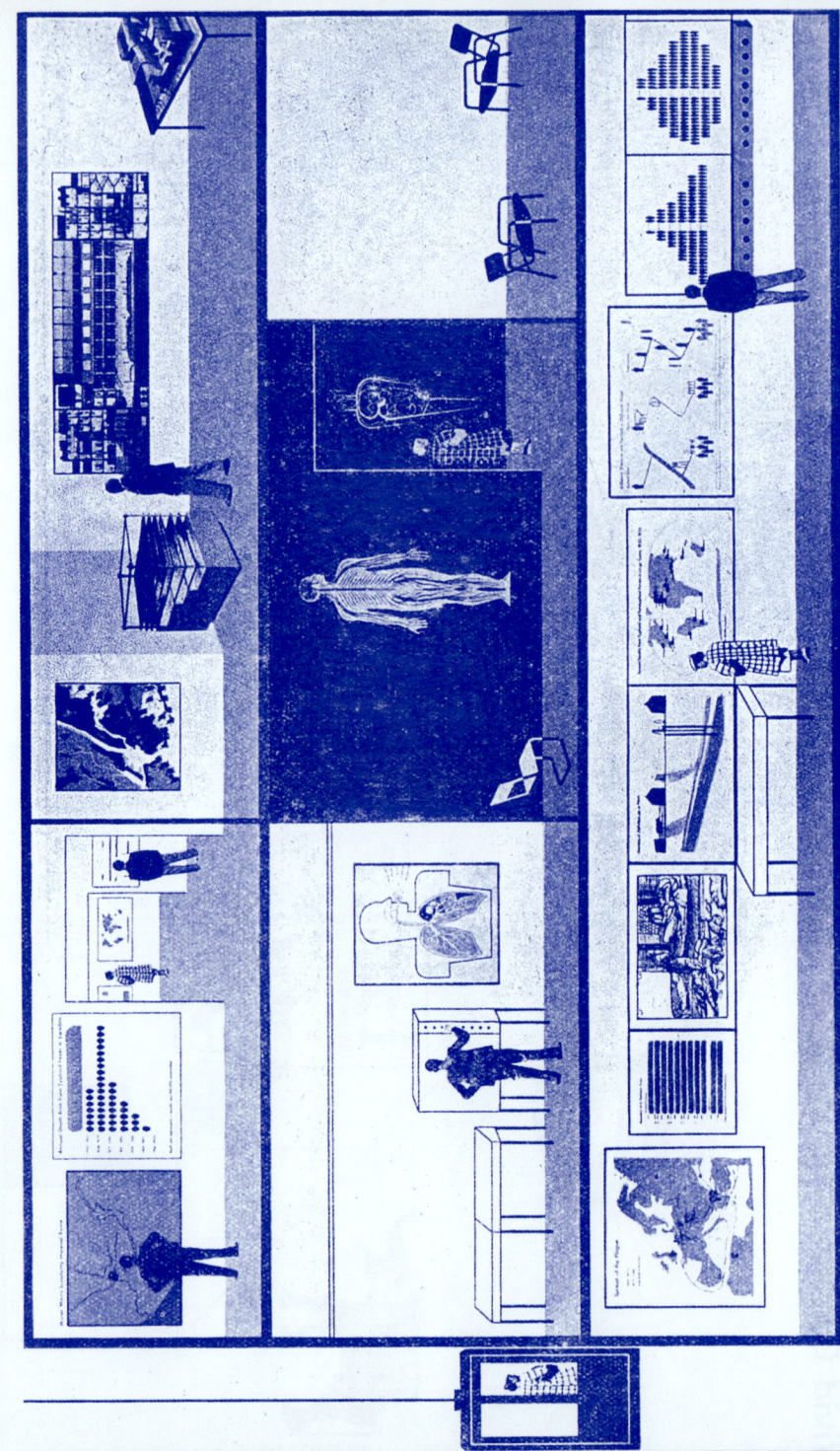

170

Rembrandt in zijn geschilderde zelfportretten

jeugd-
periode
in Leiden
1626

1631

eerste
A'damse
periode
1632

1642

twede
A'damse
periode
1643

1657

derde
A'damse
periode
1658

1669

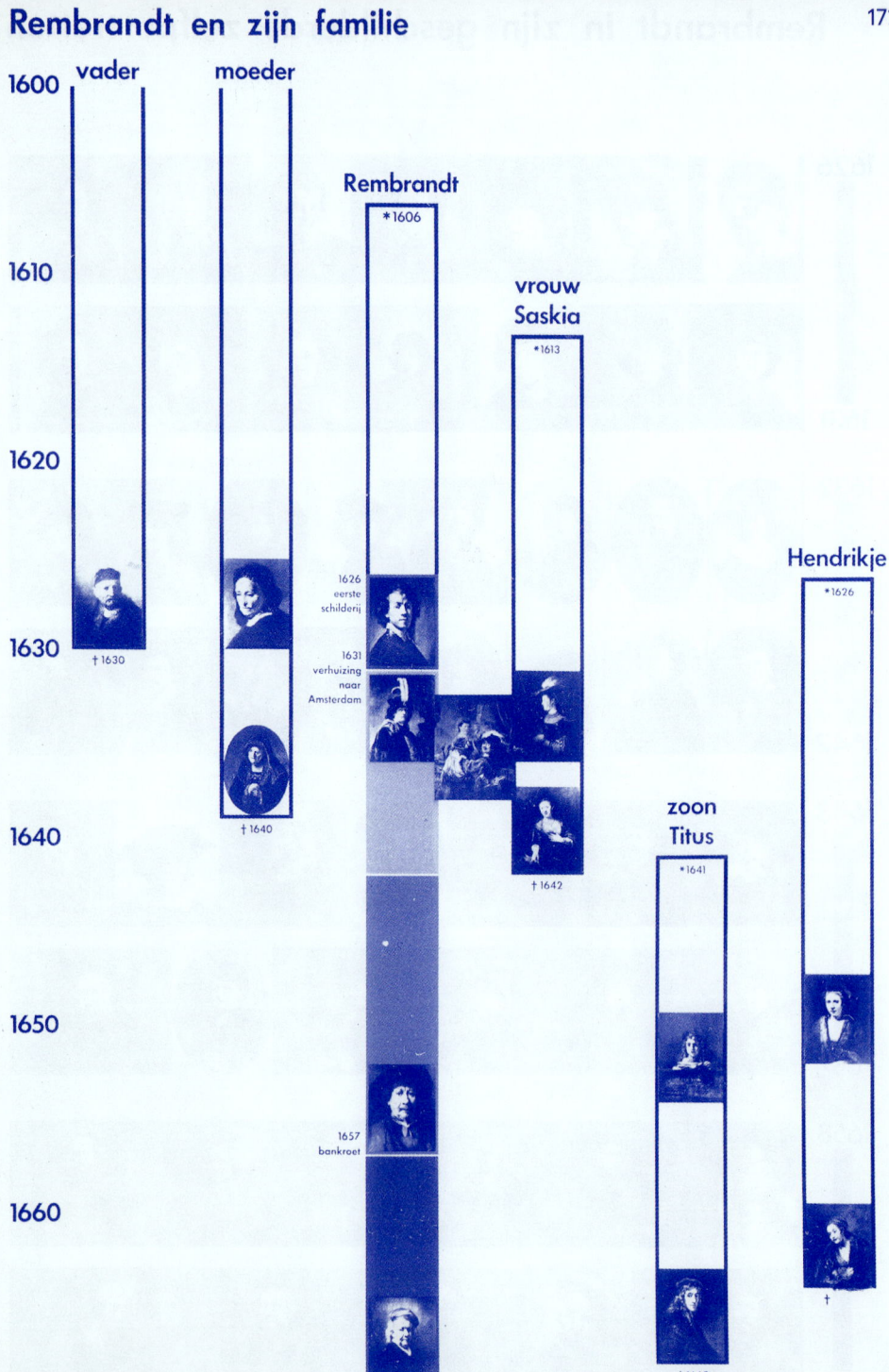

Rembrandt en zijn familie

172

1600 — vader — moeder

Rembrandt *1606

1610

vrouw Saskia *1613

1620

Hendrikje *1626

† 1630

1626 eerste schilderij

1631 verhuizing naar Amsterdam

1630

† 1640

zoon Titus *1641

† 1642

1640

1650

1657 bankroet

1660

† 1668

† 1669

†

173   **Rembrandts leerlingen en schilders door hem beinvloed**

1626 - 1631

1632 - 1642

1643 - 1657

1658 - 1669

gekleurd: leerlingen   grijs: beinvloed

Werken van leerlingen uit de vier perioden

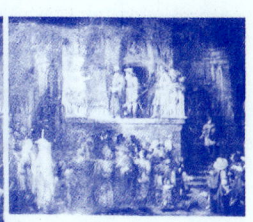

Voorstudies en uitwerking van een thema

Getekende studies voor het schilderij "de Staalmeesters"

1662

De onderwerpen van de schilderijen en hun bestemming

174

bij Rubens

altaarstukken

bijbelse onderwerpen (niet voor de kerk)

mythologische en historische onderwerpen

portretten

genre en landschap

Vlaamse kerk

bij Rembrandt

bijbelse onderwerpen (niet voor de kerk)

mythologische en historische onderwerpen

portretten

zelfportretten

genre en landschap

Hollandse kerk

Elk symbool stelt voor 5 % van het aantal schilderijen

Hollands binnenhuis

175 Schilderijen van Rembrandt in Nederland

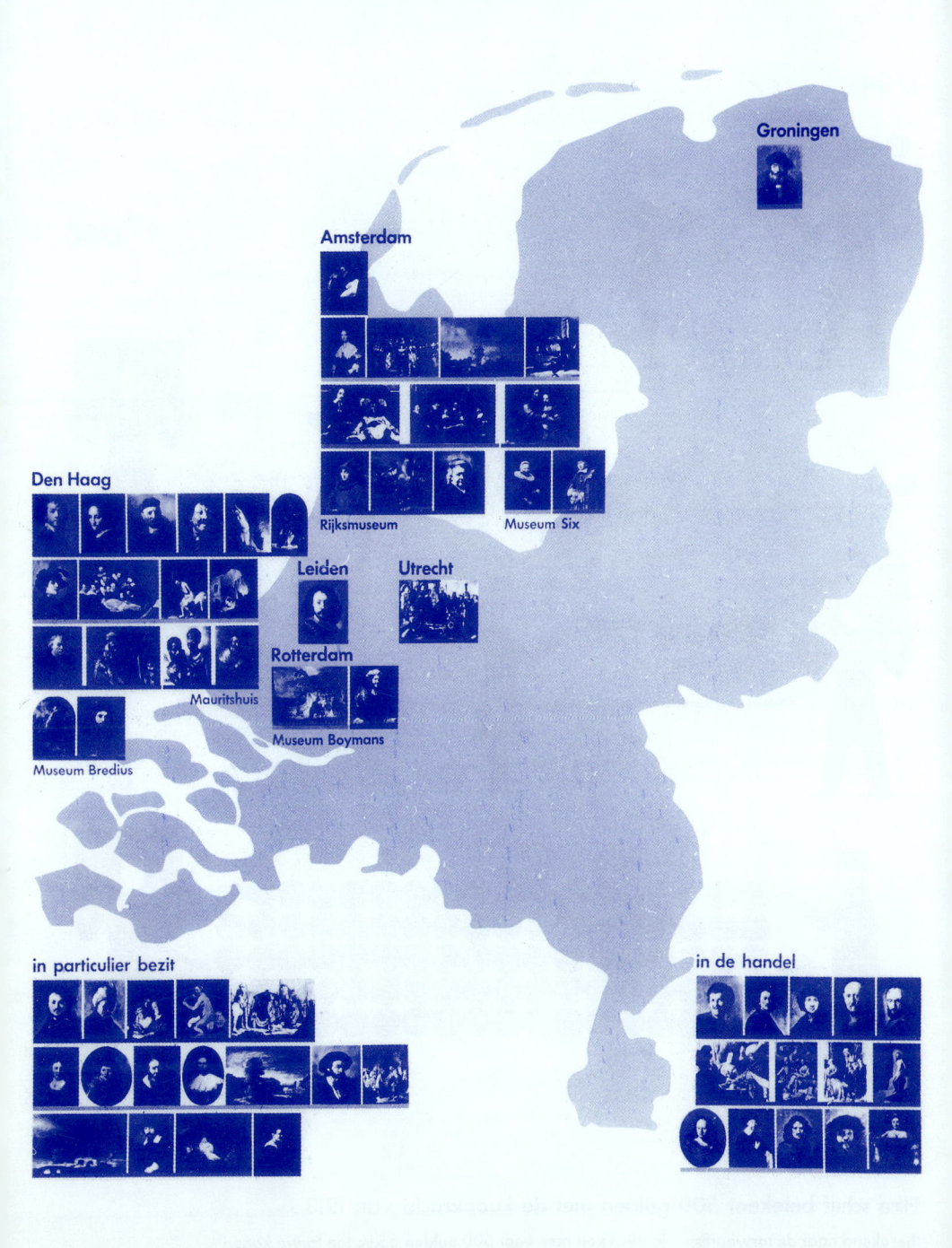

Groningen

Amsterdam

Rijksmuseum

Museum Six

Den Haag

Leiden

Utrecht

Rotterdam

Mauritshuis

Museum Boymans

Museum Bredius

in particulier bezit

in de handel

Wat er voor een schilderij van Rembrandt betaald werd in de verschillende eeuwen

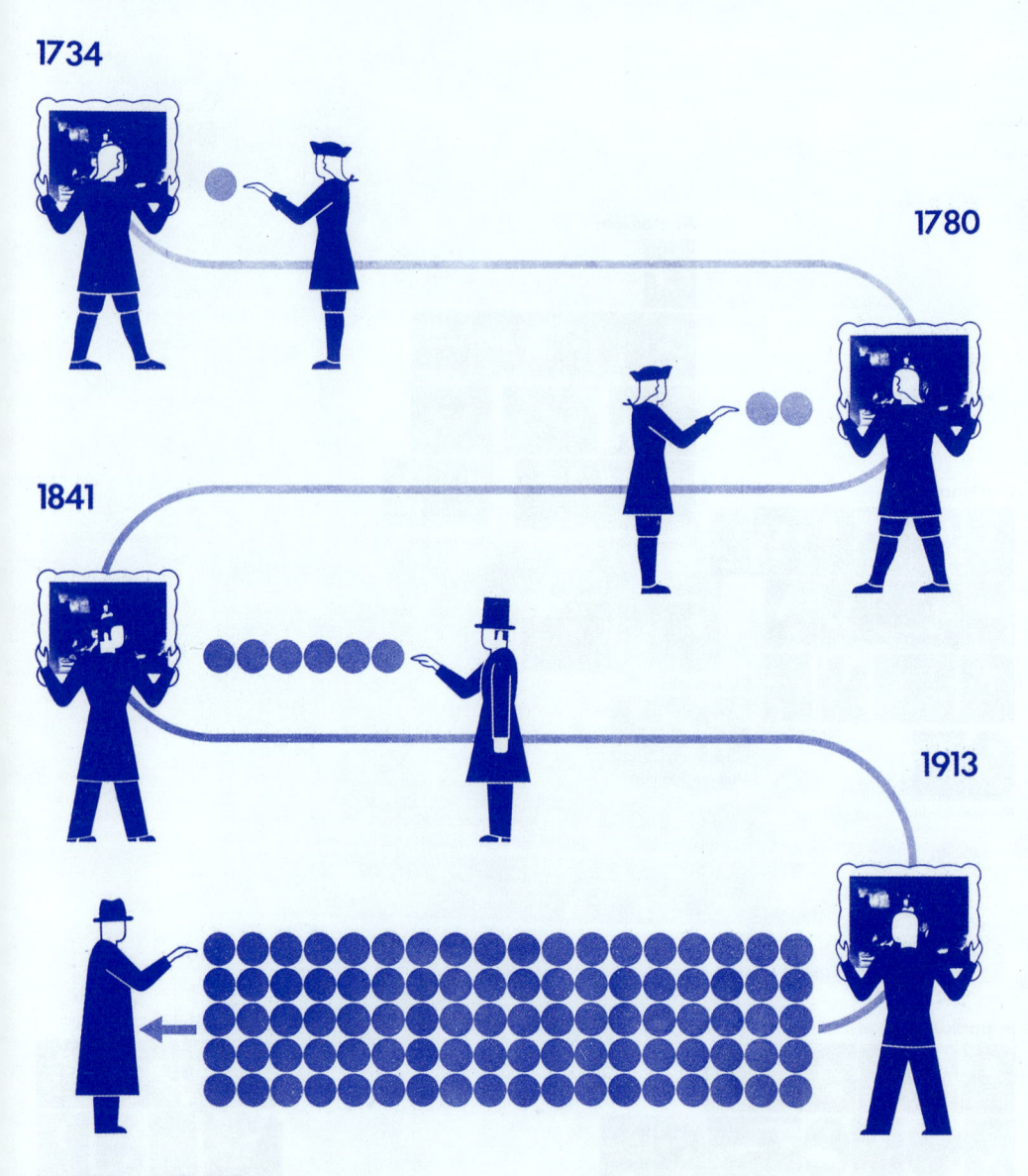

1734

1780

1841

1913

het schilderij "Bathseba" is thans in New York

Elke schijf betekent 500 gulden met de koopkracht van 1913
(berekend naar de tarweprijs)   in 1913 kon men voor 500 gulden ±5 1/4 ton tarwe kopen